Ready
Set
Sew

Published by
Butterick Publishing
A Division of American Can Company

EDITOR-IN-CHIEF
Patricia Perry

COPY EDITOR   **TECHNICAL EDITOR**
Alice Rohrbacher   Elizabeth Musheno

ART DIRECTORS
Jean Jacques DuBane
Elizabeth Shurter

PRODUCTION COORDINATORS
Harvey Factor
Connie Meyer

STAFF

Gisela Sachs   Mona London
Janet Lombardo   Ellen Culp
Susan Frye   Susanne Olson
Loretta Leiva   Doreen Williams
Norma Risman

Cover Photography by Horn/Griner
Room Photography by Jerry Abramowitz

Library of Congress Catalog Card Number 70-169061
International Standard Book Number 0-88421-004-9

Copyright © 1971 by
Butterick Publishing
161 Sixth Avenue
New York, New York 10013
A Division of American Can Company
Seventh Printing, October 1976

Ready

You've made the decision . . . you're READY to sew. Start afresh . . . whether you are, or not . . . get in on the ground floor of a whole new way to sew—the **easy** way—with Butterick.

Prepare for action . . . clear a corner of your favorite room and collect your notions and tools. Plan a place for everything . . . and put everything in its place. A big part of easy sewing is having what you need where it's needed.

Pause for some reflection—about yourself and **your** style of living. We've started at the very beginning . . . gathered lots of fashion, pattern, and fabric information . . . all in the name of getting you together in style. Put yourself on speaking terms with patterns . . . as the relationship deepens, let Butterick take you on a guided tour of the fabric department.

You're about to take a critical step . . . choosing the Butterick pattern and the fabric that will be everything you want them to be charts the course of your entire sewing project . . . future success depends on decisions made now.

The name of the game is fashion sewing—with Butterick on your side, how can you possibly lose?

A Word About Fashion

Patterns—The Cover Story

Making The Most Of Your Money

Turn On To Fabric

Dictionary Of Fabrics

Notions From A To Z

A Toolbox For Sewing

The Machine Shop

Looking Great

A Word About Fashion

Clothes with a split personality are far from rare. In fact, the difference between the looks of a dress on the hanger and on you is one of the biggest joys or sorrows in the what-to-wear issue. Design and its relationship to your figure and features are at the root of the situation. Understanding them helps make them work for you.

DESIGN DATA

Five separate ingredients go into the design formula. They emerge as a unit of interdependent parts which create an over-all success.

COLOR: Working successfully with colors begins with putting them in categories.

Hue: This is the name associated with a color—red, yellow, and blue are primary hues; orange, green, and violet are secondary hues; and double-name colors (like red-orange·) are tertiary hues.

Value: The lightness or darkness of a color results from adding white or black—white produces tints of higher value; black produces shades of lower value.

Intensity: The brightness or dullness of colors is the issue—pure colors are most intense, while adding gray produces a tone of less intensity.

Color Schemes: Successfully relating colors of different hues, values, and intensity depends on understanding color schemes. A monochromatic color scheme uses a number of values and intensities of one color, or a color with black and white; an analogous color scheme uses related hues, like red, red-orange, and orange; a complementary color scheme uses opposing hues like yellow and violet or red and green.

LINE: Create shape and guide the eyes with lines which make up the body, silhouette, and details of a garment. Whether horizontal, vertical, diagonal, or curved, lines are made dominant by such factors as length, width, brightness, repetition, and the tendency of our eyes to move in the direction we read.

Because the eyes follow straight lines quickly, these seem severe; curved lines have a slowing effect and seem softer. Remember that both patterns and fabric can have lines, and that these must work together.

PROPORTION AND BALANCE: Having to do with relationships within a design, these elements tie together color, print, texture, and lines. Proportion involves space relationships within the garment. Balance requires that equal amounts of interest exist on both sides of the natural center of interest.

PRINT: A forceful dimension of fabric, prints are really additional colors and lines which must be given as much consideration as other color and line combinations in a garment. Often a particular color or line emerges as the dominant feature of a print.

TEXTURE: Another fabric exclusive, texture is surface variation which can introduce a new line or shift emphasis to or from existing design lines.

6

DESIGN AND YOU

Armed with some knowledge of the ingredients which go into design, you're ready to learn how to make them make the most of you.

USE COLOR

Join us in the wonderful world of color! We've seen the decline of many former do's and don't's about color—like redheads never wearing purple or pink. Experiment—be bold and innovative in using colors and color combinations that are new to you.

Don't throw caution completely to the wind, however. Keep wearing those colors which have served you well in the past. Be critical of those which you are trying out for the first time. Don't buy a currently popular color or color combination before considering carefully how it affects your personal coloring.

Analyze yourself with fabrics in front of a mirror. Does the fabric color enhance your skin, hair coloring, and eyes? Don't ignore the colors of your lipstick and eye shadow. Above all, how do you feel about the color, and in the color?

There are some color substitutes which you can turn into advantageous optical illusions. Your size can seem to shrink or blossom by the skillful manipulation of colors. Flatter your figure—fill it out with warm colors like red, yellow, and orange, or pare it down with cool colors like blue and green.

Light and dark, and bright and dull colors also influence your figure pluses and minuses. Generally, lights and brights make you seem larger; darks and dulls make you seem smaller. Boldly contrasting colors make you look larger while more subtle color variances reduce your size. Be alert to these color characteristics as you plan each garment.

Accessories can brighten dull colors or tone down loud ones while making the most of your best features and the least of your less fortunate ones. A splashy scarf tied around your neck will draw attention to your face and away from a thick waist or heavy hips. A contrasting belt that rides your hips will draw attention away from heaviness above the waist. If you have heavy thighs and hips, bracelets worn on your upper arm rather than on your wrist will be more attractive.

Color and accessory plans carefully made will most certainly thrust you into the limelight—or violet, or amber, or strawberry . . .

USE LINE

Simple as they seem at first glance, lines are really a complex art form. Your garment has lines, as does your fabric if it's printed or textured. Even you have lines! Body, silhouette, fabric, and detail lines can be made to work together to create a garment that says "Wow!"

Just like color, lines can draw attention to good features and away from bad ones. This is accomplished by dominant lines—those that are longer, wider, brighter, or more often repeated than others.

Another concept about line which will be useful in creating your fashion image is that a straight line is a severe, classical line, while a curved line is a softer, more graceful, and more relaxed line. Vertical, horizontal, diagonal, or curved, you want to be on the good side of those lines.

A vertical line projects an impression of height and is effective in creating a tall and slender appearance. One vertical line in your garment is more slenderizing than two because all eye movement will be up and down rather than lateral. If in proportion with your figure, a center panel can also create the illusion of slenderness.

Horizontal lines lead the eye across to dramatize width. If you have narrow shoulders, waist, or hips, you can take advantage of this effect. For narrow shoulders, select a pattern with a yoke and/or puffed sleeves. A wide belt, or a gathered or pleated skirt will add fullness to a narrow waist and hips.

VERTICAL   HORIZONTAL

CURVED

STRAIGHT

Even if you're more broad than narrow, you don't have to shy away from horizontal lines entirely. A horizontal line near the top or bottom of your garment will exaggerate the length of the longer area. Consider combining horizontal and vertical lines too, keeping in mind what you have learned about dominance.

Diagonal lines are a cross between verticals and horizontals, and depending on angle, placement, and length, can create the illusions of either of those. To make shoulder, bust, and waist areas look wider, confine the diagonal to that area only. If a slender look is what you're after, the diagonal should be longer, perhaps from shoulder to hemline.

Curves are essential to femininity, and curved garment lines finish what Mother Nature began. Curves are not as forceful as straight lines, but can bring about the same illusions. A heavy bust and waist is minimized by a softly curving bodice silhouette. Rounded patch pockets make narrow hips seem fuller.

Line is quicker than the eye. If you do your fashion flattery homework, you'll be able to use all of these lines, confident that they are working for, rather than against you.

USE PROPORTION AND BALANCE

Something missing . . . and you can't put your finger on it? You may have neglected two principles no woman in her right fashion mind can afford to forget—proportion and balance. Intangible though they are, awareness and application of these concepts is as vital to your good looks as your desire to look good.

Proportion requires that you relate and complement the spacial divisions of your garment or outfit to one another and to your figure. Proportion is easily achieved by dividing your garment in halves, thirds, fourths, etc., but you can achieve

variety as well as unity in proportion by using close, uneven ratios of space —for example, $2:3$, $3:5$, $5:8$, etc.

Of course you can deviate from these guidelines, but when you do, strive for a pleasing relationship between your body structure and the uneven garment divisions.

When the eye is attracted equally to garment divisions, a state of formal balance, or symmetry, exists. If used exclusively, this method of achieving balance would smack of monotony.

Informal balance, or asymmetry, provides variety within unity by shifting the eye from an unbalanced focal point to another point of interest which has been emphasized. For example, a dress with neckline interest can be informally balanced by having pockets on its skirt.

FORMAL BALANCE   INFORMAL BALANCE

Although garment divisions are a piece of the proportion and balance action, your body structure also comes into play. If you have a long torso and short legs, the division lines created by a shirtwaist dress would only emphasize your imbalance. A skimmy shift is the answer to the problem.

Accessories put that last, great touch to a well-proportioned, balanced garment. Relate the size of your accessories to both your body size and the purpose your garment is to serve.

USE PRINT

Put some print power in your wardrobe plans! The variations of prints are endless: florals, geometrics, dots, plaids, paisleys, ethnics, and borders, to name but a few. Creating clothes from printed fabrics can be fun as well as a thing of beauty, if you're aware of some pertinent facts.

Prints and solid colors play by the same rules. Bold and bright colors have an expanding effect, while more subdued, quiet colors in the same print have a contracting effect.

Judge the relationship of the size and color of the print to your figure. Choose a print that's in scale with your dimensions. Unless you do, the contrast between you and your print will be unattractively exaggerated.

An unexpected windfall is in your future if you choose a print. Prints enable you to wear a lovely but otherwise unflattering color when this is combined with some colors which you know are attractive on you.

When selecting a print, consider its most dominant color—that color which is brightest or most extensively used. Also, remember that colors used in combinations create the illusion of a different color—for example, red and yellow together may have the over-all effect of orange.

Be sure the angular or curved lines of your garment and print are complementary. Clothes are prettier when print lines are similar to garment lines. Rounded print designs harmonize with curved garment lines, while angular plaids or stripes are ideal mates for straight garment lines. Remember, too, that some garments have intricate lines that are inappropriate for the complexities of prints.

If you decide that it's best for you not to wear a certain print as an entire garment, consider the possibility of using that print as a trim to focus attention where you want it.

Perhaps a printed collar on a solid-color dress will enhance your face.

When you feel daring, try mixing a couple of prints in one garment. This takes much caution and skill, but the look can be smashing. Choose prints that complement the proportion and color of each other.

USE TEXTURE

Rough or smooth, shiny or dull, clingy or stiff—this is the stuff of texture. In its own important way, texture contributes to your clothing's personality to clue people in to yours.

By understanding texture, you can create fabric illusions which flatter you. Rough, nubby fabrics like tweed and corduroy, and shiny fabrics like vinyl and metallics add bulk. Stiff fabrics look sleek over heavy hips and thighs, but can't camouflage an all-over roly-poly figure.

Clingy, transparent fabrics leave less to the imagination than those already discussed. Unless your figure is perfect, it's advisable to use these fabrics in soft, draped designs.

When you love and long to use a fabric that you know you shouldn't, go ahead and use it—sparingly. If you're on the skinny side, make a sheer fabric sash, bolero, or sleeves in a dress of heavier textured fabric. Keep in mind that the fun of wearing "forbidden" fabrics only lasts as long as they're worn cautiously.

If you're on the heavy side, try using tweed in your more slender areas, or as a trim on pockets, cuffs, or other details.

Expand your mind—use your imagination to come up with your own tricks of the trade. A fascinating wardrobe is within your grasp.

USE COMMON SENSE

If you're truly interested in a fashion look that's really all together, none of these ingredients (color, line, proportion and balance, print, and texture) can be ignored. They all react to you, your body structure, your pluses, and your minuses.

Pause for some reflection—look at yourself in a mirror or photograph. Look in your closet. Analyze yourself, and your current wardrobe. Consult a friend whose clothes-sense you trust. Then ask some questions.

What are your good points, your bad points? What do you want your fashion image to be? How can you make all the elements of design work for you?

How can you achieve a today fashion look that's in gear with your figure, pocketbook, and life-style? What accessories are best for you and your fashion look?

The best way to answer these questions is to sit down and bone up, honestly and frankly. What more fascinating and challenging subject could you ask for than yourself? Remember, practice making perfect is truer than ever, so don't expect to be an overnight hit on the fashion stage. Dress rehearsals are the name of the game.

Great fashion comes from being informed, and there are reliable guides all around you—pattern catalogues, pattern and fashion magazines, store windows and displays, and people who have already established their ability to use fashion. Make frequent use of all of these sources.

Each of us is an individual, and very few try to conform to the here-today, gone-tomorrow contemporary ideal. Concentrate on improving your good and bad features in a unique way.

Sewing frees you from the limitations of your community's fashion outlook. You can choose and create your own fashion image from all of those presented by Butterick. Be as liberated as you like!

Fashion falls into some broad-based categories. Each is a creative condition whose representatives approach fashion differently. By modifying one of these to suit the real you, your clothes look can begin to take shape.

The **conservative** soft-pedals the fashion scene, plays it cool; well-dressed means wearing classic styles and fabrics, earrings, and gloves. A **sophisticate** is with-it, and adapts fashion trends to herself in a uniquely personal manner. The **budget-oriented** demands clothes designed for double-duty—a great look is an all-day, any-day look. The **experimenter** latches onto new trends before they're hot; fashion is a larky game.

CONSERVATIVE   SOPHISTICATE   BUDGET-ORIENTED   EXPERIMENTER

Keep your approach to fashion flexible, not hard-and-fast. Adapt it to your needs, preferences, and point of view, but don't be trapped into thinking that being up-to-date means spending a fortune every season.

The clothes you have now can achieve your interpretation of today's fashion with a little bit of help from accessories—jewelry, scarves, belts, handbags, shoes, hats, jackets, sweaters, and blouses. In a word, minor additions, not major overhauls!

Follow the rules of design to the letter when you're new to the game. After serving your apprenticeship, you'll develop your own tricks . . . like combining several prints, textures, or prints and textures in one garment.

Some of the greatest looks can be achieved by combining color-coordinated checks and stripes, stripes and dots, or other seemingly adverse prints.

A combination of knitted and woven fabrics in one garment is another illusion-maker. Knits and wovens each possess personality traits which are adaptable to your figure quirks. Knits like to hug, while wovens are a bit more stand-offish. Combine a knit top and a woven skirt or pants if you have an average bust and waist but narrow hips.

Fashion is a personal thing. It's yours to use or abuse. We have given you some basic facts and suggestions to smooth your way to looking great, but it's up to you to really get it together.

People appreciate fashion-sense, and you can find yourself glowing a little in that appreciation when the clothes you're wearing are really expressive of you. Fashion sewing really gives you a piece of the action—from careful planning to final stitch.

Finding The Perfect Pattern

Patterns —The Cover Story

Butterick designs its patterns for you—fashion-conscious and young-in-spirit, adding quality and your personal touch to everything you sew. A wide selection of easy-to-sew patterns for the entire family is available from Butterick at reasonable prices. So here it is — all the incentive you need to sew up a storm!

GETTING STRAIGHT ABOUT SIZE

Choosing the correct pattern size is your first important step in determining the success or failure of your sewing project. Set aside a few minutes for some preliminary figure-work that will save you money, effort, and time, and minimize the amount of altering and fitting that will be necessary. Do NOT rely on ready-to-wear sizing, because this varies with each manufacturer and may be slightly different from Butterick's size charts.

Success depends on your taking accurate body measurements, typing your figure correctly, and being aware of current fashion influences on silhouette and fit.

After you have determined your correct pattern size, don't make the mistake of thinking that you'll wear that size forever. Gaining or losing even a slight amount of weight may cause a change in pattern size.

If you maintain your weight for years, there still may be subtle, yet quite normal changes in your body shape. Measure yourself and re-check figure types on a regular basis so that you can purchase new patterns with confidence and accuracy.

Because your pattern size is derived from your actual body measurements, we will explain the correct procedure for taking the proper measurements. Knowing how isn't quite enough, though — be prepared to be honest about those inches!

When taking most circumference and width measurements, hold the tape snugly against the body and parallel to the floor. Don't draw up the tape tightly. Before writing down your measurements, check to see that the tape is exactly where it should be for the measurements you're taking.

Keep a chart of all figure measurements. Besides using this in determining your pattern size, you'll find it a handy table to have when checking pattern dimensions for adjustments and alterations. Revise your chart whenever figure changes occur, and record the date.

Put on undergarments and shoes so that your figure and posture will correspond to your normal, everyday appearance. Tie a string closely, but not tightly, around the thinnest part of your waist.

MEASURING WOMEN

Look at the figure to note position of tape and record all of the following measurements on your chart. Even the measurements you'll need for pants are included. Take these measurements on both developing and mature figures. The string around your waist is the take-off point for many measurements.

BACK NECK TO WAIST: Measure from prominent neck bone down center back to waist string (1).

SHOULDER: Measure from base of neck to shoulder bone or hinge (2).

LENGTH: For skirts, measure from waist at center back to desired point on leg for hem (3). For pants, measure side from waistline string to center of knee, waist to calf, and waist to floor or desired length of pants (4).

BUST: Measure over fullest part of bust and straight across back (1).

WAIST: Measure at the string (2).

FRONT NECK TO WAIST: Measure from hollow between neck bones to center front waistline (3).

ARM LENGTH: With arm slightly bent, measure from shoulder bone to elbow, then to wrist bone. Record each length (4).

HIGH HIP: Measure 2″ to 4″ below string at waist over top of hip bones (5).

FULL HIP: Measure at fullest part of hips; mark the tape position with pins on the undergarment and measure down from string at waist to pins to establish hipline. This is usually 7″ to 9″ below waist. Record distance from waist to hip as well as hip measurement (6).

CIRCUMFERENCE OF LEG: Measure fullest part of thigh (7), knee (8), calf (9), and instep (10).

CROTCH LENGTH: Sitting on a hard, flat chair, measure from side waist at string to chair seat.

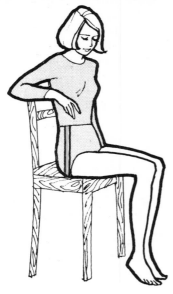

MEASURING CHILDREN

To make figure charts for toddlers, children, and girls, take the following measurements. Use the string at the waist as you did for women. If you plan on making pants for children, take the same crotch, hip, and leg measurements that you would take for women.

BREAST: Measure around fullest part of chest (1).

WAIST: Measure at string (2).

HIP: Measure across hip bones or fullest part of hip; mark the tape position with pins on the undergarment and measure down from waist to pins to establish hipline. Record both hip measurements and distance from waist to hip (3).

BACK NECK TO WAIST: Measure center back from prominent neck bone to string at waist (1).

HEIGHT: Measure height of child without shoes, standing against a wall (2).

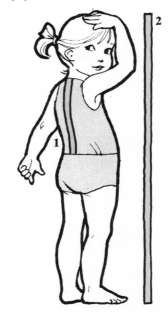

MEASURING MEN AND BOYS

Men, boys, and teenage boys need their own size charts, too. Look at the figures and follow these directions for measuring your favorite fellows. Use the string at the waist as you did for women.

NECK: Measure around the neck; add ½″ for wearing ease (1).

CHEST: Measure around fullest part of chest (2).

WAIST: Measure at string (3).

HIP: Measure at seat or fullest part of hip; mark the tape position with pins on the undergarment and measure down from waist to pins to establish hipline. Record hip measurement and distance from waist to hip (4).

BACK NECK TO WAIST: Measure center back from prominent neck bone to waist string (1).

SLEEVE LENGTH: With arm slightly bent, measure across shoulder from back base of neck over elbow to wrist (2).

TROUSER LENGTH: Measure from the waist down the outside of the leg to the knee and then to floor or desired trouser length. Record both measurements (3).

INSEAM: Measure from the crotch down the inside of the leg to the knee and then to the floor or desired trouser length. Record both measurements (4).

CROTCH LENGTH: Measure as instructed for women's pants on page 17 (not shown).

FIGURE TYPES

Each of us has a body shape that is uniquely her own. The National Bureau of Standards and the pattern industry have gotten together and established standard or average body measurements which are the basis for pattern sizes. These sizes are in turn grouped according to figure types, or the general appearance your measurements take.

On the following pages, Butterick figure types are described and listed with their corresponding pattern sizes.

Avoid the pitfall of mentally equating each figure type with an age group. Often your age will have very little to do with your overall appearance. Young people can have the very well-developed, full figures mistakenly associated only with maturity. Concurrently, older people can be as slight and trim as the smallest of teenagers.

Figure types are the product of measurements, and measurements only. Forget about your birthday, and take the word of your tape measure—keep in mind that honesty is the best policy!

Butterick figure types can help considerably in pattern selection. Pattern styles for each figure type are those that would be most attractive on such a figure.

Getting in the swing of figure types is easy once you see how much they can help in selecting pattern styles that make the most of you. After all, who in her right mind could ignore such a good thing?

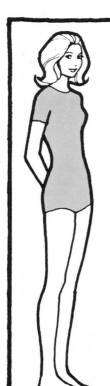

MISSES': The classic feminine figure type, misses' patterns are designed for a well-proportioned and well-developed figure whose height without shoes is 5'5"-5'6".

Misses' patterns run the full gamut, design-wise. As a rule, she can wear most designs, because it has often been her proportions that have inspired fashion designers in the first place.

Dresses, Blouses, Jackets, and Coats

Size	6	8	10	12	14	16	18	20
Bust	30½	31½	32½	34	36	38	40	42
Waist	23	24	25	26½	28	30	32	34
Hip	32½	33½	34½	36	38	40	42	44
Back Waist Length	15½	15¾	16	16¼	16½	16¾	17	17¼

Skirts and Pants

	6	8	10	12	14	16	18	20
Waist	23	24	25	26½	28	30	32	34
Hip	32½	33½	34½	36	38	40	42	44

MISS PETITE: A shorter version of the classic miss, the miss petite figure is a well-proportioned and well-developed figure whose height without shoes is about 5′2″-5′4″.

Patterns for miss petite are designed by Butterick to enhance the smallness of her figure. Lines are flattering and won't cut across a short figure in exactly the wrong place.

Dresses, Blouses, Jackets, and Coats

Size	6mp	8mp	10mp	12mp	14mp	16mp
Bust	30½	31½	32½	34	36	38
Waist	23½	24½	25½	27	28½	30½
Hip	32½	33½	34½	36	38	40
Back Waist Length	14½	14¾	15	15¼	15½	15¾

Skirts and Pants

	6mp	8mp	10mp	12mp	14mp	16mp
Waist	23½	24½	25½	27	28½	30½
Hip	32½	33½	34½	36	38	40

JUNIOR: The junior figure can be described as trim. She's well-proportioned, but lacks the fullness of figure and height of her miss counterpart. Without shoes, she stands about 5′4″-5′5″ in height.

Patterns for the junior figure are designed with her trimness and shorter proportions in mind. Soft and spare clothes make the most of a figure that's lean and active.

Dresses, Blouses, Jackets, and Coats

Size	5	7	9	11	13	15
Bust	30	31	32	33½	35	37
Waist	22½	23½	24½	25½	27	29
Hip	32	33	34	35½	37	39
Back Waist Length	15	15¼	15½	15¾	16	16¼

Skirts and Pants

	5	7	9	11	13	15
Waist	22½	23½	24½	25½	27	29
Hip	32	33	34	35½	37	39

JUNIOR PETITE: A shorter version of the junior figure, junior petite is well-proportioned, but tiny. She's trim, like the junior figure, and her height without shoes is about 5'-5'1".

Junior petite is pretty mini. Butterick has seen to it that patterns designed for her are especially appropriate for tiny figures. Design lines are located where they'll make the most of a small body and often have just enough curve to add a bit of extra femininity, too.

Dresses, Blouses, Jackets, and Coats

Size	3jp	5jp	7jp	9jp	11jp	13jp
Bust	30½	31	32	33	34	35
Waist	22½	23	24	25	26	27
Hip	31½	32	33	34	35	36
Back Waist Length	14	14¼	14½	14¾	15	15¼

Skirts and Pants

	3jp	5jp	7jp	9jp	11jp	13jp
Waist	22½	23	24	25	26	27
Hip	31½	32	33	34	35	36

YOUNG JUNIOR/TEEN: Here's a group of sizes that are specially designed to correspond to developing pre-teen and teen figures. The young junior/teen is about 5'1"-5'3" tall without shoes.

Butterick designs clothes for the young junior/teen figure that are young, and fun. There are lots of simple styles—easy-to-make things that can be stitched together real fast for a great with-it look.

Dresses, Blouses, Jackets, and Coats

Size	5/6	7/8	9/10	11/12	13/14	15/16
Bust	28	29	30½	32	33½	35
Waist	22	23	24	25	26	27
Hip	31	32	33½	35	36½	38
Back Waist Length	13½	14	14½	15	15⅜	15¾

Skirts and Pants

	5/6	7/8	9/10	11/12	13/14	15/16
Waist	22	23	24	25	26	27
Hip	31	32	33½	35	36½	38

WOMEN'S: Butterick patterns for women are designed for a fully developed, larger figure. Without shoes, she is about 5'5"-5'6" in height.

Slenderizing is the design goal of women's patterns. All the newest, greatest fashion ideas are incorporated into these patterns in a way that flatters the larger figure.

Dresses, Blouses, Jackets, and Coats

Size	38	40	42	44	46	48	50
Bust	42	44	46	48	50	52	54
Waist	35	37	39	41½	44	46½	49
Hip	44	46	48	50	52	54	56
Back Waist Length	17¼	17⅜	17½	17⅝	17¾	17⅞	18

Skirts and Pants

Waist	35	37	39	41½	44	46½	49
Hip	44	46	48	50	52	54	56

HALF SIZE: This group of sizes is planned for a fully developed figure whose back measurement from neck to waist is shorter than the women's figure. Her waist and hip measurements are larger in proportion to her bust than other figure types. She is about 5'2"-5'3" tall without shoes.

Patterns for the half size figure are designed to lengthen and slenderize her short figure. Butterick uses lines and proportion to make the most of verticality in clothes.

Dresses, Blouses, Jackets, and Coats

Size	10½	12½	14½	16½	18½	20½	22½	24½
Bust	33	35	37	39	41	43	45	47
Waist	27	29	31	33	35	37½	40	42½
Hip	35	37	39	41	43	45½	48	50½
Back Waist Length	15	15¼	15½	15¾	15⅞	16	16⅛	16¼

Skirt and Pants

Waist	27	29	31	33	35	37½	40	42½
Hip	35	37	39	41	43	45½	48	50½

GIRLS': Here are patterns especially sized for the girl who hasn't yet begun to mature. Her height is incorporated into the size chart, because this is usually directly proportional to her other dimensions.

Designs are simple and youthful versions of today's fashion trends. They range from sturdy playclothes, to coats and jackets, to the kinds of feminine dresses little girls just love. They're easy-to-sew things that can be stitched up quick-as-a-wink.

Size	7	8	10	12	14
Breast	26	27	28½	30	32
Waist	23	23½	24½	25½	26½
Hip	27	28	30	32	34
Back Waist Length	11½	12	12¾	13½	14¼
Approx. Heights	50	52	56	58½	61

CHILDREN'S: Sizes incorporate measurements and height because the two are usually inter-related in children. Children's patterns are designed for the elementary school age youngster who is more mature than a toddler, but who hasn't yet reached the pre-teen years.

Butterick has designed everything for children from sturdy playclothes to school clothes to party clothes—a complete wardrobe that can be sewn fast and effortlessly.

Size	1	2	3	4	5	6	6X
Breast	20	21	22	23	24	25	25½
Waist	19½	20	20½	21	21½	22	22½
Hip				24	25	26	26½
Back Waist Length	8¼	8½	9	9½	10	10½	10¾
Approx. Heights	31	34	37	40	43	46	48
Dress Lengths from Back Neck Base to Lower Edge	17	18	19	20	22	24	25

TODDLERS': Here are pattern sizes especially for that in-between baby and child stage of growth. Patterns are designed with easy sewing and comfortable wearing in mind. Butterick designs offer great mini-fashion for even the youngest child.

Size	½	1	2	3	4
Breast	19	20	21	22	23
Waist	19	19½	20	20½	21
Dress Lengths from Back Neck Base to Lower Edge	14	15	16	17	18
Approximate Height	28	31	34	37	40

MEN'S: Patterns for men are planned for a figure of average build who stands about 5'10" tall without shoes. Butterick tracks down the latest looks on the menswear fashion scene to design patterns for all of the casual clothes and suits your man could possibly need.

Size	34	36	38	40	42	44	46	48
Chest	34	36	38	40	42	44	46	48
Waist	28	30	32	34	36	39	42	44
Hip (Seat)	35	37	39	41	43	45	47	49
Neckband	14	14½	15	15½	16	16½	17	17½
Sleeve Length	32	32	33	33	34	34	35	35

BOYS' AND TEEN-BOYS': Here are size ranges planned for boys and young men who haven't reached adult stature. Height is incorporated in the pattern size because it's usually directly related to circumference measurements. Butterick offers a complete wardrobe for boys—school clothes, sleepwear, playwear, and even dress-up clothes.

Size	BOYS'				TEEN-BOYS'			
	7	**8**	**10**	**12**	**14**	**16**	**18**	**20**
Chest	26	27	28	30	32	33½	35	36½
Waist	23	24	25	26	27	28	29	30
Hip (Seat)	27	28	29½	31	32½	34	35½	37
Neck	11¾	12	12½	13	13½	14	14½	15
Approximate Height	48	50	54	58	61	64	66	68

PATTERN SELECTION

After charting your measurements and determining your figure type, you will have all the information needed to select the right pattern size. Remember that pattern sizes have been based on a standardized, numerically average figure.

Your personal measurements probably won't correspond exactly to all of the measurements listed under one size and figure type. The pattern size that you should choose is the one with measurements that most closely match your own.

If your figure type seems to be a combination of two or more, take a minute to analyze your body structure. Is your figure long or short? Is it slender or full? Is your bone structure small, medium, or large?

Combine this self-analysis with your understanding of figure types to select the Butterick pattern size that is just perfect for you. Take your time —it's no easy task to make such a decision, and a wrong guess could end up being a very sad and expensive mistake.

The next step in the pattern selection game is a leap into fashion. Tab dividers tell you what's in each section of the Butterick catalog; figure types and general garment categories are indicated on the tabs. All you have to do is decide what kind of clothing you'd like to make, and turn to that category for your figure type. Couldn't be any easier!

A word to the wise: never treat your pattern catalog like a smorgasbord! Picking and choosing your most favorite designs from each section devoted to a figure type could very likely result in a disastrous sewing experience.

A marvelous guide toward achieving flattering fashion and superb fit, figure types can only do their job well if you type yourself accurately, and then abide by the results when selecting patterns.

Another big consideration is the time and energy you're prepared to spend on a sewing project. Size, figure type, and style are an important part of the sewing scene, but unless you realize the extent of the task you've set for yourself, the results could be tragic.

In addition to an extensive collection of regular and specialty patterns—including some for accessories and costumes—Butterick offers **Sew and Go** extra easy patterns, **Easy** patterns, patterns that are **Great for Knits**, patterns by **Young Designers**, and **Young America Creates** patterns. A complete menu to tempt every sewing palate! Keep your taste and ambition in mind as you select.

Pattern picking is great fun when you use the proper information, your own good sense and fashion judgement, and Butterick's resources. Be a browser—but an educated one! The Butterick catalog is just loaded with fashion information. The latest fabrics and accessories are right there, along with the designs themselves. Consider you, your wardrobe, your way of living, and Butterick's way with patterns.

YOUR PATTERN HAS A MESSAGE

Good things come in small packages—your Butterick pattern is no exception. In fact, the small package itself—the pattern envelope—is no small part of Butterick's beautiful way to sew.

The envelope which contains your pattern is printed all over—both front and back—with lots of important information. Read it thoroughly, because everything is there for a reason.

THE ENVELOPE FRONT

The headline spells fashion—from Butterick to you. Besides being designed to inspire you to new heights of sewing creativity, the envelope front quickly identifies the pattern and makes it easy to find in those endlessly filled drawers in the store.

1 BUTTERICK: This is our name and your assurance of great fashion and smooth sewing.

2 STYLE NUMBER AND PRICE: In the upper right corner is the information you'll need in order to purchase the pattern for the style you chose in the catalog.

3 SIZE AND BUST MEASUREMENT: Here's a last-minute assurance that the pattern you are buying is the correct size. If yours is a skirt or pants pattern, you'll find waist and hip measurements given instead.

4 FASHION ILLUSTRATION: What made you choose a pattern in the first place? The illustration of the style—colors, variations, and suggested accessories are right there to show you how to make the most of a Butterick fashion.

Butterick illustrates every aspect of a pattern which has multiple views. We want to be sure that you know about all the good things in your pattern envelope.

Style views or versions are lettered so that you can identify them instantly.

Near the fashion illustration, you'll sometimes find a special note from Butterick. **Easy, Sew and Go, Great for Knits**, and **For Knits Only** are some of Butterick's pattern types to meet your sewing needs.

5 BACK VIEWS: Styling and construction details which can't be seen in the illustrated views are diagrammed so that you'll have a complete and accurate impression of the sewing project you're tackling.

6 SIZE RANGE: All sizes in which the pattern is available are listed.

1

Butterick
THE FASHION ONE

2

6195
65c
Canada 85c

3 SIZE 8
BUST 31½

4

great for knits

B

A

5

6   8 10 12 14 16

THE ENVELOPE BACK

Your personal shopping list—on the envelope back you'll find all the information needed to select and purchase fabric and notions. Specific yardage requirements for various fabric widths, garment design features and details, and information having to do with pattern sizes are found here. Your experiences in fabric stores or departments won't ever again be limited to guesswork, or even hesitancy!

1 DESCRIPTIVE CAPTION: Your pattern is identified by style number, figure type, and garment category. The total number of pattern pieces included is also given here. Along with this identifying data is a thorough description of the garment itself—silhouette, intended fit, and views are covered in detail.

2 BODY MEASUREMENTS: Here in capsule form, are the body measurements from which pattern sizes are computed. This is a handy reference for fitting your pattern. Wearing ease and style ease which are a part of the design are included in the pattern pieces, but not in the body measurements.

3 YARDAGE: This is a graphic list of the fabric required for each view of the garment in each pattern size. Yardages are included for the commercial fabric widths which you're likely to be using. Interfacing, lining, and underlining requirements are given when applicable. Yardages for trim and contrast fabric are included when these have been featured in the design. Nap indication for each width tells which yardage can be used for napped fabrics.

4 FABRIC AND DESIGN SUITABILITY: When pattern design lines are such that you won't be able to match the designs of certain fabrics at the seamlines, this is stated as follows: "Striped, plaid, or obvious diagonal fabrics are not suitable."

If plaids or stripes are suitable, your pattern will state "No allowance for matching plaid or stripes" because additional yardage needed varies with the size of the repeat.

5 FABRIC KEY: The abbreviations **w** and **wo** tell you whether or not the indicated yardages are for napped fabrics. In a with nap layout (**w**), pattern pieces are all placed in the same direction. Without nap layouts (**wo**) don't include the extra yardage that's necessary for napped fabrics. Layouts for fabrics both with and without nap are keyed **w/wo**.

6 GARMENT DIMENSIONS: The width at lower edge is a measurement of hem circumference which relates the fullness of the finished garment to you. The finished back length from base of neck, and finished side length from waist are measurements which are the basis for your pattern length adjustments.

7 BUTTERICK PATTERN SERVICE: Here's our address, and the locations of our offices—as you can see, Butterick fashion is world-wide!

8 FABRICS: These are Butterick's fabric selections and recommendations to help you make the most of your pattern and avoid a disappointing finished garment. Not all patterns can be made in any fabric, so only types most suitable for the design are listed.

The quality of softness or crispness is also indicated to help you achieve the intended silhouette.

9 NOTIONS: So that you'll be able to purchase your notions along with your pattern and fabric, all required and optional notions are listed. Recommended sizes of notions complement garment proportion.

10 SKETCH OF PATTERN PIECES: When there is enough room, a numbered illustration of all pattern pieces is included on the envelope back (not shown). For your convenience, this illustration is also found on the instruction sheet.

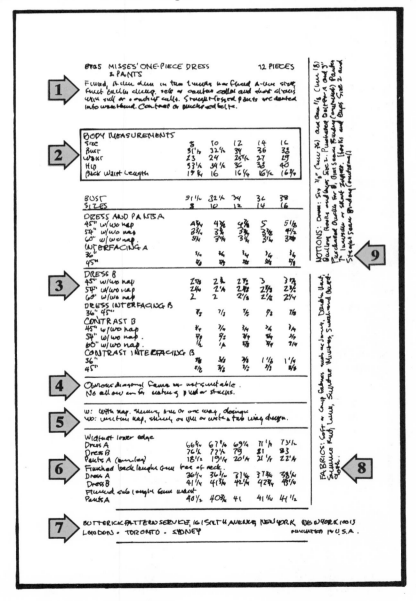

Get Fabric Savvy

Making the Most of Your Money

There you are—enthusiastic, fashion-conscious, and anxious to get busy on a new outfit that will enliven your wardrobe and give you fresh pride in your creativity. You've found the perfect pattern, and your next step—through the door of the fabric shop—is one of the most important in your whole sewing project.

DO YOU LOVE IT?

In so personal a choice, forget the deeper considerations for the time being, and give free rein to your senses.

Let your fashion head—that creative streak that led you to sew in the first place—aim you straight to the fabrics you like. Your feel for fashion was developed from living your life, and no one knows better what's right for you. Trust yourself. The fabric you choose must complement your personality, express your sense of taste, and fit comfortably into your life.

Making something you'll never wear from a wild fabric you love is impractical, but it's just as bad to be lured into the snare of over-conservatism. The tremendous variety of fabrics available enables you to select one which best expresses the real you.

STYLE

The next step is the one that requires the best of your experience and understanding. It's also the most exciting part of do-it-yourself fashion: besides reflecting and boosting your personality, a fabric must enhance and express the design of the pattern you've chosen.

The most exacting sewing job is wasted when droopy fabric tries to hold a crisp, sculpted shape; or when stiff fabric can't drape into a soft gather. You can't do yourself a greater favor than to develop that instinct for matching the right fabric to the right fashion. Thick and shaggy, firm and crisp, or soft and drapey, the fabric you choose must be right for your design.

While the pattern envelope provides some guidelines, the final decision is yours! Toss an end of the fabric over the bolt. Play with it . . . gather it in your hand . . . drape it on your finger. Soft fabrics are fluid—the folds fall in a straight line. Crisp fabrics are a bit rigid and pull into puffy folds.

Test the fabric with inner construction fabrics to get a total picture of the action. Place the fabric on top of the interfacing, lining, or underlining and handle the two fabrics as one to see how they react to each other. Combining a soft fabric with a crisp inner fabric often doesn't work—ridges show through. If the fabric doesn't do what you and the designer want it to do—don't buy it!

QUALITY

Style is a matter of intuition—but quality is a matter of fact. Learning the components of quality will pay off in many ways: you'll know a bargain when you see one, and won't have to use price as a barometer of value. Have the pleasure of sewing on good cloth, and the garment you've made will last as long as you want to wear it.

START NOW: Don't make the sad mistake of thinking that if you're new to sewing, you should "practice" on sleazy fabric. Nothing is more depressing than seeing your first masterpiece (which, to your surprise, turned out beautifully) fall apart in its first washing. Good fabric has some important bonuses—it wears longer, sews more easily, copes with your mistakes a lot better, and doesn't have to cost a lot of money!

Your best economy is a real understanding of what quality is all about. There are good and bad, durable and flimsy fabrics in all price ranges—learning the differences between these is invaluable if your goal is successful sewing.

GAUGES OF QUALITY: Hold a single layer of fabric up to the light. Does the light come through in patches, evenly, or not at all?

Thinner areas of fabric are weaker and wear out quickly. Dense or sheer, the fabric should be of a constant thickness or weight. Even when fabric is by nature slubbed or spun thick and thin, the overall effect must be consistent.

Scratch an edge of the fabric with your fingernail. If the threads shift without much effort, seam slippage will be a problem. Look for a firm, close, secure weave or knit whose threads are stable.

Check for powdery dust on fabric that indicates sizing. This is a type of starch that can be washed out, leaving the fabric limp. Cottons are frequently treated with a sizing.

Crumple a corner of the fabric tightly in your hand. Hold it a few seconds, then release and flatten it out. If it wrinkles easily, it may be one of those that will be unsightly after a very short period of wearing. Look for fabrics treated with wrinkle-resistant finishes.

Take a long critical look at the color. Some garish chemical dyes shout "cheap!" Look for bright colors that are subtle and pastels that are low-key. Train your eye to look for colors with an interesting flavor. Whether brilliant or soft, at an expensive or a pin-money price, the color of your fabric should proclaim good taste.

Rub both sides of the fabric against one of a contrasting color. Do tiny fibers come off? Sometimes fabrics are "filled" by forcing loose fibers into them; this makes them appear to be of better quality than they are. Filled fibers will eventually come out; they are a linty nuisance and leave behind a loosely-woven, weak fabric.

Hold the fabric up on your index finger. Stiff and scratchy or sloppy and limp is not beautiful . . . quality fabric, no matter how soft or crisp, falls in rich, smooth folds and feels good. You'll develop this sixth sense automatically, just from loving to touch fabrics. Maybe that's why you sew in the first place!

HOW WILL IT ACT?

In fabric selection, a lot of invisible factors come into play and should be carefully considered before making your final decision that will send the saleslady's scissors slicing across the bolt.

Think of fabric as a material to be sculpted. It has built-in character that is responsible for its behavior. The more you know about the origins of fabric, the more you'll understand this behavior.

LABEL

Each fascinating step in the creation of fabric is a clue to the simple things that add up to "performance." Your bridge to solving the mystery is the label. Respect it—because it tells you the whole story. Look for it—because without its information you may arrive home knowing little more about your fabric than its color and texture.

Labels help you figure out how to clean or press your fabric, guide

your choice of thread, and let you know how well wrinkles, rain, or stains from spaghetti sauce can be shed. The Federal Trade Commission, in the Fiber Products Identification Act, rules that a fabric label must contain this information:

- **Fiber content:** The generic name (not a trademark) of the fiber.
- **Component proportions:** Percentage by weight of each fiber which makes up more than 5% of a blend.
- **Manufacturer:** Name and address, or identification number.
- **Country of origin:** Where from, if not U.S.A.

All too often labels get lost in the shuffle of store merchandise. If you don't see it on an accessible hangtag, or written on or tucked into the end of the bolt, ask a salesperson. You have a right to the information, and knowing that you are interested keeps retailers on their toes.

Usually a manufacturer who is proud of his product prominently displays the facts about it. Many consumer protection agencies encourage manufacturers to go even further than the law requires, listing specific instruction about care, finish, and cloth construction.

Fabric manufacturers who are concerned with consumer relations often take great pains to list explicit instructions for the care of their product. They tell you whether to wash or dry clean the fabric, whether it can be bleached, how it is best dried, and whether it should be pressed. In cases where temperature may have a damaging effect on the fabric, you will usually find that the recommended wash temperatures, dryer heat settings, and iron fabric settings are also listed. As you can see, caring for fabric is a breeze if you buy labeled goods.

CARE & DURABILITY

Your creation may be a simple shift, a kicky party culotte, or a complicated suit, but it will need care and upkeep in its life as a member of your wardrobe. Some clothes are almost care-free—they're a breeze to wash and tumble-dry, and they scoff at ironing. Others demand and are worth special care. It's a pleasure to press these luxury fabrics as many times as you wear the garment. What makes the difference?

A delicate fabric is a bad choice for a sliding-down-the-bannisters jumpsuit, and a "dry-clean only" white crepe would never do for a shirt you'll want to use with everything. There are two reasons why slacks for gardening need to be of sterner stuff than the dress for the PTA. Dirt means laundry—if a dry cleanable fabric is light-colored or worn very often, it may mean break-ing into the piggy bank for the cleaning bills. Constant rough wear means wearing out, unless the weight and strength of the fabric are equal to the treatment it will get.

Some of your wardrobe is for keeps and is made up of the all-time classics that you depend on and wear constantly. These working sturdys have to be of long-wearing stuff, and deserve the strongest fabric you can find. Buying poor quality inexpensive goods for this kind of garment is false economy.

In many towns you can find department stores or a branch of a chain store that has a fairly complete fabric department. Anyway, for a fabric that will be a wardrobe mainstay, don't begrudge the few extra pennies it may cost for the best . . . remember how much you save by sewing!

Now, project yourself into the kind of service you'll ask of your fabric. It's not always true that the best available fabric will be the right choice for your purpose. One of the reasons everyone sews is for those mad, exciting, special-occasion clothes that make you feel smashing and are worn only on the most festive days of the year.

Sewing lets you take advantage of fly-by-night fashion while bringing it down to an affordable level. If you know you'll only use a dress a few times, it doesn't have to be of fabric that wears like iron. Fashion fabrics aren't always durable—but then, they don't always have to be.

CAN YOU LIVE WITH IT?

When a sewing project enters your life, it either finds a happy home or gives you problems. If you don't plan ahead, you can easily flip into a whim that spells sewing or wardrobe disaster. Consider the fab-

ric in terms of how it fits into your past sewing experience and your future wardrobe plans.

KNOW YOUR TIME— AND SKILLS

What kind of seamstress are you? Do you love spending the extra concentration involved in a hard-to-sew fabric, or would you rather have a new thing to wear in a flash? In your enthusiasm for great plaids and stripes, don't ever forget that they take extra time and care for matching. Do you want to spend it?

Can you feel confident enough of your sewing skills to take a chance on that new fake fur or vinyl, or should you stick to the great fabrics that don't need special handling for a little more practice? Don't shy away from the difficult-to-sew things, because that's the way to learn. Just remember that every new technique takes time to master.

One of the common time-consuming sewing snags is off-grain fabric. Wovens or knits can be enough askew that they need a lot of straightening—you might even find yourself wrestling with one that you'd have hesitated to buy if you had noticed the problem in the store.

Off-grain prints are a layout nightmare; noticing the problem before buying fabric saves you a lot of time and nervous energy.

Off-grain bonding doesn't usually spell garment catastrophe, but can be a sewing nuisance since the correct grain (direction of threads) isn't visible from the wrong side. Keep these factors in mind as you can evaluate the kind of project each fabric would be to sew. Refer to pages 119-121 for more information about grain.

WARDROBE WIZARDRY

Before you decide on this new tenant in your closet, make sure it has some friends. The best-dressed people have a plan—a system of co-ordinating colors, accessories, and purpose. When they bring home an imaginative new fabric whim there's no second-thought discovery that only an entirely new wardrobe can make it usable. Plan details like shoes, belts, coats, tops, or bottoms. Really wearable clothes go with more than one thing.

Are you planning a whole outfit? Coordinate it with clothes you already own, so the parts will be interchangeable. Stay clear of color monotony, however; vivid contrast is often more exciting than a perfect match.

Clothes are usually a seasonal thing. List clothes and categories for a certain season and consider your fabric needs in light of temperature. Clothes for work must be comfortable in an office environment—if it's "climate controlled" it may be cooler in summer than in winter! Don't break out the woolies, only to swelter; keep clothes practical. Careful planning is an easy route to an efficient, custom-designed wardrobe.

One of the best ways to sort out the wardrobe dilemma is to keep a small scrapbook or envelope of snips taken from inside seams and leftover cuttings of all your important clothes. Carry this record with you all the time; when you run across that gorgeous sale fabric that you're pretty certain would be a perfect match for your favorite red blouse, you'll know for sure.

Memory plays tricks when it comes to matching colors, and in clothes that are supposed to match, a near miss is major catastrophe. Besides, you may own a skirt that you'd forgotten about because it's been so long since you had anything to go with it; a tiny scrap will nudge your memory just when you can do something about it—in the fabric shop. A greater budget-stretcher never existed! Besides, think of the fun of having a really workable wardrobe.

As you probably have already guessed, the major step in getting together a great wardrobe is really devoting some time and thought to the matter. Creativity, interest, self-expression, and economy don't just happen! With fashion knowledge under your belt, you're ready to pick up a little fabric knowledge.

Turn On To Fabric

Just like people, fabrics are a combination of heredity and environment. There's an art to understanding cloth, and the more you know about it the greater pleasure it can give you. Here's the life history of fabrics—a breakdown of the basic facts from the point of view of what you need to know.

WHAT'S THE STORY?

The initial muddle of fabrics—identification, this new finish, that new knit, another new fiber—is enough to scare you away from the whole thing. Bè not dismayed! The mystery is solved when you understand a few facts about the process of creating cloth. Fibers are made into yarns, and then yarns are made into fabrics which in turn are finished and ready for you.

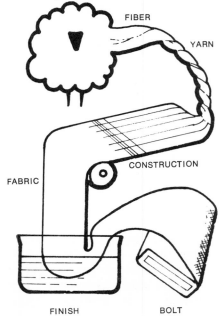

All things considered, the production of fabrics is relatively easy-to-understand once you're tuned in.

NAMES

What's most confusing about fabrics is the vast number of terms. There's a boom going on in the textile field and every day new formulas and processes are invented for fibers, yarns, fabrics, and finishes. New names for these are invented and patented, to add to the assortment that may already have your head spinning.

The key to term troubles is understanding the difference between **trademarks** and **generic names.** Orlon® is DuPont's registered trademark for an acrylic fiber, and Acrilan® is Monsanto's trademark for an acrylic fiber. They are essentially the same thing, because they belong to the same generic fiber category—acrylics.

Trademarks exist for all stages of fabric creation. Qiana® refers to the fiber, Fluflon® to the yarn, Lutesong® to the fabric, and Scotchgard® to the finish. Look on the label for the tiny line of type which tells you what the trademark means.

FIBERS

The soul or basic component of fabric is fiber. Its characteristics are the ones that affect every stage of the fabric's future. A fiber is actually a piece of matter that is many times longer than it is wide; it can be from 1½″ to hundreds of yards long. Each fiber type imparts a different quality to the cloth you buy, because each has different properties. These can be altered slightly by yarn, fabric, and finishing, but the personality of the fiber will always be evident in the final fabric.

There are two types of fiber—natural and man-made. Natural fibers—cotton, flax, wool, and silk are the most familiar—have the irregularities and subtleties inherent in natural things that give an unmistakeable character to fabrics made of them.

COTTON

Plant fibers, animal fur, minerals, and the fine threads used by silk worms to make winter homes are perfect raw materials for fabrics. People have used them since learning the craft of weaving several thousand years ago.

Recently, a new category of fibers has appeared—they come from test tubes and are called man-made. Forcing a fiber solution through tiny holes into a chemical bath or air chamber hardens it into a fiber. The resulting rope contains many fibers that can be processed into almost anything.

One kind of fiber can be changed in many ways by adding things to either the solution or the hardening bath or by changing the shape of the holes. Variations are practically limitless.

Since the creation of rayon, synthetic fibers have constantly been improved—today they feel beautiful, look smart, and behave with perfect manners. Fabric types are infinite and increasing, and the variations of each type have created a revolution in textiles. Sewing itself has moved into a new dimension as a result of this.

The following chart lists the characteristics, care requirements, and fabrics typical of each fiber group. The generic names for synthetic fibers are set by the Federal Trade Commission. Though each trademarked fiber varies slightly from others of its category, the members of a generic group must all have certain common chemical characteristics. This means that they will demand similiar care.

The most familiar trademarks and their owners are given for each of the man-made fibers. With the exception of triacetate—chemically a member of the acetate family, but with characteristics different enough to merit separate listing—all the types shown are the generic classifications according to the U.S. Government's definitions. Although there are a few other fibers, we have included only those ordinarily available in fashion fabrics for garment use.

Generally, fabrics composed of two or more fibers are cared for according to the directions for the dominant one. Blending several fibers is a great way to give the fabric the advantages of each.

THE NATURALS

Fiber And Fabric	Care
Cotton: Comes in many weights, textures, and constructions. Has considerable strength which increases when wet. Doesn't pill or slip. Comfortable, non-clinging, dyes well, and can be colorfast. Subject to wrinkling, shrinking, and damage from mildew and sunlight. Examples: organdy, broadcloth, poplin, terry, corduroy, seersucker, denim, tweed.	Wash 10 minutes in hot water at regular speed with heavy-duty detergent. Can use chlorine bleach on white cottons, but some finishes may react by turning yellow (see label). Fabric softener will reduce wrinkling. Tumble dry on regular heat setting; don't overdry. Press with hot iron while damp until completely dry or use a steam iron with a slightly dampened press cloth.
Linen: Sheer, medium, or heavyweight fabrics. Durable, lustrous, strong, stiff, comfortable, and lint-free. Colors may bleed when wet. Wrinkles, shrinks, and is subject to damage from mildew, but not moths.	Usually dry cleaned, but launders well if pre-shrunk. Wash 5-8 minutes in hot water at regular speed with heavy-duty detergent. Can use chlorine bleach but over-bleaching may weaken the fiber. Tumble dry on regular heat setting, but remove and iron while still very damp. Iron at high setting (unless treated with special finishes; see label). For maximum durability, creases should be finger pressed rather than ironed into the garment.
Silk: Sheer, medium, or heavyweight fabrics. Fine, yet strong, comfortable, and wrinkle resistant. Many cling; dyes well, but may bleed. Yellows and fades with age or when exposed to strong soap or high heat. Resists mildew and moths. Examples: crepe, brocade, chiffon, satin, jersey, tweed.	Usually dry cleaned. If marked washable, use mild suds in lukewarm water; or machine wash for 3 minutes at gentle speed. Don't use chlorine bleach. Tumble dry at low heat setting for a short time or hang to dry; avoid prolonged exposure to light. Iron on wrong side while damp with a low heat setting or use a steam iron; silk is easily water spotted, so protect the fabric with a press cloth.
Wool: Comes in many weights, textures, and unique constructions. Retains shape well and can be molded by heat and pressure. Dyes well and is wrinkle resistant, comfortable, and warm. Shrinks, pills, and is weakened by abrasion, wetness, and sunlight. Subject to damage from mildew and moths. Examples: tweed, knits, gabardine, flannel, jersey, melton, fleece.	Usually dry cleaned; brush between cleanings. For hand washables, use mild suds and cool water; or machine wash for 2 minutes at gentle speed (interrupt the agitation time for 10 minutes to let the fabric soak, then complete the cycle). Don't tumble dry; block to shape on a flat surface away from heat. If labeled "machine wash-and-dry," wash 3-8 minutes in warm water at gentle speed with mild soap. Tumble dry at regular heat setting but remove while slightly damp. Never use chlorine bleach; it will weaken and yellow the fibers. Press gently on the wrong side; use a warm iron and damp press cloth or a steam iron.

THE MAN-MADES

Fiber And Fabric	Care
Acetate: Silk-like, soft, lustrous, moderately comfortable, and warm. Takes and holds dyes well and resists stretching, shrinking, mildew, and moths. Has low strength and tends to wrinkle, cling, and gas-fade. Is damaged by sunlight. Examples: satin, jersey, lace, taffeta, brocade, tricot, crepe, faille, and blends with other man-made fibers. Trademarks: Acele□□, Avicolor△△, Avisco△△, Celanese★★, Celaperm★★, Celara★★, Chromspun♦♦, Estron♦♦.	Usually dry cleaned. If washable, use mild suds and warm or cold water at gentle speed for 3 minutes. Tumble dry at cool setting for short time or hang to dry away from heat. To hand wash, gently squeeze suds through fabric; rinse in lukewarm water. Iron on the wrong side while damp. Use light pressure and lowest temperature; a hot iron may melt the fabric. To iron on the right side, use a press cloth and steam iron. Always place brown paper between the garment and seam allowances or darts. Never use acetone (nail polish remover) or other organic solvents to remove spots.
Acrylic: Usually used in soft, fluffy fabrics. Lightweight, wrinkle resistant, quick-drying, and strong. Retains its shape, dyes well, and is colorfast; resists mildew, moths, chemicals, and sunlight. Can be damaged by excessive heat. May pill and cling. Examples: knits, fleece, pile fabrics, fake fur, and fabric blends of natural and man-made fibers. Trademarks: Acrilan•••, Creslan•, Orlon□□, Zefkrome••, Zefran••.	Remove oily stains before cleaning. Dry-clean, or launder for 3-5 minutes. For sturdy fabrics, use regular agitation with heavy-duty detergent. For delicate fabrics, use gentle agitation with mild suds or hand wash; use warm water (for bright colors, use cool water). Use fabric softener in rinse. Gently squeeze out water. Chlorine bleach may be used for white fabrics. Tumble dry at low heat setting or dry flat. Seldom requires ironing if removed from dryer as soon as the cycle is completed; otherwise, use low heat setting, never hot, and iron on wrong side.
Metallic: Gold, silver, and colors in decorative yarns used in blended fabrics and trims. Non-tarnishing if plastic-coated. Not affected by chlorinated or salt water, or climatic conditions. Trademark: Lurex••	Laundered or drycleaned if plastic coated. Iron at low setting. Mylar polyester covering withstands heat better than acetate covering.
Modacrylic: Usually in pile fabrics. Non-allergenic, quick-drying, and retains shape well. Resists wrinkles, moths, mildew, chemicals, flame, and sunlight. Can be damaged by excessive heat, and may cling. Examples: pile fabrics, fleece, and fake fur. Trademarks: Dynel♦♦♦, Verel♦♦.	Have a furrier clean fur-like garments; other fabrics may be dry cleaned or laundered. If washable, follow directions for acrylics. If ironing is necessary, use lowest temperature to prevent stiffening or glazing. Finger press fake furs. Do not use acetone to remove spots.
Nylon: Comes in many textures, weights, and constructions. Strong, elastic, easily washed, quick-drying, and warm. Holds dyes well; texture or shape can be heat-set. Resists wrinkling, moths, mildew, and non-oily stains. Fades in sunlight, pills, and melts under high heat. Trademarks: Antron□□, Blue C•••, Caprolan★, Cedilla★★, Celanese★★, Enkalure□, Qiana□□, Touch★.	Remove oily stains, then machine wash for 3-5 minutes (regular agitation for sturdy fabrics, gentle agitation for delicate fabrics). Use warm water (for bright colors, use cool water). Wash whites separately, and bleach to prevent yellowing. A fabric softener in the rinse will reduce tendency to cling. Drip, or tumble dry on wash and wear setting. Hand wash delicate items in warm water; rinse well. May not require ironing if removed from dryer immediately. Otherwise, use low temperature and iron on the wrong side.

Fiber And Fabric	Care
Olefin: Wool-like, waxy, lightweight; adapts to textured, bulky yarns. Resists wrinkling, shrinking, pilling, staining, insects, and dyeing. Non-allergenic and quick-drying; damaged by excessive heat. Examples: pile fabrics, fake fur. Trademarks: Herculon★★★, Marvess□□□.	Machine wash in lukewarm water; add a fabric softener to final rinse. Drip dry or machine-dry on very low setting; remove at end of cycle. Iron on lowest possible temperature setting, or not at all. Stains can be blotted away with absorbent tissue. Do not dry clean.
Polyester: Comes in many weights, textures, and constructions. Strong, quick-drying, warm, and colorfast; resists wrinkles, abrasion, stretching, shrinking, mildew, and moths. May pill, yellow, cling, and attract lint. Occasional seam slippage. Retains heat-set pleats and creases. Examples: permanent press fabrics, knits. Trademarks: Avlin△△, Blue C●●●, Dacron□□, Encron□, Fortrel★★, Kodel♦♦, Quintess□□□, Trevira○○○, Vycron△.	Remove oily stains before cleaning. Machine wash for 3-5 minutes (regular agitation for sturdy fabrics, and gentle agitation for delicate fabrics). Use warm water (for bright colors use cool water). Rinse well; a fabric softener in the rinse water reduces tendency to cling. Chlorine bleach can be used for whites before the spin cycle; others can be tumble dried at wash and wear or low setting. May not require ironing if removed from dryer immediately. Otherwise, use a medium-warm setting or steam iron.
Rayon: Comes in many weights, textures, and constructions. Soft, comfortable, warm, takes dyes well, and is colorfast. Has low strength and is subject to mildew, wrinkling, shrinking, stretching, and sunlight. Trademarks: Avicolor♦, Avril△△, Bemberg○, Coloray○○, Cupioni△, Englo□, Enkrome□, Zantrel□.	Usually dry cleaned; wetness will weaken, ravel, or shrink fabric. If washable, use mild detergent in warm water at gentle speed for 3-5 minutes. When hand washing, use mild lukewarm suds, gently squeeze them through fabric, rinse in lukewarm water. Never wring or twist. Do not soak colored fabrics. Chlorine bleaches can be used; but some finishes may be sensitive to chlorine bleach. Tumble dry or hang to dry away from sunlight. Iron while damp on wrong side. A moderate temperature will prevent shine.
Spandex: Lightweight, stretchable, strong, durable, quick-drying, resistant to oily stains. Yellows in sunlight. Trademark: Lycra□□.	Hand or machine wash in warm water for 3 minutes with gentle agitation. Do not use chlorine bleach. Rinse well. Drip dry or tumble dry at cool setting. Don't over-dry. Iron at a low temperature.
Triacetate: Resists wrinkling and shrinking. Shape and texture can be heat-set. Clings, but may have an anti-static finish. Takes dyes well and is colorfast. Has low strength and washes easily. Examples: tricot, sharkskin, flannel, taffeta, and blends. Trademark: Arnel★★.	Machine wash and tumble dry. Permanently pleated garments should be hand washed and hung to dry. Usually requires ironing; can withstand higher temperature than acetate. Do not use acetone (nail polish remover) or any other organic solvent to remove spots.

TRADEMARKS

★	Allied Chemical	★★	Celanese	★★★	Hercules
○	American Bemberg	○○	Courtaulds	○○○	Hystron
●	American Cyanamid	●●	Dow Badische	●●●	Monsanto
□	American Enka	□□	DuPont	□□□	Phillips
♦	American Mfg. Co.	♦♦	Eastman Chemical	♦♦♦	Union Carbide
△	Beaunit	△△	FMC Corp., Amer. Viscose Div.		

YARNS

All kinds of yarn—from the bulky kind grandmothers use, to some that are thinner than sewing thread—go into the manufacture of fabrics. Yarn gives fabric two important characteristics—texture and strength. It must be carefully designed and chosen so that it will impart exactly the right properties to the fabric. Yarn can be made from two forms of fibers—staple and filament.

Staple refers to fibers less than 12″ long that must be spun or twisted together to build a long strand of yarn. This usually makes yarns that feel fuzzy because they have tiny fiber ends. All natural fibers but silk exist only in staple form because animal hair and plant fibers are limited in length.

Filament is fiber as it is unreeled from the cocoon of the silk worm, or as it is extruded from a chemical solution. These are always many yards long and, in the case of the man-mades, may even be of unlimited length.

Several filaments form a **yarn** when twisted together; or, they can be chopped into staple lengths and spun to imitate natural fibers. **Ply yarn** is formed when two or more yarns are twisted together.

Woolen yarn is made from wool fibers that have not been aligned and combed. Worsted yarn is crisper and is made from longer combed wool fibers.

Fabrics with an interesting feel or hand often get it from the yarn. The oldest ways to give texture to yarn are by varying the twist or composing a multiple ply yarn of several textures twisted together.

New ways to give yarns an exciting touch are the result of the modern fiber technology. Texture can be imparted to man-made fibers by the use of a heat-setting process. The filament is actually slightly melted and given a three-dimensional coil or crimp that changes the way it feels. This often results in added body and stretch.

The strength of the yarn determines how a fabric will wear. Yarns with longer fibers, smooth construction, and/or higher twist will be stronger. Crisp worsted gabardine wears better than lumpy boucle of similar weight and quality, because novelty yarns are seldom strong.

FABRICS

Preparation of fiber and yarn are preliminaries. The birth of a fabric is actually marked by its construction. Creative sewing depends on your sensitivity to fabrics—the best way to understand what fabrics can do for you is to know a bit about how they're put together.

The millions of variations in fabric style and structure are easily sorted into a few basic types. Study a little scrap; pull at a thread and try to take it apart. What you can't tell by feeling, learn to know by looking.

If the surface is textured, is it created by textured yarn, by brushing the fabric surface, or by extra fibers rising from the ground fabric? If the surface confuses the issue, look at the back for a clue. Are there really two attached layers? If so, can you separate them, or are they held together by threads? Remember to ignore the color—that counts as decoration, not structure.

The main factor that will affect sewing is **grain.** How the yarns lie determines grain, and grain, in turn, determines how the fabric handles and drapes. Grain refers to the relationship of the yarns to each other, their thickness, density, and direction. Pull the fabric in all directions, including the diagonal. Does it stretch? If so, how much?

Grain is established in the construction of fabric, but can be distorted before it gets to you. The line that indicates the crosswise grain must be at right angles to the lengthwise grain indicated by the finished edge. Loosely constructed fabric—one in which the yarns aren't closely packed—is more flexible and tends to droop more than firm fabric.

WEAVING: If you can pull a single thread straight across an edge of your scrap, leaving a fringe, it was made by weaving. No matter what's going on the surface of the fabric, its foundation is formed by threads coming together at right angles to each other. The variations all follow this rule and differ only in the plan by which the threads intersect. Thousands have been invented since making cloth became one of Man's most practical art forms.

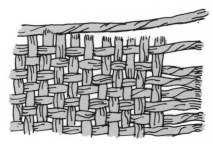

Weaving is done on a loom. The yarns which will form the warp are stretched from the front to the back of the loom. They are raised and lowered by a series of harness frames. A weft, or filling yarn is inserted at right angles to the warp, between the high and low sets of warp yarns.

Each weft will be beaten into position against the previous yarn.

The warp is changed as each weft yarn is drawn through, enfolding the filling yarn in alternating up and down warps, and making the space for the next filling yarn. The selvage is where the filling reverses its direction, forming finished edges along both long edges of the cloth.

Lengthwise grain is the warp threads. They must be strong, smooth, and stable because the warp is under great tension. Lengthwise grain is used in a garment area where strength is needed.

Crosswise grain, or filling, isn't subjected to tension or friction and can be of weaker, softer yarns. It may tend to stretch.

The importance of understanding and carefully checking fabric grain before cutting out garment pieces can't be stressed enough. There have been too many sorry experiences resulting from the pieces of a garment being cut with grainline slightly off the straight grain of the fabric.

The forces of everyday wear, hanging, and gravity take advantage of the fabric and pull the lines of the garment out of shape. Such distortion is hardly the fashion image you'd like to have—especially in an outfit you've made yourself!

Variations in the patterns of up and down warps, and some special gadgets which were invented to complicate weaves are responsible for the many kinds of woven fabrics on the market. Right-angle construction is in part responsible for their quirks; it creates bias which can work for you or give you trouble. True bias is the 45° angle from any straight thread when the warp and weft are at right angles to each other (see page 119). It is the direction in which woven fabrics have the most stretch.

Bias may seem erratic, but it acts as it does for a simple reason: the square spaces between yarns turn into diamond shapes when woven fabric is pulled diagonally. Straight yarns don't go anywhere—they stretch very little when they are pulled in the direction of the grain. But when the fabric is pulled on the bias, it can stretch as much as the yarns will let it.

WEAVING WORDS

basket weave A variation of the plain weave in which paired or multiple yarns are used in the same alternating pattern. Less stability than similar weight plain weaves may cause seams to slip. Examples: oxford cloth, monk's cloth, hopsacking.

dobby weave A patterned weave made by a special loom attachment; a small-figured fabric, usually in a geometric design, is produced. Thick "stuffer" yarns may be used on the back to raise the surface texture. Example: piqué.

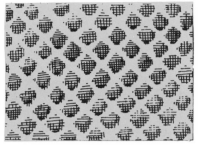

herringbone weave A twill weave in which the diagonal ridges switch direction back and forth, making a zigzag pattern.

jacquard weave A patterned weave made on a special complex loom; programmed by punch cards. Practically any design can be used, including very large repeats and elaborate textures. Examples: brocade, matelassé, damask.

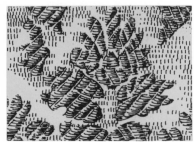

leno weave A lacy and open, yet stable, fabric produced by a spe-

cial attachment which crosses the warp yarns. Example: marquisette.

pile weave Fabric woven by one of several techniques that permit extra yarns or fibers to rise from the surface to form a fuzzy texture. Examples: velvet, terrycloth.

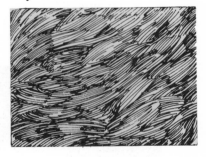

plain weave The simplest weave. Each yarn in both warp and filling goes alternately over, then under one of the cross threads. Basically sturdy, but this can vary with weight and compactness of the yarns. Examples: percale, voile.

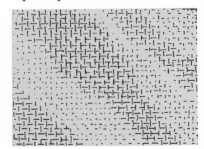

rib weave A plain weave in which the yarns in one direction are thinner or closer together than those in the other. Examples: faille, grosgrain.

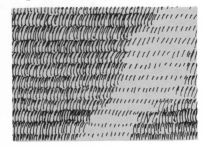

satin weave The weaving structure that produces fabrics with a shiny smooth face. Usually a filament, each warp yarn passes over many filling threads before going under one. Examples: crepe-backed satin, double-faced satin, sateen.

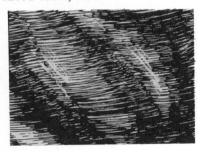

twill weave A strong weave with a pronounced diagonal ridge. Durable because yarns are packed close together. Examples: denim, gabardine.

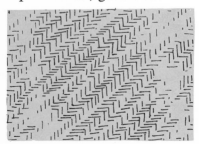

KNITTING: Your fabric is probably a knit if you can't pull a thread out of the scrap, or if it comes out along the crosswise direction in loops without leaving any other lengthwise threads behind. Knits have as many variations as wovens, but they're all made of loops.

Twining in and out of each other in every pattern and direction, the loops hold the fabric together in a strong but flexible construction. They give knits the stretch which accounts for most of the difficulties in sewing them. Each loop opens out when pulled. Some knit constructions control or prevent the movement of the loops by the way they are interlocked, but nearly all of them have some degree of stretch (see Knits, pages 144-147).

Knits have no real bias. They often have more crosswise than diagonal stretch. The main distinction is that between weft knits and warp knits.

Weft knits are put together like hand knitting, with a single continuous yarn that loops its way across the fabric. **Warp knits** are made of many yarns which loop up the fabric in a lengthwise direction.

The knitted version of **grain** is created by a tiny, crochet-like hook that links the loops. You can follow the lengthwise and crosswise yarns pretty easily in a woven fabric, but the grain may be harder to find in knits.

The lengthwise grain is a line called a **wale,** that is made by the action of a single needle forming a continuous row of interlocked loops.

RIGHT SIDE

WRONG SIDE

Crosswise grain is a line called a **course,** that is a row of side by side loops. In weft knitting, the course is formed by a single yarn.

RIGHT SIDE

WRONG SIDE

If a single loop depends on only one loop for support, the knit can run. The run occurs when one loop loses the support of the next one; it in turn releases the one depending on it, and a whole row of loops can be pulled apart. This is less likely in knits of fuzzy fibers like wool.

Complicated machines produce fabric in flat or tubular form. As it comes to you on the bolt, the knit can be distorted in shape, so think about whether it can be straightened. Synthetic knits and knits with permanent finishes are difficult to straighten and may even have a permanent crease where they're folded on the bolt.

KNITTING WORDS

denier A unit of weight which indicates the fineness or coarseness of a fiber filament. The higher the denier number, the coarser the yarn.

double knit A stable form of weft knitting that resists runs. It can be made reversible, or patterned on complex jacquard machinery (see page 144).

gauge The number of knit stitches per 1″ of fabric describes the fineness or coarseness of the knit.

knit A stitch in weft knitting produced by pulling a yarn loop through the front of another loop. Or, any fabric produced by a series of interlocking loops of yarn.

pattern knit A knit fabric having a design created by alternating, dropping, adding, and combining the knit and purl stitches. Usually means a weft knit. Example: fisherman knit sweater.

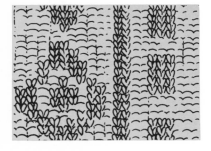

plain knit A simple and familiar weft knit composed of a flat face and a back of short horizontal loops. Called stockinette in hand knitting. Example: jersey (see page 144).

purl Weft knitting stitch in which the yarn is drawn through the back of another loop. Also, a weft knit of alternating horizontal rows of knit and purl stitches. Stretches in both directions and looks like the wrong side of a plain knit.

raschel knit A versatile warp knit that incorporates many textured yarns and fiber types. Complex designs usually have a fine, chainlike yarn on wrong side to stabilize pattern yarns and control stretch.

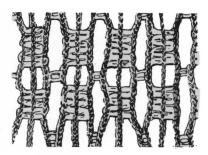

rib knit A knit construction which produces pronounced vertical ridges. Usually means weft knits composed of alternating knit and purl stitches in each row; has crosswise stretch unless controlled by a knitting technique or bonding.

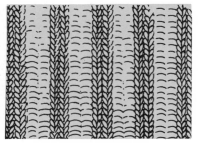

stable knits Have been constructed in a way that prevents stretch. This is accomplished during either the knitting or the finishing process. These knits can be used whenever a woven fabric would be used.

stretchable knits Have built-in stretch and recovery. They're usually used in a stretched condition over body curves for a closer fit. These knits should be used with patterns designed especially for them.

sweater knit Stretchy, single weft knit—like the fabric in a knitted sweater.

tricot knit A warp knit construction that looks like a plain knit on the front. On wrong side there are crosswise ridges in a tiny herringbone pattern. Usually very fine yarn, often used for lingerie. Good crosswise stretch; very little lengthwise stretch (see page 144).

NON-WOVENS: Felting makes fabric from wool without first spinning fibers into yarns. The scaly texture of wool fibers permits them to shrink and lock together under heat, friction, moisture, and pressure.

Fibers other than wool can be made into non-woven fabrics by arranging them in a mat. Then they are heat-fused either with an adhesive or when some of the fibers melt at a lower temperature than others.

Non-woven fabrics have no grain; their edges need not be finished. They are strong, but don't shape well or recover when stretched.

Don't confuse the non-wovens with the bonded fabrics which are explained on pages 142-143.

NETTING: Developed as a machine reproduction of hand-made nets and laces, the netting process gives us tulle, fishnet, and magnificently complex laces and lace embroidery.

HOW DOES IT END?

The transformation of fabrics from their actual construction to their finished appearance is like the classic difference between the caterpillar and the butterfly.

Functional finishes applied to fabric can give it resistance to staining, burning, shrinking, and wrinkling. Because consumers are more aware than ever of the tremendous advantages imparted to fabric by such finishes, these are in great demand.

The most noticeable part of the entire finishing process is the decorative touch—the all-important steps that make fabric a pleasure to look at as well as to feel. Color and pattern in fabric have challenged countless artists—their work is a mobile and wearable art form.

THE PRACTICAL ANGLE

Functional finishes may be hard to see, but the results are impressive and important. Many are such standard practice that you never hear about them. Others are the highly advertised pride of the manufacturer. These finishes can allow natural fibers to compete with new man-mades in performance and ease of care. They also allow man-mades to overcome certain disadvantages.

Remember that when a fabric's label says the finish is permanent, it means only for the normal life of the fabric under normal conditions, and only if you treat it as the manufacturer recommends. Here's a list of terms you're likely to find on labels—and what they mean to you.

colorfast Color won't fade with normal use, if laundered as recommended.

crease resistant Fabric has been treated to resist and recover from wrinkling caused by normal wear.

durable press Another term for Permanent Press (see below).

fire resistant Fabric resists the spread of flame.

mercerized Cotton or linen treated under tension with caustic soda to swell the fibers; improves dyeing capacity, strength, and luster of fabric.

oil repellent Fabric won't absorb oil-based stains.

permanent press Fabric can be machine washed and dried; sheds wrinkles and retains shape without ironing (see pages 143-144).

pre-shrunk Fabric which has undergone a preliminary shrinking process. Residual shrinkage must be declared. This is the percentage of possible shrinkage remaining in a fabric after it has been pre-shrunk.

sanforized® A trademark which means fabric won't shrink more than one percent in washing.

sanforized plus® A trademark which means fabric has also passed standardized tests for wash-and-wear performance.

shrinkage controlled Fabric has undergone compressive shrinkage in manufacturing. This increases its durability by compacting the weave.

soil release A treatment which makes possible the removal of oil stains from permanent press fabric. It makes water resistant fibers absorbent so the washing solution can penetrate the fiber and remove soil.

stain and spot resistant Fabric finished to repel water and oil-based stains.

wash and wear Fabric can be washed and re-worn with little or no ironing. This property may be produced by heat-setting or resin treatment and varies in permanence. Also termed easy care or minimum care.

water repellent Fabric treated to reduce its affinity for water while still remaining porous.

THE DECORATIVE APPROACH

The beauty of a fabric is probably what attracted you to it in the first place. Color, texture, print—think of what made you reach for it. Here's how its beauty came about.

COLOR: Though much of the decoration on fabric is applied after its construction, color can be imparted at any stage of manufacturing. Raw fiber can be dyed before spinning to make tweed yarn from several colors of fiber, or pigment may be added to the spinning solution of a man-made fiber so its color is really built-in.

Yarn is often dyed before the fabric is made, so several colors will form a design in the cloth—plaid is an example of this. When dyeing is done after weaving, the finished fabric can be stored, then dyed to suit fashion trends as it's needed.

New and complex chemical formulas have created dyes that will take the punishment of being laundered and worn. Dyes aren't always fast, however, so put your trust in guarantees if you're making something that will be exposed to hot water or strong sunlight.

PATTERN: Designs may be endless but techniques for creating them each have specific applications and are best suited for certain types. Some are copies of old hand processes, others are offspring of the Machine Age.

Screen Printing: This is elaborated stenciling. Dye is forced through a fine mesh fabric except where a pre-cut plastic film forms a barrier. When the film is cut by a photographic process, very delicate patterns are possible. Screen printing is especially well suited to extremely large prints.

Resist: Fabric is treated before dyeing to refuse dye in certain areas. Several processes accomplish this, the most familiar one being batik. Wax or resin is printed on the fabric where the dye should not penetrate. The fabric is dyed, and the resin melted out. This is repeated for over-lapping colors. Tie dyeing involves wrapping, folding, or gathering fabric, then fastening with waxed thread to refuse dye in a certain pattern.

Roller Printing: A design is engraved on a series of metal rollers, one for each color. Fabric is fed between the revolving rollers and a large drum. The design is formed as the pattern on each roller coincides with that of the others. In discharge printing, the fabric has been previously dyed; the rollers apply bleach, leaving a white design. Fabrics of yarns which are made of more than one fiber type can be printed with a chemical that dissolves part of the yarns; this technique is called burn-out. Printing glue on a fabric and then dusting cut fibers on the surface makes a textured design called flocking.

TEXTURE: The exciting way a fabric catches light, the soft fuzzy feel of fleece or flannel, and the richness of embroidered lace can all result from special finishing.

Calendering: This versatile technique is applied in some form to nearly all fabrics. The calender is a large heated roller that acts like an iron when a fabric is to be pressed flat. Ciré is produced by rotating a heated roller rapidly to melt the surface and glaze it. When two layers of ribbed fabric are calendered together and a little off grain, the result is an oil-on-water moiré effect. Embossing is produced by calendering with a textured roller.

Napping: Tiny fiber ends are picked up to form a soft, fuzzy surface. Flannel and fleece are familiar examples formed by drawing the fabric under a series of revolving wire brushes.

Schiffli: Beautiful and elaborate embroidery and eyelet are formed on a ground fabric by these special machines. Hundreds of needles stitch in a programmed pattern and cut eyelet holes automatically.

Dictionary of Fabrics

You've never had it so good— here's a condensation of everything you'll want to know about fabrics. We've divided the story into four parts—names of fabrics and designs; types of laces, embroidery, and trims; technical data; and words relating to furs, fibers, and yarns. You get the whole picture at a glance!

At the end of the dictionary is a list of special shaping fabrics. To take the mystery from these undercover agents, we've pinpointed what they are and how they're used.

FABRICS AND DESIGNS

Antique satin Heavy, dull-face satin.

argyle plaid Plaid design composed of large, solid color diamonds, with contrasting diagonal overstripes.

Bark cloth Nonwoven fabric made in the tropics of inner tree bark, soaked and beaten thin, dyed and/or ornamented with printed patterns. Also, a modern fabric imitating the rough appearance of the above.

batiste Soft, sheer cotton, linen, or synthetic fabric of plain weave, usually in white or pastel colors. Fine batiste is used for handkerchiefs, lingerie, blouses, and children's wear. Coarser weave often used for linings. Wool batiste is a lightweight fabric with an even weave, usually thinner than challis and used for dresses, negligees. Also, silk called *batiste de soie.*

beaver cloth Woolen fabric with a soft finish and thick nap, made to resemble beaver fur. Also, a plushy pile fabric used in millinery.

bengaline Finely woven fabric with pronounced crosswise ribs similar in appearance to poplin or faille, but heavier;

usually used for coats, suits, dresses, trimmings.

birdseye All-over pattern of small diamond shapes, each having a center dot resembling a bird's eye, woven into cotton, linen, or synthetic fabrics. Also a type of piqué with this design.

blanket cloth Heavy, reversible fabric characterized by two-color jacquard weave with soft, thick filling. Also, a heavy, napped overcoating fabric.

blazer cloth Striped flannel.

broadcloth Closely woven fabric with very small crosswise ribs, made in many weights, fibers, and blends, and often resembling fine poplin. Worsted and woolen broadcloths have a glossy finish and velvet-like texture with the nap running in one direction.

brocade Jacquard-woven fabric with raised, all-over interwoven designs giving an embossed effect, often emphasized by contrasting surfaces and colors and gold or silver threads. Ground may be satin, twill, or a combination of weaves.

burlap Coarse and heavy plain weave fabric made of jute, hemp, or cotton. Used mainly for wrapping, bagging, wall covering, drapery, and sometimes for clothing.

butcher linen Coarse homespun linen originally used for French butchers' aprons. Now widely imitated in many man-made fiber fabrics.

Calico Plain-woven cotton fabric, lightweight and similar to percale, printed with small-figured pattern.

cambric Fine, closely-woven white or solid–color cotton with glazed or glossy-looking right side; inexpensive.

canvas Heavy, strong, firmly-woven cotton, linen, or synthetic fabric, either soft-finished or highly sized. *Ada* or *Java* canvas is stiff, open weave fabric used for needlework. *Awning stripe canvas* has printed or woven stripes.

challis Soft, supple, lightweight fabric usually printed with delicate floral, Persian, or cravat effects. May be wool, rayon, cotton, or blends.

chambray Fine quality plain weave fabric with a linen-like finish, combining colored warp and white filling yarns. Comes in stripes and checks.

charvet Soft tie fabric of silk or rayon with crosswise stripes, dull finish, and satin-like texture.

check Pattern of small woven or printed squares, similar to a checkerboard.

cheviot Wool fabric in twill weave, with short, close nap and rough surface, similar to serge but heavier and less smooth. Also, heavy cotton shirting, either striped or checked, of coarse yarns.

chiffon Delicate, transparent fabric in plain weave, of silk, rayon, etc., usually soft, but sometimes with a stiff finish. Often used double. The word also connotes lightness and softness, as in chiffon wool or chiffon velvet.

china silk Plain-weave silk of various weights. Lighter weights are used primarily for lining, heavier for blouses and custom shirts.

chinchilla cloth Heavy fabric, usually wool, with a spongy texture and tufted, nubby surface achieved by a special finishing process.

chino Cotton fabric in twill weave, of combed yarns; has been mercerized and pre-shrunk. Used for sportswear.

chintz Glazed, plain-woven cotton fabric, brightly printed with figures, birds, flowers, etc. Often used for slipcovers, draperies, etc.

ciré Shiny, patent leather effect produced on fabrics, ribbons, laces, etc., by the application of wax, heat, and pressure.

cisele Velvet with contrasting cut and uncut loop pile, forming a pattern.

corduroy Cut pile fabric in either plain or twill weave, with wide or narrow wales, cords, or ribs.

covert Durable, hard- or soft-finished fabric of medium to heavy weight, in diagonal twill weave. Made of tightly twisted two-ply yarns, one woolen or worsted, the other, contrasting wool, cotton, silk, or synthetic, giving cloth a finely speckled surface.

crash Coarsely woven, rough-textured fabric, made of thick, uneven yarns. Includes plain-weave linen or cotton, used for dresses, blouses, etc.; plain-weave linen mixed with jute, used for curtains; an absorbent, linen-cotton mixture, used for towels. Also, a rough-textured novelty wool fabric.

crepe Fabric with a pebbly, crinkled, or puckered surface, which is achieved by embossing, weaving, chemical treatment, or the use of hard-twisted yarns. Crepes may be of silk, cotton, wool, synthetics, or combinations of fibers in weights that range from light and sheer to heavy and opaque.

crepe-back satin Fabric with satin face and crepe back.

crepe de chine Lustrous, plain-weave crepe, usually made of silk. Can be light, medium, or heavy in weight.

crepon Fabric with lengthwise crinkles or "treebark" texture, resembling crepe, but thicker and firmer in texture and sometimes patterned with jacquard designs.

cretonne Medium-weight unglazed fabric usually made of cotton or linen in a variety of weaves and finishes, printed with large floral designs. Used chiefly for curtains, slipcovers, etc.

Damask A reversible, firm, glossy, jacquard-weave fabric woven in patterns. Similar to brocade, but flatter.

denim Strong, coarse, washable twill-weave cotton fabric, usually inexpensive. Although usually made with colored warp and white filling, denim can be woven in plaids, stripes, etc.

diaper cloth White cotton fabric, absorbent and soft, which may be dobby, plain, or twill weave.

dimity Sheer fabric, usually made of combed cotton, with fine lengthwise cords, stripes, or checks.

doeskin Properly, leather made from the skin of the doe. Term also describes a heavy satin-weave cotton fabric napped on one side; or a heavy, short-napped woolen fabric used for menswear.

donegal Originally a thick, homespun woolen tweed handwoven in the county of Donegal, Ireland; characterized by colorful thick spots or slubs woven irregularly into the fabric. Now, any tweed with these characteristics.

dotted swiss Fine, sheer cotton fabric with woven or flocked dots. Usually is crisp and stiff.

drill Strong, twill-weave cotton fabric that is similar to denim. Called khaki when dyed that color.

duck Heavy, tightly woven fabric usually of cotton or linen, made in various weights in plain or rib weaves. One of the most durable of all fabrics.

duvetyn Smooth, close-napped twill-weave fabric that has been sheared and brushed for a velvety or suede-like appearance.

Eiderdown Warm, lightweight fabric, either knitted or woven, napped on one or both sides; used for infant's wear, negligees, etc.

Faille Fabric with light, flat, crosswise ribs or cords, usually soft and slightly glossy. Often of silk, synthetics, or cotton, faille belongs to the grosgrain family of cross-rib materials.

fakes Those man-made textile products which simulate natural substances (see Fuzzys, pages 136-137).

feather cloth Fabric, usually wool or a blend, to which feathers have been added for softness or decoration.

felt Non-woven fabric produced by processing a mat of fibers with heat, moisture, and pressure. Usually wool, fur, or mohair, as these fibers possess natural felting properties; may contain cotton or rayon.

flannel Soft fabric, either plain- or twill-weave, usually of cotton or wool, with slight nap on one or both sides.

flannelette Soft, plain-weave cotton fabric with a nap on one side. Also called kimono flannel.

foulard Lightweight twill- or plain-weave fabric, often of rayon or silk, usually printed with cravat figures. This is the fabric that is commonly used in neckties.

Gabardine Firm, tightly-woven, twilled fabric often finished with a high sheen. Can be made of many different fibers and blends. Excellent for tailoring because it molds and shapes beautifully.

gauze Thin, sheer, woven fabric similar to cheesecloth.

georgette Sheer, dull-textured crepe fabric, with a pebbled or crinkly surface. Heavier than chiffon.

gingham Firm, light to medium weight cotton fabric, yarn-dyed and woven in checks, plaids, or stripes of two or more colors.

gossamer Soft, filmy, gauze-like fabric often used as veiling and for bouffant gowns. May also describe a sheer, thin fabric.

grosgrain Firm, closely woven fabric or ribbon with pronounced crosswise cords or ribs.

Haircloth Stiff, wiry fabric, with a warp of cotton, linen, or worsted, with horsehair filling. Used for interfacing or stiffening garments and upholstery.

harlequin plaid Fabric with diamond shapes in contrasting colors, creating a vivid plaid design.

harris tweed This name refers only to woolens hand-woven on the islands of the Outer Hebrides off the coast of Scotland.

homespun Loosely spun woolen fabric in plain or twill weave, usually of coarse yarn, having rough hand. Woven by hand, can be imitated by machine. Also, coarse fabric of jute, linen, cotton, or mixtures.

honeycomb Heavy, textured fabric woven to resemble the cells of honeycomb. Sometimes called waffle cloth.

hopsacking Rough-surfaced cotton, linen, or rayon fabric, of plain weave; usually coarse.

houndstooth check Four-pointed star check in a broken twill weave.

Illusion A term for very fine, sheer tulle, net, or gossamer fabric used for veils, dresses.

Jersey A knitted fabric which originated on the Isle of Jersey; usually in tubular form, in the stockinette stitch.

Khaki A sturdy cloth of cotton or wool, often used in military uniforms and sportswear. Also, a light yellowish-brown color.

Lace fabric A fine, open-work fabric with patterns of twisted, knotted, or looped threads on a ground of mesh or net. Usually made of cotton, rayon, or nylon.

lamé A fabric made of metallic threads, sometimes combined with silk or other fibers, in plain or fancy weaves.

lansdowne A light-weight dress fabric in twill weave, with rayon or silk warp and cotton or worsted filling.

lawn A sheer, thin cloth of combed or carded cotton. Has a crisp finish. Sometimes woven with satin stripes or a crinkled plissé effect.

leatherette An imitation leather, made of paper, cloth, or plastic material, and embossed to copy the grain and texture of real leathers.

loden A thick, coarse woolen of Tyrolean origin. Characteristic color is called loden green. Wind and water resistant.

longcloth A fine, plain-weave cotton cloth with a soft finish, bleached white, and often used for underwear and infants' clothes. It was one of the first fabrics to be woven into long rolls.

Mackinaw cloth A heavy, durable cloth for outerwear, usually all-wool or wool blended with other fibers. Often double-faced, with one side napped, and with front and back in different colors, or one side in plaid.

mackintosh A waterproof, lightweight cloth, originally of rubber-coated cotton.

madras Fine, hand-loomed cotton fabric from India in natural color, or dyed with bleeding vegetable dyes and woven in plaids or stripes. Also, gauze or curtain madras, a leno-weave fabric with a dobby figure effect formed of heavier filling yarns.

marquisette A lightweight, open, leno-weave fabric. Used for dresses, curtains.

marseilles A firmly woven cotton fabric, reversible, with raised design such as in piqué. Used for trimmings, vests, etc. and in its heavier weights, for bedspreads.

matelassé A double fabric with raised woven designs, often jacquard, having a surface that looks puckered or quilted. In lighter weights of silk, synthetics, etc., and often combined with metallics; used for evening wear.

matte jersey Tricot with a dull surface made of fine crepe yarns.

melton A short-napped, non-lustrous, heavy and thick material finished without glossing or pressing. Usually in all-wool or with cotton warp and woolen weft.

merino A soft, luxurious fabric resembling cashmere, originally made from the fleece of Merino sheep. Now refers also to a superior, fine woolen or wool and cotton blend fabric, and to wool and cotton yarns used in knitwear and hosiery.

mesh An open-textured fabric with even spaces between the yarns. Can be knitted, knotted, or woven, in fine or coarse threads or yarns.

metallic cloth A tinsel-like, shiny fabric incorporating metallic threads. Often combined with silk or other non-metallic fibers. Metallic threads may be all metal, plastic-coated metal, or a core fiber surrounded by metal.

middy twill A firm, compact, twill-woven cotton cloth, used for middy blouses, shirts, uniforms, slipcovers, etc.

milanese A warp-knit fabric made with two sets of yarn knitted in diagonal directions, creating a diamond effect. Stretchable, wrinkle and run resistant, absorbent.

moiré An irregular, wavy finish on corded or ribbed fabrics of silk, cotton, and many man-made fibers. Produced by engraved rollers, steam, heat, or chemicals.

moleskin A strong, fine cotton fabric lightly napped and sheared on the right side for a velvety finish.

monk's cloth A coarse, heavy, basket-weave fabric, usually made of cotton or linen, with warp and filling threads the same. Can be difficult to sew, because yarns have a tendency to slide.

muslin A wide variety of plain-woven cotton fabrics ranging from sheer to coarse. It appears bleached or unbleached, dyed in solid colors or printed. The finer grades are used for undergarments, shirts, pillowcases, etc.

Nainsook A lightweight, soft, mercerized cotton cloth, plain-woven, with a lustrous finish. Used mostly for children's clothing, lingerie, and curtains.

needlepoint canvas A stiff canvas with clearly defined meshes, used as a base for needlepoint embroidery. Finer mesh size is petit point and larger is gros point.

net An open-work fabric that may be sheer and fine, such as tulle, or coarse and open, such as fish net. Constructed in three basic types—bobbinet, tricot, and raschel —and in various fibers.

ninon A good quality, sheer, smooth fabric of hard-twisted yarns, in plain or novelty open weaves, with a clear, transparent surface. Sometimes called triple voile.

Oilcloth A waterproof fabric consisting of heavy cotton muslin, coated on one side with a glossy finish of oil, clay, and pigments.

oiled silk Silk fabric that has been treated with an oil preparation to make it waterproof. Has a transparent look.

oilskin A cloth such as cotton, linen, synthetics, or silk, treated with oil to make it waterproof. Used for raincoats.

ombré A rainbow-colored effect in fabrics, either dyed or woven in, with colors graduated usually from light to dark. Effect can be in varying shades of the same color, or a mixture of different colors.

organdy, organdie A very fine, thin, transparent cotton cloth with a crisp finish, woven of tightly twisted yarns.

organza A fine, transparent fabric similar to organdy, using highly twisted yarns. Made in silk and synthetics.

ottoman A heavy cross-corded fabric with the ribs larger and more rounded than in bengaline or faille. A variation of the plain weave. Made in wool for coats, dresses, suits, etc., and in silk or synthetics for evening wear, trimmings, etc.

outing flannel A soft, lightweight, plain- or twill-woven fabric with nap on both sides. Made of cotton or rayon, and used for infant's wear, sleepwear, diapers, etc.

overcheck A textile or design with two superimposed check patterns in different sizes or colors.

overplaid A textile or design with two superimposed plaid patterns.

oxford cloth A cotton shirting fabric in plain or basket weave, with two fine warp yarns and a heavier filling yarn. Has a lustrous, soft finish. Also, a dark gray woolen cloth made of yarns that are mixtures of black and white fibers.

Paisley An intricate, all-over design incorporating abstract, curving figures. The term also applies to a fine, soft woolen cloth printed with a paisley design.

panama cloth A fabric suggesting the texture of Panama hats. Sometimes lightweight and made of hand-twisted worsted yarns; other times, coarser, as in a basket weave, in cotton or other fibers or blends.

panne A finish for velvet or satin produced by pressure. It flattens the pile on velvet, giving it a lustrous sheen. Satin is made smoother and more lustrous.

parachute fabric Plain-weave fabric of silk, cotton, nylon, or rayon, used for making parachutes and sometimes, clothing. Lightweight, compact, and closely woven, it has a silky sheen.

patola An East Indian sari woven especially for a bridal dress in the chiné (Chinese) technique. A pattern is printed, dyed, or painted on either the stretched warp or weft threads before weaving.

pattern In fabrics, this applies to the decorative design or motif, also the repetition of any design or weave.

peau de soie A French term meaning "skin of silk." Originally made in silk with a satin weave, but may now be made in the synthetic fibers. Either single or double face.

percale A fine, lightweight, plain-weave cotton fabric with a firm, balanced construction (i.e., an equal number of threads per inch in warp and weft).

piña cloth A soft and lustrous transparent fabric woven from the silky fibers of the pineapple plant.

pinstripe A fine, slender stripe on a fabric, approximately the width of a straight pin. Term also refers to fabric with such a stripe.

piqué A term referring to a fabric that has raised, lengthwise cords, welts, or wales in various plain or patterned effects. A dobby weave.

plaid Refers to a pattern of colored stripes or bars crossing each other. From the Scottish term for a shawl-like garment woven in a traditional tartan or clan plaid pattern.

polished cotton A cotton fabric having a shiny face achieved through either satin weave or waxed finish.

pongee A plain-woven silk fabric that is thin and naturally tan-colored, having a rough-weave effect. Term also refers to a finely-combed cotton used in underwear.

poplin Plain-weave fabric that has a fine rib running from selvage to selvage. Similar to cotton or rayon broadcloth but with a slightly heavier rib.

press cloth A strong fabric used for filtering or other industrial purposes. Also, a cloth used between an iron and a garment being pressed, to protect the garment fabric.

Quilting Fine hand or machine stitches running through two thicknesses of material with a third layer of padding between.

Traditionally in a design such as diamonds, scrolls, etc. Also, material used for quilts.

Rajah A silk fabric with a rough surface, similar to pongee, and used in clothing.

Sack cloth Coarse fabric of cotton, linen, or goat's hair used in making sacks or bags. Worn traditionally as a symbol of penance or mourning.

sailcloth A very heavy, strong, plain-weave fabric made of cotton, linen, or jute.

sateen Cotton fabric characterized by satin weave.

scrim Lightweight, loosely woven, open fabric of cotton or linen, used for curtains, needlework, and theatrical stage drops.

seersucker Lightweight cotton blend with crinkled stripes woven in the warp direction by setting some of the warp yarns tight and others slack.

serge A crisp, flat fabric with an even, right-hand twill, woven in several weights from natural fibers. Used for suitings.

shantung Originally a name for a hand-loomed, plain-weave fabric with an irregular surface, made in China of wild silk. Today, the term refers to a plain-weave fabric with heavier, rougher filling yarns, which may be cotton, silk, or man-made fibers.

sharkskin An even twill-weave, wool fabric whose warp and filling yarns are alternated, white with a color, usually black, brown, or blue. Also, a sleek, hard-finished, pebbly-surfaced fabric made of tightly-twisted yarns of cotton, linen, silk, or man-made fibers woven in either a plain or basket weave construction.

suede cloth Woven or knitted fabric of cotton, man-made fibers, wool, or blends, finished to resemble suede leather.

surah Soft, fine, twilled fabric, often of silk or man-made fibers, available in plaids, stripes, or prints.

Taffeta Basic group of fine, plain-weave fabrics, smooth, crisp, usually lustrous. Called faille taffeta when woven with a fine rib, or changeable taffeta when warp and weft are different colors, causing iridescent effect.

tapestry A heavy, decorative, hand-woven fabric whose design is formed by the filling threads which completely cover the warp. Also, a machine-made imitation whose pattern is woven in by means of colored weft threads.

tartan The twilled woolen or worsted plaid design associated with a specific Scottish clan, i.e., dress Campbell.

tattersall An over-check pattern in two colors on a white or contrasting ground.

terry cloth Woven or knitted fabric with loop pile on one or both sides. Usually cotton, very absorbent.

ticking Strong, durable, closely-woven fabric, usually in a twill weave. A distinctive red or blue, yarn-dyed, warp stripe is traditional.

tie silk Wide range of silk fabrics suitable for men's ties. Often confused with Thai silk, a plain-weave fabric woven in Thailand, often in a large, brightly colored, yarn-dyed, plaid design.

tropical suiting Lightweight summer suiting made in several fibers and weaves.

tulle A fine silk, cotton, or synthetic machine-made net with hexagonal mesh. Used for veils.

tweed A wide range of rough-textured, sturdy fabrics characterized by fiber-dyed, mottled color effects.

Uncut velvet A type of velvet made with terry pile, with the loops left uncut.

Velour, velours A soft, closely woven, smooth fabric with a short, thick pile. May be woven in several structures, or knitted, usually of cotton, wool, or mohair.

velvet A warp pile fabric with short, closely woven cut pile, usually silk. May be woven two ways: 1) double cloth, woven face to face with the pile ends interchanging between layers, and cut to produce two layers of velvet; 2) single layer, the pile of which is cut by wires inserted with the filling and withdrawn.

velveteen An all-cotton fabric with a short, close filling pile cut to resemble velvet.

vinyl Includes several thermoplastic fibers of varying chemical composition. Made in monofilament, yarn, staple, and film form. Also, vinal.

voile A lightweight, sheer fabric with a crisp, wiry hand. Made from hard-twisted yarns in a plain weave.

Whipcord A rugged fabric with a sharply defined, upright, warp twill, usually of cotton or worsted.

Yarn dyeing Coloring the yarn before it is woven or knitted. Yarn dyeing is used to produce woven check and plaid patterns, and is a common form of dyeing.

Zephyr Any of several sheer, lightweight fabrics, often containing silk. Used for shirting, shawls, embroidery.

zibeline A woolen overcoating with a long, hairy, lustrous nap pressed in one direction, hiding the basic satin weave.

LACES, TRIMS AND EMBROIDERY

Alencon Needlepoint lace, usually worked in floral designs, outlined with heavy thread on sheer net ground.

antique lace Handmade bobbin lace of heavy linen thread. Designs are darned on large, irregular square-knotted mesh.

appenzell Fine Swiss hand embroidery worked in a buttonhole stitch.

Beading Lace, embroidery, or openwork trimming through which a ribbon can be interlaced.

belgian lace Pillow lace with machine-made ground from Belgium, including Antwerp, Brussels, Mechlin, and Valencienne.

bobbinet Fine machine-made net with hexagonal mesh. Used for dresses, foundations, and gowns, and as a base for embroidered and appliquéd laces.

braid Narrow fabric for binding or trimming. Usually woven or plaited flat, but can be round or tubular. Includes rick-rack, soutache, military, etc.

bretonne (breton) lace Net designs embroidered with heavy thread, often colored.

Chantilly Bobbin lace on fine hexagonal mesh ground. Pattern is usually elaborate floral and/or scroll designs and is outlined in heavy, silky thread. Used for dresses, draperies, etc.

cluny lace Bobbin lace made with heavy linen thread in large open designs; wheat ear and wheel designs are characteristic.

Eyelet embroidery A lightweight fabric characterized by decorative stitching around cutout areas.

Filet lace Lace with darned or woven square patterns on a square-knotted mesh ground. It is often used for dresses, tablecloths, etc.

fringe Short lengths of thread; can be loose, twisted, plaited, or tasseled. Used as a border or trimming. Also, a raveled fabric edge.

Galloon A narrow tape or braid of cotton, wool, or silk. Also a double-edged lace.

gimp Flat, narrow, openwork strips of twisted strands of silk, wool, cotton, etc., run through with metallic wire or coarse cord for body. Used as a trim. Also, in lacemaking, coarse thread or cord used to outline or emphasize the design.

Milan lace Bobbin lace with scroll or floral motifs made of tape or braid on a net ground.

Passementerie A general French term referring to edgings and trimmings made from gimp, cord, beads, etc.

picot A decorative woven edge consisting of tiny loops on the selvages of ribbon, lace, etc. Effect is also achieved by cutting through the center of machine hemstitching.

point d'esprit A type of cotton bobbin net that has square dots scattered on the surface.

Renaissance lace A lace having woven tape motifs joined by various flat stitches.

ribbon A relatively narrow piece of a woven fabric like silk, satin, or velvet. Usually has a cord finish instead of a selvage along both edges.

rose point Venetian needlepoint lace worked in relief. Has floral and scroll designs delicately connected by small bars. Also, gros point and Venetian rose point.

Valenciennes A flat bobbin lace worked in one piece, with the same thread forming the ground and pattern. Commonly known as val lace, it can be hand or machine made.

venetian point lace A heavy, needlepoint lace with a floral design in relief.

TECHNICAL TERMS AND PROCESSES

Blend Combination of two or more fibers and/or colors in one yarn, resulting in new fabric and performance characteristics or a tweed effect.

botany Generic term for finest grade of worsted wool yarns and fabrics. Used interchangeably with merino.

Carding Process by which fibers of cotton are separated and brought into line as a thin web, then compacted into a continuous strand or sliver. Removes most impurities.

coated fabric Woven fabric whose surface has been impregnated with substances such as lacquer, varnish, plastic, paraffin, rubber, etc., for water- or heat-proofing.

crochet Interlocking loops or stitches in plain or fancy designs;worked with a hook to form a fabric, article, trim or lace. Also, fabric, article, trim, or lace made in such a way.

Double cloth Fabric made of two layers woven simultaneously on the same loom and held together by binding threads. Face and backing may contrast in weave and color.

double-faced Term applied to fabric that can be used on either side; includes double cloth and some of the bonded fabrics.

Ecru Light tan or beige; the color of unbleached cotton, wool, or silk fabrics and laces.

embroidery Ornamental needlework done by machine or hand on fabric with either silk, cotton, metal, or other threads.

end An individual warp yarn, thread, or cord.

Fabric The product of knitting, weaving, braiding, felting, or bonding fibers or yarns.

face The side of a fabric which looks better because of weave or finish.

fiber The basic unit in the production of textile yarns and fabrics. A small strand of matter, either formed naturally or produced by man, whose length is many times its diameter. Usually refers to staple, or short, spinnable lengths, but may also include continuous filament.

filament Continuous single strand of silk, rayon, acetate, or synthetic fiber.

filling Crosswise yarn in a weave, sometimes called weft or woof. Also, a term for sizing substances which give body or weight to a fabric.

fleece Woolly coat of the sheep, usually shorn in one piece from the animal. May also be used to describe the woolly coat of any animal (such as the goat or camel) whose hair is used to make fabric. Also, any heavy napped or pile fabric with a deep, fleece-like surface.

float In weaving or knitting, a portion of yarn which extends over a series of cross yarns before being caught under adjacent yarns. The surface of satin fabric is produced by floats.

Gray (or greige) goods Fabric in an unbleached, undyed, or unfinished state. Also, a color between gray and beige.

Hand Feel, drape, or handling qualities of fabric; refers to texture and quality.

high-count fabrics Closely-woven fabrics.

high-pile A long pile, like plush, distinguished from low-pile velvets and velveteens.

Knitting Method of constructing fabric by interlocking a series of loops of one or more yarns. The three classes of knits are warp knit (which includes tricot, milanese, and raschel), circular knit, and flat knit.

Laine French word for woolen or worsted cloth.

lappet A weaving process for small-figured cloth like dotted swiss, in which the pattern is embroidered into the body of the fabric as the cloth is woven.

lock-stitch A machine stitch in which the top threads and bobbin threads lock together with each stitch.

loom The machine or frame for weaving cloth by interlacing warp and filling yarns.

luster The quality of shine or sheen of a fiber or fabric.

Mat (matte) finish A dull-surfaced fabric.

mixture A blend of two or more fibers of different colors or types, as in homespuns and heathers.

Nap A soft, fuzzy finish which can be raised on various fabrics, usually by brushing cloth against a cylinder covered with short, protruding wires. Gives fabric a soft hand and downy appearance, and makes it warmer and more durable.

natural A yarn or fabric in its original unbleached or undyed state.

novelty weave Any weave which varies or combines the three basic weaves: plain, satin, and twill.

Padding Soft, bulky materials like wool or cotton wadding, used to stuff or pad such things as quilted coat linings and shoulder pads.

pebble weave A fabric with a rough, pebbly surface produced by a special weave or highly twisted yarns, as in pebble crepe.

pick In weaving, one throw of the shuttle across the loom, interlacing the filling threads with the warp. Also, an individual filling thread.

pinwale A narrow edge or rib found in fabrics like corduroy.

Ravel To pull away the yarns and make a fringe on the fabric edge. Also, to unwind.

reversible fabric A fabric that is finished and usable on both sides.

rubberized fabric Fabric with a rubber coating on one or both sides which renders it waterproof.

run-proof A knit construction in which locked loops prevent running.

run-of-the-mill Textile products that are often sub-standard and may be referred to as seconds.

Tubular knit Fabric knitted in tubular form on circular machinery. Examples are jersey, hosiery, tubular belts, etc.

FURS, FIBERS AND YARNS

Alpaca Soft, lustrous, strong fiber made from the hair of the South American alpaca; classified for labeling as wool. Term also applies to lightweight fabric made from cotton and either alpaca or rayon.

angora Smooth, soft hair of angora goat, often known as mohair; also, the fine, silky hair of the angora rabbit. Angora is classified for labeling as wool.

Bouclé Woven or knitted fabric with a loopy, knotted surface and usually, a springy, spongy hand.

Camel's hair Lustrous, extremely soft underhair of the camel, used either alone or combined with wool; spun or knitted into textiles for coats, sweaters, blankets, etc. Classified for labeling as wool. Also, lightweight coating fabric; thick and

warm, usually in twill weave with a high glossy finish. Made entirely or partly of camel's hair, mohair, or in cheaper grades, cow hair. Usually light tan.

cashmere Soft, flossy hair of the cashmere goat, spun and either knitted or woven into very soft, fine fabrics. Often combined with silk, cotton, or wool. Kashmir, cassimere, and cashmere also often refer to the pattern or design known as paisley or Persian.

chenille Fabric containing tufted, velvety, pile yarns similar in appearance to fuzzy caterpillars.

cotton Fibrous substance, soft and downy, obtained from seed pods of the cotton plant, which is spun into yarn and then woven into textiles. Also, fabric made of cotton.

crimp Natural or manufactured wrinkles or waviness in fibers. Lends bulk and resilience.

Flax Soft, silky fiber of the flax plant, which is processed and used to make linen.

Hair fibers Textile fibers which include the hair of alpaca, angora goats, camels, llama, etc., often used in combination with wool. Classified as specialty fibers; lower grades may be used for felt.

hemp A lustrous, coarse, and durable textured fiber from the hemp plant. Used for weaving into coarse fabrics like sailcloth; also for cordage, twine. Fibers are steel gray to creamy white.

Jute A glossy fiber from India used for sacking, burlap, twine, and rug and carpet backing.

Kapok A filling for mattresses, pillows, life preservers, etc., made of the silky fiber seed coverings of the kapok tree of Malaya.

kemp Coarse, wavy fibers of wool or mohair. Used in mixed wools for special novelty effects.

Lamb's wool The soft, elastic fleece obtained from a 7-8 month old lamb's first shearing. Can be woven into a superior fabric. Used in padding, interlinings, etc.

linen Fabric made from natural flax fibers, outstanding for its luster and strength. Usually in a plain weave, but also appears in damask and other patterns.

lisle A tightly twisted, smooth cotton yarn. Used mainly in knit hosiery, gloves, and underwear.

Marl Yarns of two different colors or lusters twisted together for novelty effect.

mohair Long, silky, lightweight, resilient hair of the angora goat.

monofilament A single, untwisted strand of a synthetic filament like nylon, in any diameter or strength which can be used in the normal weaving process.

multifilament Man-made yarns composed of many fine filaments—usually 60 or more —twisted together.

Natural fibers Animal, vegetable, or mineral materials which occur in fibrous form in a natural state.

novelty yarns Yarns of irregular or unusual textures. Used for creating special effects in weaving or knitting.

Pearl (or perle) cotton A mercerized cotton thread or yarn in various colors and sizes, used for embroidery and other needlework as well as knitting and crocheting.

pima cotton A high quality cotton with great strength; developed from certain Egyptian cottons.

ply yarn Yarn composed of two or more strands or filaments twisted together.

pure silk Refers to silk fabric that does not contain metallic weighting or finishing materials exceeding ten per cent. In black silk, fifteen per cent is allowed.

Rabbit hair This natural hair is normally of a pale brown hue and soft texture. It is often combined with other fibers in weaves or knits for a softening or special effect.

raffia Natural or colored straw from the raffia palm of Madagascar. Used to make hats, draperies, or articles like baskets.

raw silk Silk fibers as they are taken from the cocoon, before the natural gum has been removed.

Shetland Soft, lightweight, warm fabric woven or knitted from the wool of the Shetland sheep.

silk Continuous protein filament produced by silkworm larvae (Bombyx mori) when constructing their cocoons. The filament is reeled off and boiled to remove a stiff natural glue, then woven into luxurious fabrics noted for their soft luster and strength.

synthetic fibers Trade group of man-made fibers made by the chemical synthesis or "building up" of one or more simple chemical compounds. Does not include rayon or cellulose acetate.

Textured yarns Continuous filament man-made yarns which have been treated to give them loft and/or stretch qualities.

Vicuña A wild relative of the llama which yields the finest animal fiber.

virgin wool Wool which has not previously undergone any manufacturing process.

Wild silk Silk obtained from the cocoons of silkworms which feed on other than mulberry leaves.

wool The fine, soft fiber covering of the sheep. Also includes the hair of the angora or cashmere goat, and may refer to the specialty fibers from the hair of the camel, alpaca, and vicuña. Wool is distinguished from hair by a covering of minute scales, which give it unique felting and insulation properties. Reused wool must be so labeled and is taken from cloth which has been used or worn. Reprocessed wool is reclaimed from manufacturing scraps of cloth.

woolen A method of yarn-making in which the fibers are carded and then spun directly without combing. The nature of the fibers used is less critical than in any other system. Yarns are bulkier, more randomly oriented, and less tightly twisted than those produced by the worsted process. Also, fabrics made of such yarns; this includes most bulky, heavily fulled, or napped wools.

worsted Fabric woven from yarn spun from combed wool. Also, a yarn spinning system. Yarn is fine and strong; fabrics are usually smooth, tightly woven, and crisp.

Fabrics For Shaping	Type			Weight			Color				Use				Care	
	Woven	Non-woven	Iron-on	Light	Medium	Heavy	Black	White	Natural	Colors	Interfacing	Underlining	Lining	Interlining	Washable	Dry-cleanable
◇ **About Face**	✓		✓						✓		✓				✓	✓
◇ **About Face** Basic Liner	✓		✓	✓		✓	✓	✓		✓	✓				✓	✓
★ **Acro**—Hair Canvas	✓		✓	✓					✓		✓	✓			✓	✓
★ **Armo**—Hair Canvas	✓			✓	✓				✓		✓					✓
★ **Armo**—Lamb's Wool	✓			✓			✓		✓					✓		✓
★ **Armo Press**	✓		✓					✓			✓				✓	
⁑ **Ascot**—Regular, Permanent Press	✓	✓	✓	✓	✓	✓	✓	✓	✓		✓				✓	✓
⁑ **Ascot All Bias**		✓				✓	✓	✓			✓				✓	✓
⁑ **Bataan Batiste**	✓			✓					✓			✓	✓		✓	
Batiste	✓			✓					✓			✓			✓	
□ **Bravo Canvas**	✓			✓			✓	✓			✓					✓
□ **Bravo-Set**	✓			✓				✓			✓				✓	✓
Brocade	✓				✓				✓				✓			✓
□ **Butterfly**	✓			✓					✓				✓		✓	✓
China silk	✓			✓					✓			✓	✓			✓
★ **Ciao**	✓				✓				✓			✓	✓		✓	
Crepe—(for stretch)	✓			✓		✓			✓			✓	✓		✓	✓
⊟ **Earl Glo**—Sheath Lining	✓			✓					✓			✓	✓		✓	
⊟ **Earl Glo**—Acetate Faille, Crepe-Back Satin, Rayon Twill, Crepe	✓				✓				✓				✓			✓
⊟ **Earlaire of Reemay**		✓		✓	✓			✓	✓	✓					✓	✓
⁑ **Empress Satin**—Plain, Seasonal-All	✓			✓					✓				✓	✓		✓
◇ **Face Flex**	✓	✓	✓	✓	✓		✓	✓	✓		✓				✓	✓
◇ **Face Form**	✓	✓	✓	✓	✓		✓	✓	✓		✓				✓	✓
◇ **Facelon**		✓	✓	✓	✓	✓	✓	✓			✓				✓	✓
Fakes—i.e. pile fabric	✓	✓				✓			✓					✓	✓	✓

FOR TRADEMARK IDENTIFICATION, SEE PAGE 65.

Fabrics For Shaping	Type			Weight			Color				Use				Care	
	Woven	Non-woven	Iron-on	Light	Medium	Heavy	Black	White	Natural	Colors	Interfacing	Underlining	Lining	Interlining	Washable	Dry-cleanable
★ Fino	✓			✓			✓	✓	✓		✓	✓				✓
★ Finolight	✓		✓						✓		✓					✓
★ Formite—Sheer Canvas	✓		✓				✓	✓	✓		✓	✓			✓	
□ Hymo Canvas—Regular, Special	✓				✓				✓		✓					✓
★ Inside Out	✓				✓					✓		✓				✓
★ Instant Armo Iron-on—Dress Weight Cotton	✓		✓			✓				✓					✓	
★ Instant Armo Iron-on—Canvas Finolight, Formite	✓		✓		✓	✓			✓		✓					✓
□ Interlon		✓		✓	✓	✓	✓	✓			✓				✓	✓
□ Interlon Bias		✓		✓				✓	✓			✓			✓	✓
⚹ Intimate	✓			✓						✓	✓	✓			✓	
⚹ Intimate Quilted	✓				✓					✓			✓	✓		✓
⊙ Keynote Plus	✓			✓						✓			✓		✓	
† Kyron		✓		✓	✓	✓			✓	✓	✓				✓	✓
⚹ Lana	✓				✓	✓								✓		✓
Lawn	✓			✓						✓		✓	✓		✓	✓
○ Love-Life	✓			✓						✓		✓	✓		✓	
Marquisette	✓			✓						✓		✓			✓	✓
⊟ Marvelaire	✓			✓						✓		✓	✓		✓	
⧫ Milium	✓				✓					✓			✓	✓		✓
Muslin	✓			✓			✓	✓			✓	✓			✓	✓
Organdy	✓			✓					✓	✓	✓				✓	✓
Organza	✓			✓	✓					✓		✓	✓		✓	✓
†† Pellon		✓		✓	✓	✓	✓	✓			✓	✓			✓	✓
†† Pellon All Bias		✓		✓				✓	✓		✓	✓			✓	✓
†† Pelomite Detail		✓	✓		✓			✓	✓		✓				✓	✓
Percale	✓			✓						✓		✓	✓		✓	✓

FOR TRADEMARK IDENTIFICATION, SEE PAGE 65.

Fabrics For Shaping	Type			Weight			Color				Use				Care	
	Woven	Non-woven	Iron-on	Light	Medium	Heavy	Black	White	Natural	Colors	Interfacing	Underlining	Lining	Interlining	Washable	Dry-cleanable
⁑ Polee	✓			✓						✓			✓		✓	
◇ Prima Canvas	✓			✓				✓		✓						✓
◇ Saja	✓			✓						✓		✓	✓		✓	✓
□ Shape-Flex—Iron-on	✓	✓	✓	✓	✓		✓	✓	✓	✓					✓	✓
★ SiBonne	✓			✓						✓		✓	✓		✓	✓
★ Siri	✓			✓	✓				✓	✓	✓				✓	✓
○ Solo	✓				✓	✓			✓			✓	✓		✓	
□ Sta-Shape—Hair Canvas, Durable Press, Lightweight Canvas	✓			✓	✓	✓	✓	✓	✓						✓	✓
Taffeta	✓			✓					✓			✓	✓			✓
⁑ Taffeta Supreme	✓			✓					✓			✓	✓		✓	
□ Thermolam—Lamb's Wool	✓			✓	✓	✓			✓					✓	✓	
⁑ Touch of Gold	✓			✓					✓				✓		✓	
⁑ Touche	✓			✓			✓	✓	✓	✓		✓	✓		✓	
Tricot—(for stretch)	✓			✓					✓				✓		✓	✓
⁑ Tritessa	✓			✓	✓	✓			✓			✓	✓		✓	✓
□ Undercurrent	✓			✓	✓				✓			✓	✓		✓	✓
□ Veriform	✓			✓	✓	✓				✓	✓				✓	✓
□ Veri-Super	✓			✓	✓	✓				✓	✓				✓	✓
Voile	✓			✓					✓			✓	✓		✓	✓
⁑ Whisper	✓			✓					✓			✓	✓		✓	
□ Worsted Canvas	✓			✓			✓	✓	✓							✓

★ Trademark of the Armo Company

⁑ Trademark of Ascot Textile Corporation

○ Trademark of Fabricators

⊖ Trademark of Klopman Mills

◇ Trademark of Hayden Textile Inc.

◇ Trademark of Deering Milliken

□ Trademark of Stacy Fabrics Corporation

□ Trademark of N. Erlanger, Blumgart & Co., Inc.

†Trademark of J. P. Stevens & Co., Inc.

††Trademark of Pellon Corporation

Notions Essentials

Notions From A To Z

It takes more than a pattern and fabric to finish a garment. Notions provide the perfect finishing touch. Stock an assortment of notions staples —snaps, hooks and eyes, and elastic.

The notions needed for a garment are listed on the back of its pattern envelope. Purchase these with your pattern and fabric so you'll have everything when you start to sew.

Adhesives are special glues which can be used in place of stitching. Some can be used on leather, suede, and trims. Test on fabric scraps first. See Fusible Adhesives.

Appliqués are available in many designs. They can be glued, fused, machine zig-zagged, or hand sewn to almost any garment for a decorative touch.

Belting in widths from ½″ to 3″ is a flexible shaper for custom-made belts. Regular and iron-on belting come in black or white, and are sold by the yard or in pre-cut and packaged lengths.

Bias tape is made of cotton and comes in ¼″, ½″, and 1″ widths. The 1″ width has edges folded ¼″ to the wrong side. Single-fold bias tape has folded edges that meet in the center on the wrong side.

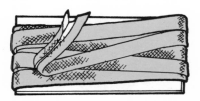

Double-fold bias binding has an additional, slightly off-center fold.

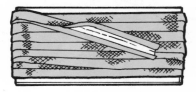

Bias tape is used as a stay, hem finish, or facing. Choose a color from the many available that matches or is a shade darker than the garment color. Bias tape used as a trim should match or contrast garment color.

Blanket binding is available in 2″ to 3″ folded widths. It is made of acetate or nylon satin and is available in a range of colors. Use it to replace worn blanket bindings or as a decoration.

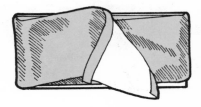

Boning is stiff to maintain and mold shape. Also called feather boning, it's made of flexible, fabric-covered nylon. Boning comes by the yard or in various shorter, pre-cut and packaged lengths. See Stays.

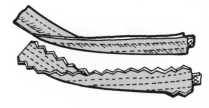

Bra cups are made of molded foam. Use them to shape swimsuit tops and other similar garments. They come in 32″, 34″, and 36″ sizes. Cup size is adjustable.

Buckles are available in many styles and widths. Cover-your-own buckle kits are sold in ½″ to 3″ widths.

Novelty buckles in countless sizes and shapes are found at notions counters of many stores.

Buttons are both a design accent and a fastening. They come in all shapes and sizes. Cover-your-own button kits are available, too.

Buttons are sold by lines as well as inches—40 lines equal one inch. Here's a simplified listing of button sizes for general purposes: Line 20 or 24 - shirt or shirtwaist dress size; Line 30 - size of a dime; Line 36 - size of a nickel; Line 40 - size of a quarter; Line 60 - size of a silver dollar. Exact sizes are shown in the chart below.

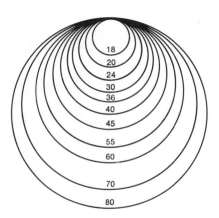

18
20
24
30
36
40
45
55
60
70
80

Cording is of cotton, cellulose, or synthetic fibers. It's available in diameters from ⅛" to 1". You can buy it by the yard or pre-cut and packaged. Use it to fill piping, tubing, or buttonholes.

Coat and jacket hangers are short lengths of chain or nylon braid. Sew them at the inside of a jacket or coat back neckline to simplify hanging the garment on a hook.

Elastic is sold by the yard or in pre-cut and packaged lengths. It is available in white, black, and some basic colors, and ranges in width from ¼" to 1¼". The most common elastic is made of nylon or rayon and rubber. Elastic ranges in style from the standard type to pajama webbing. Buy the type called for by your pattern. For swim wear, make sure elastic will recover after being wet.

Elastic thread is small and cord-like. Use it for shirring or specialty features.

Embroidery floss is made of 6-strand cotton or silk and comes in a complete range of colors. It's used for decorative hand embroidery.

Eyelets are small, round pieces of metal that are punched through fabric to make a reinforced hole. Use them wherever belt eyelets or lacing are needed. Eyelets are often available in kits with buckles or belts, or are packaged with an eyelet punch. They are available in many sizes; very large eyelets are called grommets.

Fur tacks act like studs to hold collars and fur pieces to coats and suits.

Fusible adhesives secure two layers of fabric by the application of heat and pressure instead of sewing. The adhesive is a fiber mesh that is available by the yard at 18" wide or in pre-cut and packaged lengths that are ¾", 1½", or 5" wide.

Grosgrain ribbon ranges in width from 3/16" to 3⅛" and is available in a wide range of colors. Use it to stay waistlines or for decorative purposes. Some grosgrain bleeds and shrinks when wet; if you plan to wash it, take proper precautions.

Hammer-on snaps have either plain, round heads or any of a variety of decorative heads. These two-part snaps are strong enough to withstand hard wear and are ideal for children's clothes, sportswear, pajamas, and work clothes. They are often packaged and sold with an applicator.

Hem facing is a cotton or rayon bias strip that can be used for facing. The 2" width has both long edges folded in ¼" and is sold in pre-cut and packaged lengths. Stretch lace also comes as hem facing.

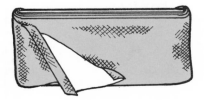

Hooks and eyes come in a variety of designs for special holding purposes. The standard type is made of brass, nickel, or black enamel-coated metal. Use nickel or brass hooks and eyes on light colors and black ones on dark colors.

Sizes range from 00 to 5. Larger sizes for heavyweight fabrics come in nickel or black. Covered hooks and eyes to match garment are used on coats, furs, and other similar items. Specially shaped, adjustable or skirt hook and eye closures are a secure fastener for waistbands. See pages 210-211 for applying hooks and eyes. Actual sizes are as follows:

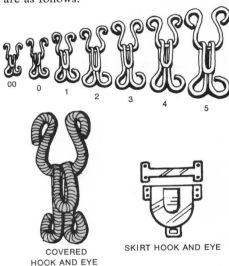

COVERED HOOK AND EYE

SKIRT HOOK AND EYE

Horsehair braid is the ideal hem facing to achieve soft flare in sheers or to finish and stabilize hems in heavy fabrics. It comes in black or white in widths from ½" to 6". See page 243 for application.

Iron-on mending tape is available in narrow strips or larger fabric pieces. It can be cut in any shape and pressed onto your fabric for an instant patch. Also use it to reinforce an area where a button will be sewn or which might otherwise be strained.

Labels personalize your wardrobe workmanship and autograph the gifts you make.

Lace seam binding finishes seams and hems attractively. It is cotton or a man-made fiber and comes in many colors and in widths from ½″ to ¾″. It comes in pre-cut and packaged lengths or by the yard.

Lingerie strap-holders are available in black or white. Or, make your own from ribbon seam binding. They are attached at garment shoulder seams and, when fastened, keep lingerie straps from wandering. Thread loops can also be used to make lingerie strap-holders (see page 214).

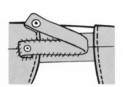 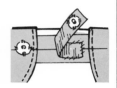

Metallic thread is decorative and can be sewn by hand or machine. It is available in gold, silver, and a few colors. Heat and steam can tarnish or otherwise damage metallic threads.

Nylon tape fastener consists of a pile and a hook strip that interlock when the two are pressed together. It is sold by the yard and can be attached in strips or in shapes to fit a closure area. Use it for a lightweight, jam-proof fastening on an area that won't be strained.

Patches for knees and elbows are found in the notions department or can be cut from scraps remaining from earlier sewing projects. Use fabric or leather patches on children's clothes, sweaters, or jackets.

Piping is a small, corded bias strip with a ¼″ seam allowance. It is available in a variety of colors in pre-cut and packaged lengths. You can use piping as a trim. To make a piped seam, refer to the instructions on page 170.

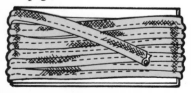

Rickrack is a trimming strip that's available in pre-cut and packaged lengths. It's woven braid in a zigzagging shape and ranges in size from a mini to a jumbo type.

Rickrack comes in many colors and metallics. For its application, refer to page 284.

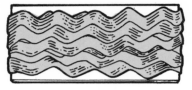

Seam binding is rayon and comes in wash and wear, iron-on, and bias versions. A complete range of colors is sold in pre-cut and packaged lengths of ½″ and 1″ widths. Choose seam binding that matches or is one shade darker than the garment.

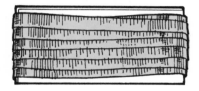

Shoulder pads camouflage sloping or narrow shoulders and support garment shoulders for correct draping. They are available in black or white in dress and coat weights. Shoulder pads have squared or rounded ends and are fabric-covered or plain.

Snaps are available in many sizes and types. Dress fasteners come in nickel or black enamel-coated metal and range in size from 4/0 to 1. Larger sizes 2 to 4 are for heavy-duty use; covered snaps are for coats and suits. Clear, see-through nylon snaps are available. Use nickel or brass snaps on light colors and black ones on dark colors. Read pages 209-210 for the application of snaps. Here are the actual sizes:

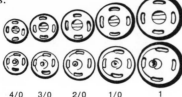

| 4/0 | 3/0 | 2/0 | 1/0 | 1 |

Stays are 4″, 6″, or 8″ plastic strips or metal spirals for shaping, molding, and vertical reinforcement. Short plastic stays support the points of shirt collars. Also, see Boning.

Thread is used for all sewing. Choose it to suit fabric and purpose. See the chart on page 77 to select appropriate threads and needles. Thread color should match or be one shade darker than the fabric.

Twill tape is a woven cotton tape that is used as a stay in tailored garments and waistlines. It is available in pre-cut and packaged lengths. Colors are black or white, and widths are from ¼″ to 1″.

Weights control and improve the drape of your garment. Lead weights ranging in size from ¾″ to 1⅛″ in diameter are encased in fabric, then sewn into the garment. Lead weight strips consisting of lead pellets encased in fabric are sold by the yard. Chain weights come in different weights and widths and are usually sewn along hem allowances.

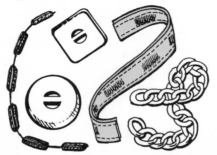

Yarn fills buttonholes and other garment areas which require similar slight padding.

Keep a stock of light and dark yarn on hand. You can also use it to make decorative fringe, tassels, or pompons (see pages 271-273).

Zipper adhesive is double-stick tape. Apply it to the zipper tape, position the zipper on garment and press in place with fingertips. Then stitch zipper to garment.

Zipper lubricant is a colorless, stainless stick of wax. Rub a little on zipper teeth so slider will glide smoothly.

Zippers come in many types, colors, and styles. Select the one you need by the performance expected of it. Many of the three major types are available with metal teeth or polyester coils: **Regular zippers** have teeth visible on both sides; the choice for most garments, they're also available in a heavy-duty weight. **Covered zippers** have small tape extensions that lap over the zipper chain; they're ideal for fabrics whose surfaces might catch in the zipper. **Invisible zippers** have coils or teeth on the wrong side and provide an inconspicuous, seam-like finish.

Zipper length depends on type, style, and brand; select the one closest to your needs from the supply in your store and shorten it if necessary (see page 203). Color should match or be a shade darker than your garment.

Skirt or neckline zippers (4″-24″) have an opening at one end and a stop at the other; use these at garment edges. Dress zippers (12″-14″) have stops at both ends; use these for openings within a garment seam. Trouser zippers (11″) are similar to skirt zippers; they open at one end and have slide supports and wide tapes for reinforcement. Separating jacket zippers (10″-24″) open at both ends; the zipper tape is reinforced at the ends to withstand wear.

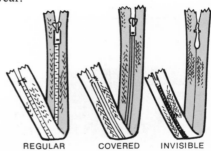

REGULAR   COVERED   INVISIBLE

And Indispensable Tools

A Toolbox For Sewing

Fill your sewing basket from the bottom up. Ease that pocketbook pain by purchasing basic tools first and then buying the extras as you need them. Get the best quality you can afford and take care of your tools so they'll last longer. Good tools make sewing easier and more enjoyable. Many manufacturers include instructions for care with their packaged products. Keep these suggestions and the instructions for use in a special file for future reference.

NECESSITIES

Bring your basic tools together in the form of a portable sewing kit. This can be easily moved from one area to another. Eliminate confusion by storing other tools according to the jobs they perform. Take the organization one step further by grouping notions and trims so you can locate them immediately at that crucial moment.

Here's a list of basic supplies for your sewing kit. These and other useful items are described on the following pages along with recommendations and general uses.

Tape Measure
Ruler
Yardstick
Sewing Gauge
Tracing Wheel
Dressmaker's Tracing Paper
Tailor's Chalk
Bent Handle Shears
Scissors
Assortment of Thread
Needles
Thimble
Dressmaker's Silk Pins
Pincushion

Here's what you should keep within easy reach in your sewing area.

Sewing Machine
Waste Container
Cutting Surface
Steam Iron
Ironing Board
Press Cloths
Tailor's Ham
Full Length Mirror
Extension Cord

MEASURING TOOLS

Measurements must be accurate if you want a perfectly fitting garment. To measure correctly, have the right tools, use them often, and always re-check figures.

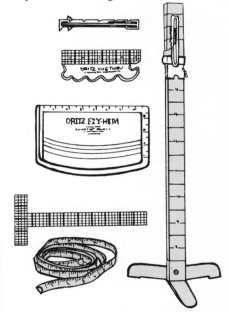

Tape measures are used for circumference as well as length and width measurements. Select a 60″ tape that has numbers and fractional markings clearly printed on both sides. Because they don't stretch, plastic or fiberglass tape measures with metal tips on the ends are your best choice.

Sewing gauges are 6″ rulers. They have a sliding marker that is adjustable to fractions of an inch and are available in plastic or sturdier metal. Sewing gauges help in measuring hems, spacing buttons, and in other detailed work.

Rulers are made in a variety of materials, but the best ones are transparent and have clear markings every ⅛″. A 12″ ruler is a must, but it's advisable to have a 6″ and an 18″ one, too. Use a ruler whenever a straightedge is required.

Yardsticks are 36″ long and are made of smoothly finished hardwood or metal. They should be clearly marked on both sides with designated fractions of a yard. Use your yardstick to check grainlines, mark bias, and establish hem lengths.

Hem gauges are usually made of metal and are multi-purpose. The curved side is like the hem shape and is marked for standard hem depths. The straight side is marked like a ruler.

Dressmaker's gauge is usually made of transparent plastic. One side is shaped for marking scallops; the other side is straight for measuring pleats and tucks.

Skirt markers are available for use with pins, chalk, or a combination of the two. The pin type is the most accurate, but requires another person's assistance. The chalk type is self-operative but may leave permanent markings. The pin-chalk combination has the best features of each. Buy one with a sturdy base that's adjustable to all fashion lengths.

Triangle is helpful in measuring and marking true bias; get one that has one 90° angle and two 45° angles. The clear plastic kind is your best choice.

French curves are an aid in altering patterns and in redrawing construction lines. You can get one wherever draftsmen's or artists' supplies are sold.

T-squares are used to locate cross grains and to alter patterns. The best type to get is a plastic one that's 9″ long with a 4″ span; be sure markings are clearly printed.

CUTTING TOOLS

Any type of cutting tool is easier to operate if it slides rather than saws. It is especially important that cutting tools be in top condition.

Shears of the best quality are of hot, drop-forged steel and have been hardened and tempered. Another good buy is Molybdenum that has been nickel-coated and chrome-plated. Test shears before purchasing to see that they cut smoothly and evenly along the entire blade. Be sure the pair you select has an adjustable screw to personalize the cutting tension.

Give your cutting tools monthly attention. Place a drop of sewing machine oil at the screw; open and close shears a few times, then wipe away the excess oil with a soft cloth. Have shears sharpened as soon as they show signs of dullness.

Never use fabric shears to cut paper heavier than tissue; set aside an old pair for that job. Don't drop shears, because this can disalign the blades.

Dressmaking shears for cutting fabric can be purchased in either the straight or bent-handle variety. Bent-handle shears with a 7″ or 8″ blade are the best since they allow the fabric to rest on the table as it is cut. The combined small and large ring handles are better controlled, and fit the hand more closely. Left-handed shears are available.

Scissors have straight blades and identical rings for handles. Get a pair that is 5″-6″ long for trimming, clipping, and detail work. 3½″-4″ scissors are optional.

Pinking or scalloping shears trim the fabric in the shape that the name implies. They range in blade length from 7½″ to 9″ and are fastened with a ball bearing pivot. Use them to finish seams and raw edges of fabric that will not ravel easily. They weren't designed to withstand long-distance, heavy cutting.

Buttonhole scissors have a screw and nut arrangement that adjusts the blade length. They allow you to begin cutting within the body of the fabric and continue for a pre-determined length. These scissors are best used for machine-made buttonholes.

Thread clips are a palm-sized variation of scissors. Slip the ring over your little finger and squeeze for a quick, neat job of snipping threads.

Electric scissors speed the cutting process and can be used as a general substitute for shears. They are available either with a cord or cordless and should fit the hand comfortably.

Seam ripper is a pen-like object with a small blade. Use it carefully to remove stitching.

MARKING TOOLS

To accurately transfer pattern symbols to fabric, use the appropriate marking tool and refer to pages 125-127.

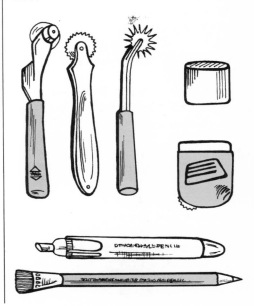

Tracing wheels have either a serrated edge for most light to medium weight fabrics or a needlepoint edge for heavy fabrics. Use a smooth edged wheel with tracing paper on most fabrics or without tracing paper for light or sheer fabrics. Apply slight pressure as you roll the wheel along a pattern marking.

Dressmaker's tracing paper is used with a tracing wheel and comes in packages of assorted colors. Double-faced tracing paper is available and enables you to mark two layers of fabric at one time.

Tailor's chalk comes in chalk or wax types in colored squares or convenient refillable pencils with sharpener. Test types and colors for removability because the wax type can be difficult to remove from hard-surfaced fabrics.

Needle and thread are used for tailor's tacks and basting. Depending on your fabric, use either silk thread or mercerized cotton thread in white or a slightly contrasting color.

Dressmaker's marking pencils are a pencil form of tailor's chalk. They usually have a brush at one end and are not refillable. Test chalk and wax types before using.

Pins are a fast but impermanent method of marking. See Hand Tools.

HAND TOOLS

Here are the items you'll need for simple and perfect hand sewing. They're all uncomplicated and very inexpensive, so try to accumulate everything we suggest to make your hand sewing effortless.

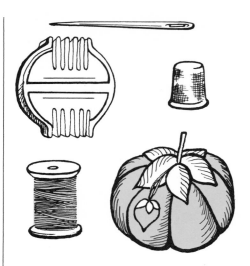

Pins to buy are fine and slightly larger brass or steel dressmaker's silk pins. Colored plastic heads make pins easy to see and handle.

Thimbles are for protection. Sizes run 6-11; choose one that fits the middle finger securely yet comfortably. Using a thimble eliminates the danger of puncturing your finger.

Magnets pick up pins and needles.

Beeswax blocks are available in a case for strengthening and keeping thread tangle-free for hand sewing.

Pincushions vary in size and shape. A wrist pincushion is handy for sewing and fitting, while a larger one stores the bulk of your supply.

Emery bags sharpen needles; they're often attached to large pin cushions.

Needle threaders simplify an eye-straining chore. Insert the threader through eye of needle, put thread through the larger threader eye, and pull threader and thread back through needle.

NEEDLES AND THREADS

| Fabric Weight and Examples | Thread Type and Size | | | Needle Size | | Number of Stitches Per Inch |
	Cotton and linen fabrics	Silk and wool fabrics	Man-made fabrics	Hand	Machine	
Very Sheer chiffon, net, silk organza	mercerized cotton 90-100	Silk A	nylon, polyester, cotton-covered polyester (extra-fine)	10	9	16
Sheer organdy, voile, fine lace	mercerized cotton 70-80	Silk A	nylon, polyester, cotton-covered polyester (extra-fine)	9	9-11	14-16
Light lawn, dotted swiss, tricot	mercerized cotton 60	Silk A	nylon, polyester, cotton-covered polyester (regular)	8-9	9-11	12-14
Medium denim, wool crepe, linen	mercerized cotton 50	Silk A	nylon, polyester, cotton-covered polyester (regular)	7-8	11-14	10-14
Medium Heavy sailcloth, corduroy, wool flannel	mercerized cotton 40 heavy-duty cotton 36, 40	Silk A	nylon, polyester, cotton-covered polyester (regular)	6-7	14-16	10-12
Heavy duck, wool fleece, velveteen	mercerized cotton 24, 30, 36 heavy-duty button and carpet	Silk A	nylon, polyester, cotton-covered polyester (extra-strong)	4-5	14-18	8-10
Very Heavy canvas, wool melton, tapestry	mercerized cotton 8, 10, 20 heavy-duty button and carpet	Silk A	nylon, polyester, cotton-covered polyester (extra-strong)	1-2-3	16-18	6-8

SPECIALTIES

These are the things that make some of the more time-consuming sewing operations easy.

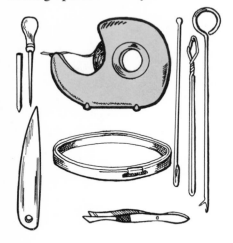

Tweezers are useful in plucking out short, loose threads and basting.

Loop turners quickly turn tubing or cording to the right side. The turner has a latch hook on one end.

Bodkins are used to insert elastic or drawstrings in casings and other similar jobs. One type has a safety pin closing; another looks like a large needle with a ball-point end.

Awl is a sharp, pointed tool used for making eyelets and round holes. Also called a stiletto, it should have a snug protective cover.

Pointer and creaser is a small, flat, wooden tool. The pointed end pushes out corners, while the rounded end helps flatten seamlines.

Transparent tape mends torn patterns, secures alterations, guides topstitching, and holds zippers in place for stitching.

Tissue paper is used in making pattern adjustments and alterations. It's also used when working with special fabrics like sheers.

Embroidery hoops hold fabric taut for embroidery and beading. They consist of two round wooden or metal rings. One fits inside the other. Your best choice is the metal type with an adjustable spring and a cork-lined outer hoop.

Lap boards are small, contoured table tops. Balance one on chair arms if you prefer working in an armchair rather than at a table. Some varieties have legs for greater stability.

Dress forms are a fitting aid which reproduces your body shape. The various types include wire forms, sectional forms, and covered foam forms. They range in price, ease of adjustment, and degree of accuracy. The easiest and most accurate form to adjust is a polyurethane form with a personally fitted and zippered cover.

PRESSING EQUIPMENT

Treat your garment to the pressing care it deserves. Use pressing equipment throughout construction. Your iron should be one that combines steam and dry features. Steam vents are ideally located at the front of the sole plate for concentrated steam. Choose an iron with a wide temperature range and a spray device.

An ironing board should be level, sturdy, and adjustable to a comfortable height. Pad the board with cotton batting or pre-cut purchased padding. Slip on a silicone-treated cover to prevent scorching or sticking. Keep the cover soil-free and smooth to avoid pressing stains and wrinkles into your fabric.

Press cloths should be similar to fabric weight. Have at least two: a cotton one that reverses to wool for general pressing, and a transparent one for details. Cheese cloth is a good general press cloth. Use a large fabric scrap to press right side of garment.

Tailor's ham is an oblong, firmly stuffed cushion with rounded ends. Use it to press curved areas of your garment. Hams come in different sizes; one side should be covered in cotton and one side in wool.

Press mitt is a version of the tailor's ham that fits on your hand. Use it for hard-to-reach places, or slip it over the end of a sleeve board to press sleeve caps. One side of the mitt should be covered in cotton, the other side in wool; it should have pockets on both sides.

Sleeve board is two small, narrow, connected ironing boards for pressing garment areas that won't fit over a regular board. Pad and cover it like a regular ironing board.

Seam roll is a cylindrical stuffed cushion with rounded ends for pressing small curves or long seams in narrow areas; one side should be cotton-covered, the other, wool-covered.

Point presser is a wooden tool with shaped surfaces for pressing points, curves, and straight edges. It also prevents ridges from showing on the right side of the fabric.

Pressing pad is a ½"-¾" thickness of soft fabric. Press monograms and sequinned or textured fabrics right side down on the pad.

Pounding block or clapper is made of wood and is used with steam to flatten edges. It's a necessity in tailoring. Steam edge and pound firmly, adjusting pressure and motion for various edges.

Needleboard is a bed of needles. Pressing pile fabric right side down so the pile falls in between the needles prevents flattening.

Sponge dampens small areas for pressing and mops up spills.

Brown paper strips are placed under folds of darts or edges of pleats to avoid pressing ridges into the right side of garment.

Clothes brush raises nap to freshen fabric or remedy slight overpressing. It also removes stray threads and lint after final pressing.

The Machine Shop

Your most vital piece of equipment is your sewing machine. Select a machine to meet your sewing needs.

YOUR SEWING MACHINE

Compare and test the three basic machines and decide which meets your sewing needs. **Straight Stitch** machines stitch forward or backward. **Zigzag Stitch** machines stitch forward, backward, and from side to side. **Automatic Stitch** machines have built-in discs or cams for straight, zigzag, chain, or decorative stitching; additional cams are often available.

Look at both portable and cabinet models to see which fits into your sewing area. Find out the accessories included in the price, if they are easily replaced, where the machine can be serviced, and whether it has a guarantee or warranty. Don't be misled by gadgets—a straight stitch machine meets most sewing needs. Unless you sew a lot and like to experiment, it's wise to stick to a basic machine.

Once you've purchased a machine, get to know it! Carefully read your instruction manual for information on parts and operation. Review the section on machine sewing (pages 159-163) for further details.

WHAT GOES WITH IT

Many new machines come with accessories for their use and upkeep. Check your equipment box before buying any of these materials.

Needles come in sizes 9-18, the smaller size being a finer needle. Buy needles which will fit your machine. Refer to the needle and thread chart (page 77). On zigzag machines, double or triple needles mounted on a single base make close parallel stitching. Ball point needles avoid snagging lingerie, elastic, knits, and stretch fabrics. Wedge or cutting needles stitch leather. Self-threading machine needles are available.

Bobbins are metal or clear plastic and should be purchased to fit your particular machine. Keep several bobbins filled with colors of thread used most often, and others empty so they can be filled with special colors. Avoid winding new thread on a partially filled bobbin.

Brushes clean lint from machine parts.

Small screwdrivers enable you to open the machine and change attachments.

FEET

You won't need all of the feet available for your machine, but study the list and decide which will make your style of sewing easier.

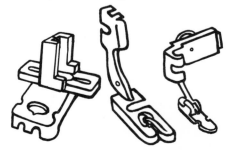

Straight stitch presser foot is hinged to go over variations in fabric thickness. Use it for general straight stitch sewing.

General purpose presser foot is hinged and is used for general straight and zigzag stitching.

Special purpose presser foot has a raised center section which allows closely spaced zigzag stitches to feed evenly. Small holes in the front hold an optional filler cord. Use it for buttonholes, appliqués, and ornamental stitching.

Zipper foot allows you to stitch close to a raised edge. It can be adjusted to the right or left side of the needle. Use it for corded seams, tubing, and zipper insertion.

Invisible zipper foot is purchased to suit the style of invisible zipper used and the type of sewing machine you have. Made of several plastic parts, it comes with complete directions.

Hemming foot turns and stitches a narrow hem in one step.

Button foot holds a flat sew-through button for zigzag stitching. To form a thread shank, put a toothpick in the groove of the short, open foot.

Gathering foot locks fabric fullness in each stitch to gather or shirr.

Roller foot feeds leathers, vinyls, synthetic fabrics, and knits evenly through the machine.

Quilting foot has an adjustable space guide for making parallel rows of straight stitching. It's easy to use for lightly padded fabrics or various stitching designs.

Binder foot applies bias binding to an unfinished edge with straight, zigzag, or decorative stitching.

ATTACHMENTS

The following are optional attachments to speed your machine work.

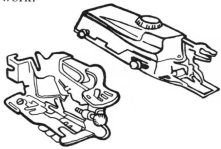

Seam guide adjusts to stitch seams of uniform width.

Circular stitcher guides fabric in a perfect full or half circle. It adjusts from 2″ to 10″ diameters.

Buttonholer makes durable, uniform buttonholes. Templates are included for buttonholes from 5/16″ to 1½″. Most buttonholers make eyelets and keyhole buttonholes, too.

Gauge presser foot is for topstitching. It is gauged to 1/16″ and can be used on the right or left side of needle.

Ruffler gathers or pleats ruffles and can attach them as they are made.

Tucker forms, and straight or decoratively stitches tucks ⅛″-1″ wide.

Edge stitcher uses straight stitches to join or insert lace, or make French seams and seam finishes.

Set

You're all SET . . . the get-acquainted stage has arrived. We're going to introduce you to patterns . . . sample some perfect fit . . . and dive into fabric hands first!

Make a clean sweep in your sewing area . . . space is the most important thing on your horizon. Spreading out patterns and fabric takes a lot of room. Find a big flat table, and collect the tools you'll need.

Between you and Butterick patterns, there are no secrets . . . we explain it all—on intimate terms. The goal is mutual understanding and respect. Beautiful fit is another aim—flattery will get us everywhere. Learn the most particular details to help make your garment a fitting masterpiece . . . whatever shape it takes.

And then to the real stuff . . . cut and mark with confidence on fabric that you know is well-prepared. Or take the plunge and tackle a special project . . . one of those very new, very super, very interesting fabrics that begs for your idea of fashion.

Butterick gives you the inside word—the beautiful beginnings of a great ending!

Patterns—The Inside Line

Fit Is Beautiful

Fabric Perfect

Layout Wise

Making Your Mark

Fabrics That Groove

What's In It For You

Patterns—The Inside Line

The beginnings of a great new wardrobe are tucked away in the pattern you've just bought. Take a long look at the contents of the envelope before doing anything else.

The instruction sheet and pattern pieces are carefully planned to simultaneously explain and illustrate how to make the garment you've chosen. Cutting and sewing will be simple, quick, and accurate when you follow the instructions keyed to your particular pattern.

THE INSTRUCTION SHEET

Inside the pattern envelope, you'll find an instruction sheet prepared for you by Butterick. This guide, created by sewing experts at Butterick, brings all of their knowledge and skill to you.

Butterick professionals have figured out the most economical use of fabric and the easiest, fastest, and best sewing procedures to use on your particular garment. Sewing the foolproof Butterick way begins with reading and understanding your instruction sheet.

The instructions are separated into two areas, and on the following pages, each division of the sheet is thoroughly explained. A pattern with multiple views may have more than one sheet of instructions; in such a case, pages are numbered for your convenience.

One side of the instruction sheet is devoted to all the special information you'll need to cut and mark your garment pieces, while the other side covers actual garment construction.

INSPIRATION

Read from left to right across the top of the outside, or first page, of your instruction sheet. You'll see that there are four blocks of information. These are designed to acquaint you with the fashion you've chosen and to help you get busy with the shears without any worries!

1 BUTTERICK PATTERN IDENTIFICATION is your assurance of the newest, greatest styles and of the information you'll need to really get them together. The style number is easy to see in the upper left corner. Beneath are illustrations of all the versions you can make from your pattern; each fashion view is lettered so that you can quickly select the information which relates to it from the complete data on your instruction sheet.

2 PATTERN PIECES eliminates any confusion as to which piece is what and goes where! Here, also in a box, you are shown the shape of each pattern piece along with its name and number. If more than one garment can be made from your pattern, you'll find the pieces grouped according to the garment in which they will be used.

3 STEP-BY-STEP GUIDE gives you some important reminders about adjusting the fit of your pattern, preparing and arranging your fabric for cutting, understanding Butterick pattern symbols, and marking and sewing your garment—all in all, the special make-or-break details.

4 CUTTING LAYOUTS are one of the best things that ever happened to sewing. They fill the bottom half of the first page and sometimes, because of their completeness, go onto an additional page or pages.

Saving is the object of Butterick's cutting layouts—and your time and money are what we've set out to preserve. For each garment or version in any fabric width and pattern size you might be using, Butterick experts have carefully planned cutting layouts for the least possible amount of fabric.

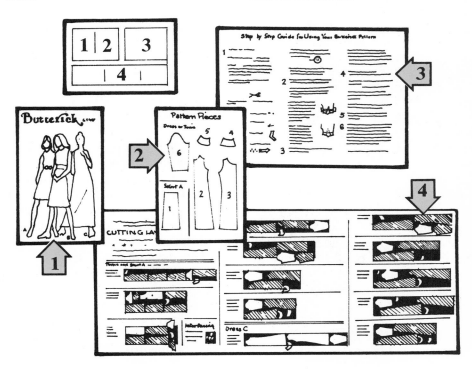

All the ins and outs of planning cutting layouts have been taken care of for you—no need to wrack your brain figuring out how to fit all those little pattern pieces on that uncooperative length of fabric!

Some cutting layouts may look a little strange—pattern pieces hanging off the fabric, or the fabric itself folded, or not folded, quite differently from what you'd expect. It's all in the interest of economy. We don't want you throwing away a lot of fabric scraps or wasting energy cutting pieces you don't need.

Special cutting information is given when you have to cut pattern pieces which require additional layout preparation. Situations involving this are marked in the diagram of your cutting layout with a special key symbol on the affected pattern piece.

Cutting layouts are also included for any interfacing or lining to be used, and for contrast fabric when this is a feature of the design.

Locate the fashion view that you're planning to make, then find the cutting layouts for fabric width.

Next, choose the layout for your pattern size from those which are on the proper fabric width. It's a good idea to circle your layout so you can refer to it quickly and easily as you work.

1 SEPARATE LAYOUTS have been planned for each garment version, which has also been lettered for your convenience in identifying it. Next to the name of each version are the numbers of the pattern pieces to be used so you can quickly select the ones you need.

2 COMMERCIAL WIDTHS of recommended fabric types each have cutting layouts for the various garment versions. Also, there are notations for which pattern sizes a layout can be used.

The problem presented by napped fabrics is solved for you by Butterick. All cutting layouts state whether or not they can be used for napped fabrics. Don't worry—the layouts are still economical! Refer to page 135 for more information about cutting out napped fabrics.

3 FABRIC is indicated in a cutting layout by dark shading. Because it can be folded in many different ways, folds and selvages are labelled so they can be quickly and accurately identified. Always fold your fabric exactly as illustrated.

4 PATTERN PIECES are indicated as white when they are to be placed printed side up on the fabric. If pattern pieces are to be placed printed side down, they are shaded with diagonal lines. It's easy to slip up here, so keep close track of which pieces face up and which face down.

5 SPECIAL CUTTING INFORMATION is given when a pattern piece is shown extending beyond the fold. Cut all other pattern pieces first, then unfold the fabric and cut this piece last from a single thickness of fabric. Be very careful to place the pattern piece on the indicated grain.

If you're cutting sleeves singly, place the pattern piece face up once and face down once so that right and left sleeves will be opposites. This is noted in your cutting layout, but it's easy to forget unless you've made the mistake in the past!

Refer to pages 122-124 for more about cutting layouts.

Dress and Pants A

USE PIECES 1, 2, 3, 4, 5, 6, 7, 8, 9, 10

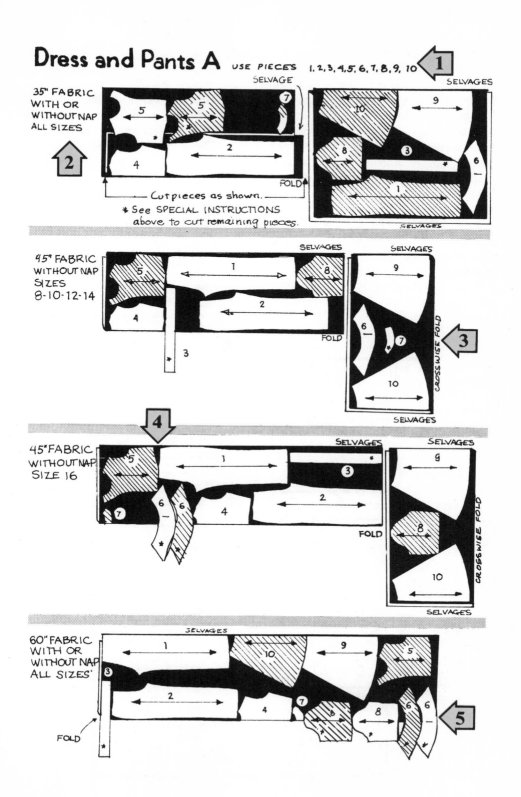

35" FABRIC WITH OR WITHOUT NAP ALL SIZES

SELVAGE
SELVAGES

— Cut pieces as shown.
* See SPECIAL INSTRUCTIONS above to cut remaining pieces.

FOLD
SELVAGES

45" FABRIC WITHOUT NAP SIZES 8-10-12-14

SELVAGES
SELVAGES
CROSSWISE FOLD
FOLD
SELVAGES

45" FABRIC WITHOUT NAP SIZE 16

SELVAGES
SELVAGES
FOLD
CROSSWISE FOLD
SELVAGES

60" FABRIC WITH OR WITHOUT NAP ALL SIZES

SELVAGES
FOLD

87

CREATION

Getting you in step with sewing is what the flip side of the instruction sheet is all about. Butterick pattern style number in the upper left corner identifies your garment. Throughout this sewing book, we use exactly the same general and key information that is presented on every Butterick instruction sheet.

1 FABRIC ILLUSTRATION KEY explains the meanings of shade and texture as these are used in the illustrations. The right side of the fabric is indicated by a gray tone, the wrong side by white, interfacing by dots, and lining by diagonal shading lines.

2 GENERAL INSTRUCTIONS follow the key and are some important points to remember when sewing. There are hints about fitting, stitching, trimming, and pressing.

3 SEWING GUIDE fills the remainder of the page. If your pattern has many versions, these instructions may run onto additional sheets. This is done so that no details will be left out which may be important in achieving a professional-looking finished garment.

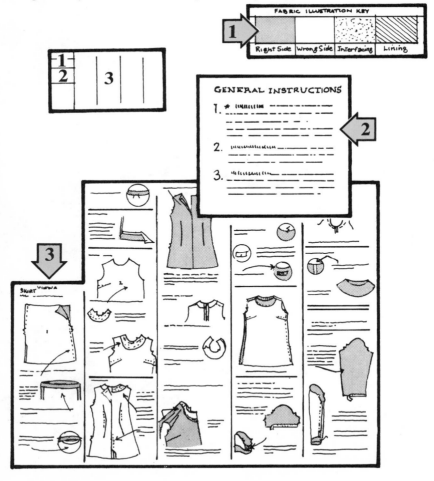

Titles separate and identify the instructions for each view or lettered garment version of the pattern. Numbered steps indicate each unit of construction which goes into a particular version of the garment. A title next to each step tells you which part of the garment this aspect of construction will complete.

Directions and illustrations within each garment unit explain sewing procedures a step at a time; arrows show you which illustration relates to which block of instructions.

Enlarged views are magnified illustrations to clarify especially important or complicated details of garment construction. They're circled so you'll know immediately that extra care is in order.

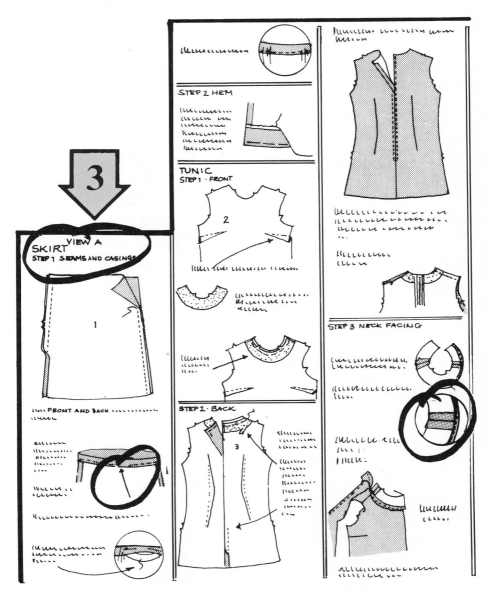

PATTERN-TALK

Open the folded pattern tissue and separate the pieces. On each pattern piece there is a system of shorthand; this is a number of symbols and markings which, once learned, save a lot of reading time. Each symbol represents a whole idea of garment construction. Some symbols will appear in every garment that you make. Don't panic—you'll be surprised at how logical the symbols are; in no time at all, pattern-talk will be second nature to you!

Butterick pattern identification is found near the center of every piece and includes number, piece name, version, and size. The large number tells you the order in which garment pieces will be put together. Special cutting instructions are given in a near-by box for easy location whenever a pattern piece is to be cut other than twice or from another fabric.

1 GRAINLINE is heavy, solid, and has arrowheads at both ends. When pinning your pattern piece to the fabric, this line should parallel the straight grain. In most cases, you should pin the pattern grainline parallel to the selvage along the lengthwise grain; exceptions to this are always noted on each pattern piece.

2 CUTTING LINE is the heavy and solid outermost line of the pattern piece. It's got scissors on it for quick identification. If you see a cutting line within the pattern piece, this indicates a cut-off line for a style variation.

3 SEAMLINE is a long, broken line, and unless otherwise specified, is ⅝″ inside the cutting line. A presser foot on the line tells you at a glance exactly where to stitch.

4 EASING LINE is a broken line between notches, with arrowheads at both ends. It indicates a seamline that is to be drawn up on a row of stitching before it can be joined to another seamline; notches on other seamline show finished length of eased area.

A gathering line is similar, but consists of two broken lines instead of one; it indicates that a greater amount of fabric is to be drawn up with two rows of stitching.

5 ●'s, ●'s, ■'s, and/or ▲'s on pattern pieces must be carefully transferred to the fabric. Matching these symbols on corresponding pattern pieces helps you to join garment sections accurately. They are also used as aids in matching plaids, stripes, or printed fabrics. Always sew through or to the center of each symbol, depending on its location on a seamline.

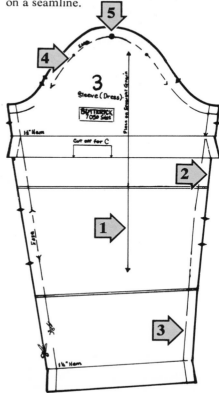

1 DARTS consist of two broken lines with ●'s which correspond on each. Transfer all markings to fabric, then match and stitch carefully.

2 NOTCHES are black, diamond-shaped symbols which extend beyond the cutting line. Cut around them so that you can use them in matching seams. Notches are numbered so that you will know the order in which seam-lines will be joined.

3 FOLDLINES are solid lines which show you where the garment is to be folded during construction to form an edge. When labelled Roll Line, the fold is to be softly rolled rather than creased.

4 BUTTONS and **BUTTON-HOLES** are marked by lines which show the exact location and size of the button, and the exact location and length of the buttonhole.

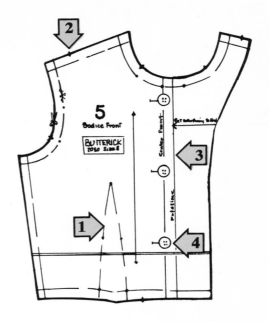

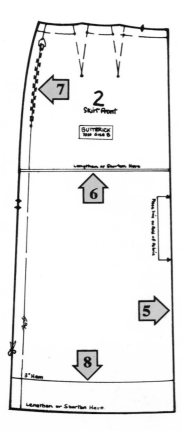

5 CENTER FRONT and **CENTER BACK** are solid lines. They tell you which part of the garment is to be along a vertical center of the body. Brackets indicate that a center line of the pattern piece is to be placed along a fold of fabric in the cutting layout. Always mark center lines on fabric for use as reference points in checking grain when fitting and for locating buttons and buttonholes.

6 ADJUSTMENT LINE is a double line which indicates where to adjust the fit of your pattern by lengthening or shortening it within the garment area. Lengthening and shortening information is also found at hem edges. In this case, this is the area in which you need to make an adjustment.

7 ZIPPER PLACEMENT is indicated by marks which represent the zipper chain. A pull tab at the top and a stop at the bottom show the exact location of the zipper.

8 HEMLINE is a finished edge of the garment. Along this line you'll find information concerning appropriate hem depth.

A Little Effort: A Lot Of Fit

Fit Is Beautiful

Perfect fit makes clothes your very own. Since almost no one corresponds exactly to the statistical averages used in pattern sizes, personalized fitting is necessary. Fitting a pattern before cutting out your fabric falls into two distinct categories.

ADJUSTMENTS: 5-minute minor changes are made on pattern before pinning it to fabric. Make equal changes on all related pattern pieces —front, back, facings, and linings. Divide the amount of circumference adjustment by four to change each quarter of your pattern equally.

ALTERATIONS: 15-minute changes are localized and often don't affect related garment sections. To find and correct figure flaws, make a basic fitting shell in muslin from Butterick's Personal Fitting Pattern for a fitted or an A-line garment.

FITTING CHECK-LIST: Think of these rules as you analyze fit and plan adjustments or alterations.

- Purchase patterns according to body measurements taken carefully and often (see the Pattern section for more information).
- Press pattern with a warm, dry iron to remove wrinkles.
- Make changes on pattern.
  Additions: (1) at edges, draw new construction lines, extending pattern with tissue if necessary; (2) within garment, slash pattern as indicated for change, placing tissue underneath and spreading cut edges as needed (pleat pattern if necessary so it will lie flat).

Subtractions: (1) at edges, draw new construction lines; (2) within garment, tuck pattern as indicated for half the amount of change, tapering if needed (clip pattern if necessary to make it lie flat).

- Make changes on muslin fitting shell (these are then transferred to pattern by the methods of addition and subtraction).
  Pin Out: Tuck muslin until problem is corrected.
  Spread: Slash muslin in problem area and insert a strip of fabric cut on same grain under cut edges. Spread muslin as needed and baste strip in place.
  Extend: Insert a strip of fabric cut on same grain under garment edge in problem area; baste. On curved edges, use a shaped bias strip.
- Re-draw disrupted grainlines; correct construction lines by equalizing them on both sides of the change to taper smoothly into the original contour.
- Only pattern pieces most affected by a fitting change will be shown; make corresponding changes on related pattern pieces.
- Changes are shown on pattern pieces for a basic fitted garment. When applying changes to another style—A-line, princess, or raglan—involves different procedures, they're illustrated.
- Mount your adjusted and altered pattern on cardboard or non-woven interfacing. It's a permanent record of fit to transfer to all Butterick patterns.

93

5-MINUTE FIT

Flat pattern adjustments involve length and circumference. Compare your measurements with those on envelope back; record variations. Change pattern accordingly.

LENGTH ADJUSTMENTS: These are made using center back measurements from base of neck to waist and from waist to hip and hip to hem edge. Make equal changes on front and back pattern pieces, shortening or lengthening as needed.

Shorten: Subtract amount of change at adjustment lines, if any. To raise hipline, subtract amount of change between waist and hip. To shorten at lower edge, cut away excess pattern parallel to original cutting line.

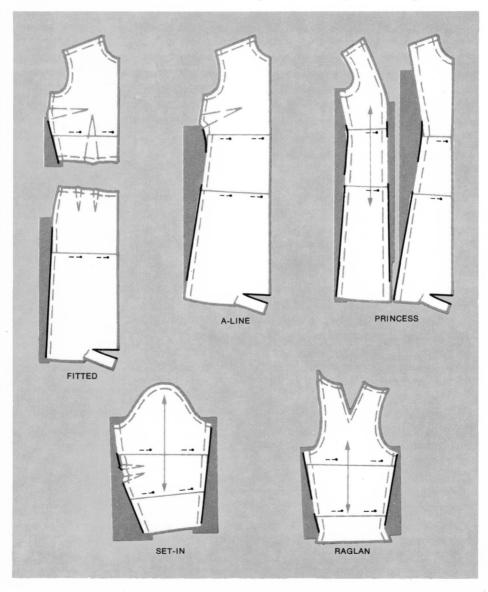

FITTED

A-LINE

PRINCESS

SET-IN

RAGLAN

Lengthen: Add amount of change at adjustment lines when these are given. To lower hipline, add amount of change in area of pattern between waist and hip. To lengthen at a lower edge, extend pattern as you would for an addition; continue original seamlines and cutting lines on the tissue which you added. At the lower edge of pattern, draw a new cutting line that is parallel to the original cutting line.

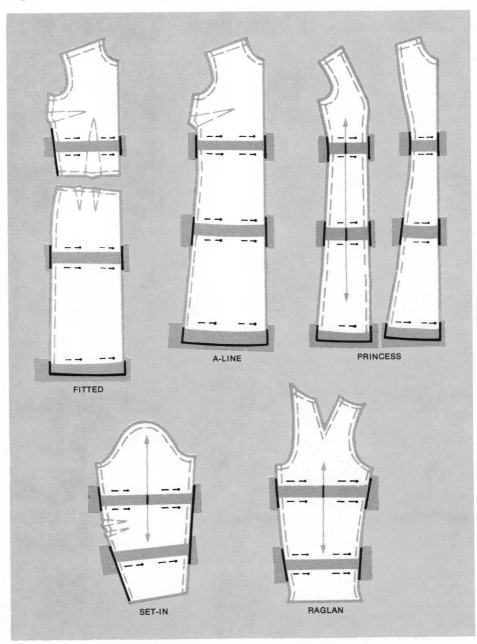

FITTED

A-LINE

PRINCESS

SET-IN

RAGLAN

CIRCUMFERENCE ADJUST-MENTS: Make equal changes on front and back pattern pieces, taking in or letting out ¼ of the amount of change at side seams of front and back. For a princess style, divide amount of change by the number of seams, then adjust each seam.

Reducing Waist and Hips: To take in less than 1″, mark change on side seam at waist and hip; draw new construction lines (not shown).

To take in more than 1″, subtract change (taking in A-line styles more than 1″ may distort design lines).

change. Be sure to slash far enough into the pattern for it to lie flat.

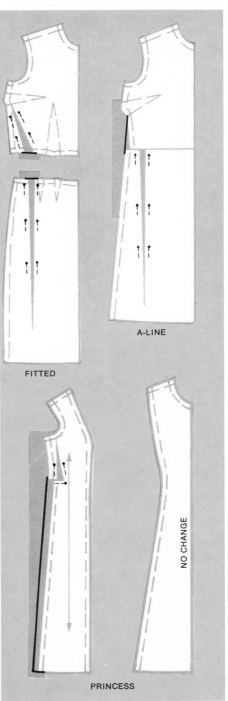

A-LINE

FITTED

PRINCESS

NO CHANGE

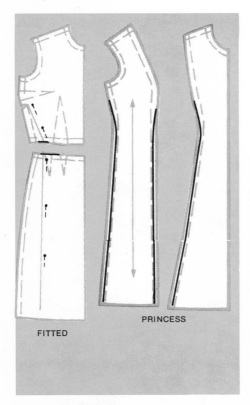

FITTED

PRINCESS

Enlarging Waist and Hips: To let out less than 1″, add change to side seams at waist and hips; draw new construction lines (not shown).

To let out more than 1″, add

Reducing Waist Without Adjusting Hips: Take in side seams at waist by drawing new construction lines. Taper these new lines to the waist and hip (not shown).

Enlarging Hips: To let out less than 2″, add change to side seams below waist.

To let out more than 2″, add by slashing skirt from waist to hem along straight grain. For A-line styles, slash from hem to hip along straight grain, then slash at a right angle to side seam. If waist was made larger, add darts or take in seams; retain hip adjustment.

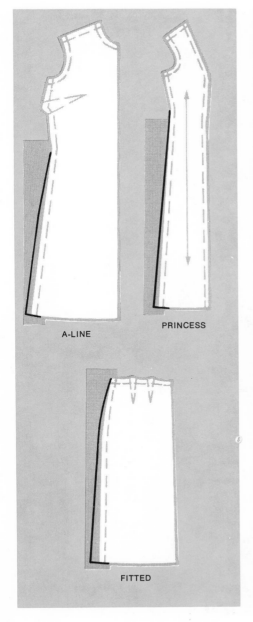

A-LINE   PRINCESS

FITTED

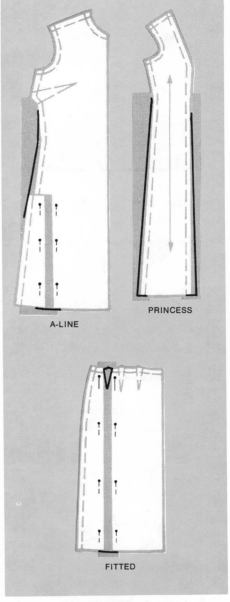

A-LINE   PRINCESS

FITTED

15-MINUTE FIT

On your completed muslin fitting shell there may be areas which need a bit of altering to fit properly. Pattern tissue adjustments can't compensate for the individualized fitting you may need. Make alterations in your fitting shell as directed for specific problem areas; don't over-fit, as this accentuates figure flaws.

NECKLINES: The fitting shell neckline should encircle the base of neck smoothly. There should be no pulling or looseness. Alter front, back, and facing pattern pieces accordingly.

Too Tight: Draw a line on garment where neckline should be. Stitch along line, then clip to stitching at ½″ intervals until neckline is comfortable.

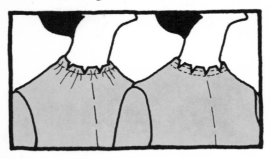 

Too Large: Extend garment neckline until it is high enough to encircle the base of the neck. Take care to keep the extended section close to the body.

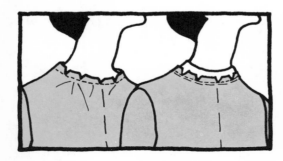 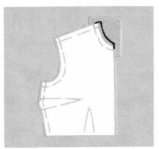

Gaping: Test changes for gaping necklines in muslin before cutting into your fashion fabric.

If the problem is *excess fabric,* pin out wrinkles, tapering to armhole seam and shortening center.

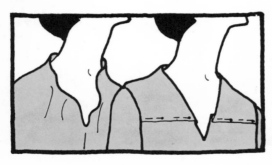 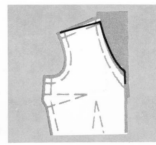

If the problem is *pulling at armhole,* slash from neckline to armhole seam; spread armhole area as needed.

Too little room across bodice is remedied by alteration for bust with large cup (page 105).

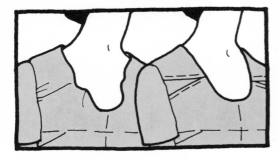

Too Low: Cut neck facings in muslin; stitch them together and along neck seamline. Turn seam allowance to inside along stitching, clipping at ½″ intervals; baste. Try on facing. Extend neckline to desired depth.

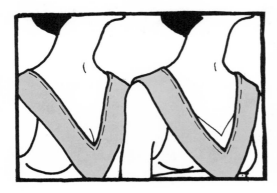

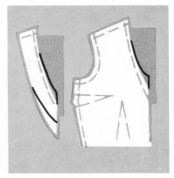

SHOULDERS: Fabric should be smoothly molded over shoulder area. Seams should be centered on top of the shoulders, and should extend from the base of neck to the arm hinge. Alter front and back pattern pieces accordingly.

Sloping: Inserting shoulder pads may correct this. If not, remove sleeves and pin excess fabric out at shoulders, tapering to neckline; lower armhole seamline the same amount.

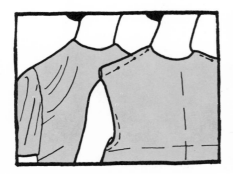

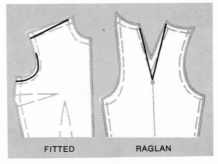

FITTED   RAGLAN

Square: Remove sleeve and slash front and back near shoulder seam from armhole edge to neckline; spread until wrinkles disappear.

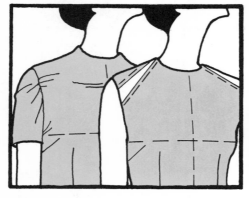

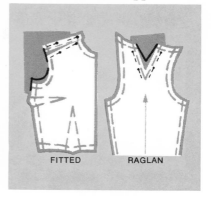

FITTED   RAGLAN

Narrow: Pin a dart in both front and back. Be sure that dart is deep enough to pull the armhole seam into the proper place.

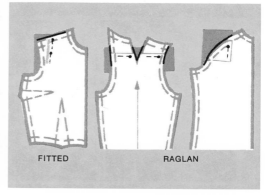

FITTED   RAGLAN

Broad: Slash front and back from the shoulder seam to the armhole seam; spread cut edges until they are smooth.

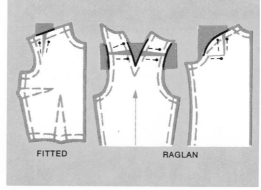

FITTED   RAGLAN

SLEEVELESS ARMHOLES: Cut and construct bodice in muslin; stitch along armhole seamline. Turn seam allowance to inside along stitching; clip at ½″ to ¾″ intervals and baste in place. Armhole should fit smoothly, with underarm seam 1″ below armpit. Alter front, back, and facing pattern pieces accordingly.

Too Large: Pin out fabric at shoulders. If alteration is extensive, extend under the arm.

If only bodice front gapes, use the alteration for a bust with a large cup; if only bodice back gapes, use the rounded back alteration.

Too Tight: Draw new line at armhole. Stitch along line; clip to stitching at ½″ intervals until armhole is comfortable (not shown).

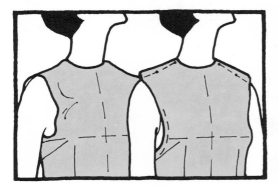
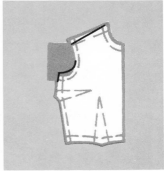

SLEEVES: Improper sleeve fit usually results from the shape of the sleeve cap not corresponding with the shape of the top of your arm. The alteration can be as simple as readjusting an improper distribution of ease in the sleeve cap or correcting a sleeve cap that's the wrong length. In order to alter, you'll have to re-move the sleeve cap from the armhole between notches.

Improper Distribution of Ease: Re-distribute ease until wrinkles disappear. If wrinkles started at front of cap, move ease forward. For wrinkles that started at back of cap, move ease backward. Re-baste sleeve into armhole to check appearance.

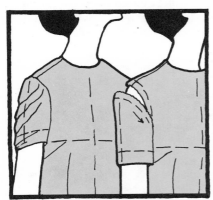

Skimpy Sleeve Cap: Slash horizontally across entire width of sleeve cap and spread the amount needed to lengthen cap.

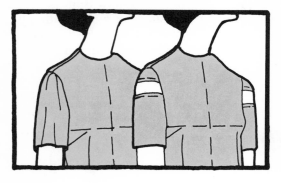 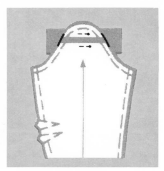

Sleeve Cap Too Long: Pin out excess fabric in tucks on sleeve cap; taper ends of tucks to nothing at the seam of the sleeve cap.

 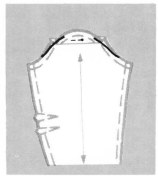

Excess Ease in Sleeve Cap: Smooth sleeve cap and pin a shallow vertical dart at top of sleeve; re-baste sleeve in place.

On pattern, make a 3″- 4″ slash at shoulder marking; lap edges amount to be decreased; clip in 1½″ at ends of eased area. Maintain width across sleeve cap where ease ends; shorten sleeve cap slightly.

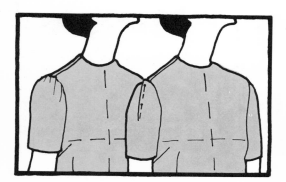 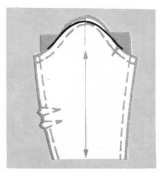

Thin Arm: Pin out excess fabric in a lengthwise tuck from cap to lower edge; taper tuck at lower edge in order to allow enough room for hand to pass. The sleeve cap will have less ease.

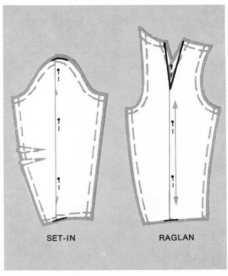

SET-IN   RAGLAN

Large Arm: Slash along lengthwise marking and spread amount needed. Easestitch 1″- 2″ beyond markings. Re-baste sleeve in armhole.

If sleeve still binds, make the alteration for square shoulders.

Thick Elbow: Remove stitching from elbow area. Slash across sleeve between darts to grainline, then to upper edge of sleeve; spread amount needed. Add a dart between original ones; restitch seam (not shown).

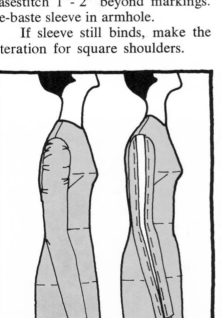

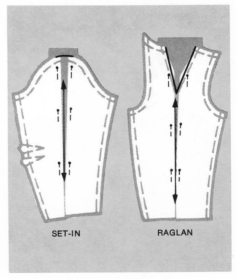

SET-IN   RAGLAN

BUST: Purchase patterns according to bust measurement so you'll have the circumference needed. Bust alterations usually involve re-positioning or re-shaping darts, or accommodating a bust with a larger or smaller than average cup size.

When a very broad back takes away some of the girth needed in front, use back alterations.

High or Low Bust: Align darts with fullest part of bust by raising or lowering them. Mark line on muslin where dart should be. Open dart and side seam and re-stitch dart in correct position. If necessary, lengthen or shorten front darts.

For a princess style, add amount to be raised or subtract amount to be lowered at a point above armhole notch on pattern. Make opposite change on pattern below bust to maintain original bodice length.

Bust Dart Length: End underarm bust darts ½"-1" from the fullest part of bust. Shorten or lengthen by marking muslin where dart should end; open dart and seam and re-stitch dart in proper length (not shown).

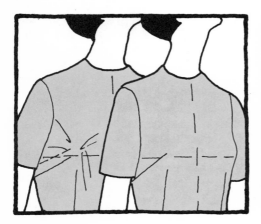
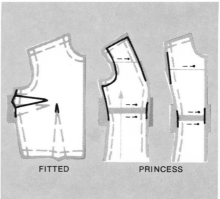

HIGH BUST

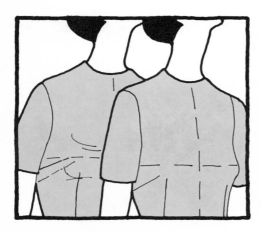
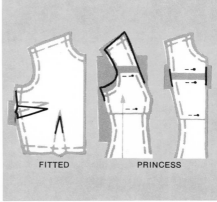

Bust with Small Cup: Pin out excess fabric in horizontal tucks which taper to the side seams and in vertical tucks which taper to shoulder and waistline.

For an A-line style, taper vertical tucks beyond waistline into the skirt area; add amount of change to side seams in the skirt area (not shown).

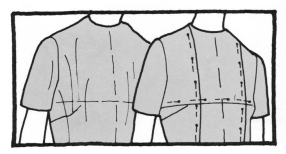 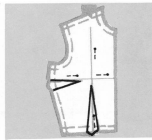

Bust with Large Cup: Slash through bust darts and across front. Slash front from shoulder to waistline; spread as needed.

For an A-line style, slash beyond waistline into skirt area; subtract amount spread from side seams in skirt area (not shown).

 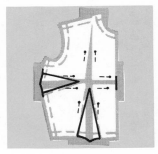

CHEST: Bone structure causes many of the problems in this area. Garment should be smooth, without tightness or wrinkling.

Hollow: Pin out wrinkles in tucks which taper to armhole or shoulder seams, decreasing length at center front.

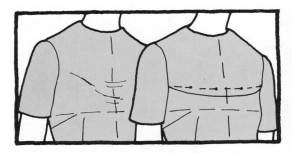 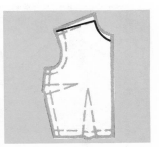

Pigeon: Slash across front above bust and continue up to shoulder seam through center of shoulder area; spread amount needed.

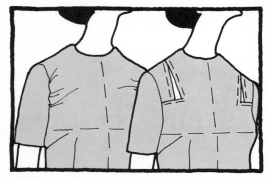 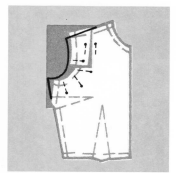

BACK: Garment back should be smooth from neck to hem, and hem should be even. Bone structure and poor posture cause problems.

Very Erect: Pin out wrinkles in tucks which taper to armhole or shoulder seams, decreasing length at center back.

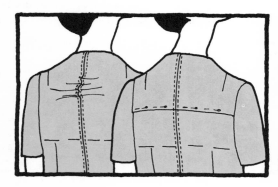 

High, Rounded: Slash across back between armhole seams and remove stitching from zipper above slash; spread as needed, allowing for center back opening. Pin darts in neck edge to fit contour; add more strips to extend back edges to center opening.

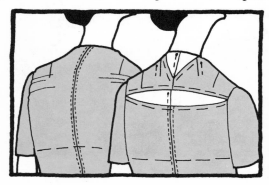 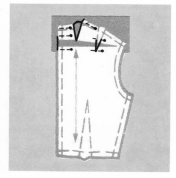

Narrow: Pin out excess fabric in a vertical tuck which extends from shoulder darts to waist darts. Back darts will then be continuous and will look like a seam. For A-line garments, use same procedure. Back darts will be continuous from shoulder into skirt area.

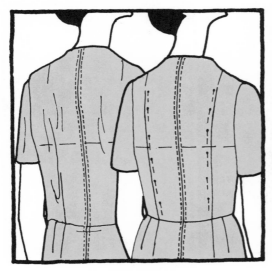
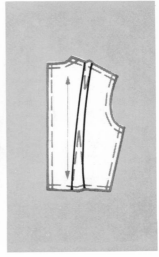

Broad Back or Prominent Shoulder Blades: Remove stitching at shoulder seams, shoulder darts, and side seams. Slash across bodice back below armhole and continue up through center of shoulder dart; spread pattern as needed. Deepen the existing darts or add new ones to conform to the body contour at shoulders. Restitch seams.

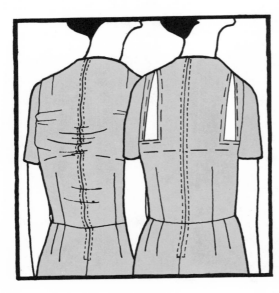
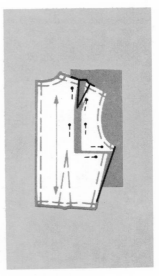

Sway: Pin out excess fabric in a tuck which tapers to side seams, decreasing length the appropriate amount at center back; darts will be shorter.

For an A-line garment, make a diagonal tuck in at center back. Tuck should be equal to amount pinned out and should taper to nothing at side; darts will be shorter.

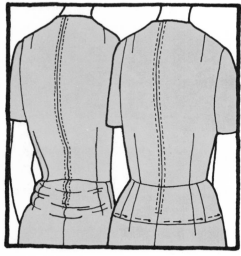
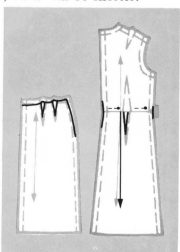

HIPS: Bone structure and posture are the usual causes of hip alterations. Fabric should mold smoothly over buttocks and hip bones.

Flat Buttocks: Pin out sagging excess fabric across hips until hem is even. Release darts, then re-pin to make shorter, narrower darts which conform to body contour. Re-stitch darts and seams.

For an A-line style, release back darts and zipper below back bustline. Pin out excess fabric at side and center back seams. Pin shorter and narrower darts. Re-stitch seams and darts (not shown).

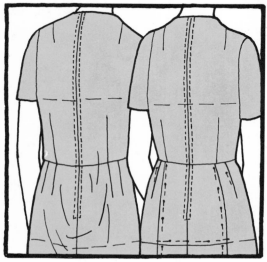
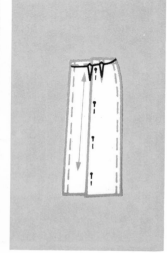

Large Buttocks or Large Back at Top of Hips: Remove stitching from darts below waist and waist seam. Re-pin darts to fit contour, adding to sides if necessary. Re-stitch darts and seams.

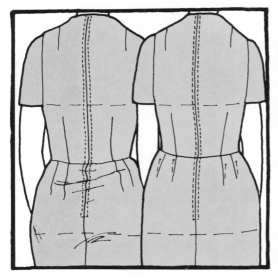
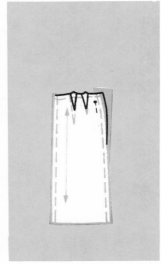

For an A-line garment, release the darts, seams, and zipper below bustline on back section. Spread center back and side seams to bring side seams into position; baste. Re-pin darts to fit contour.

Protruding Hip Bones: Refer to the Pants section for this alteration.

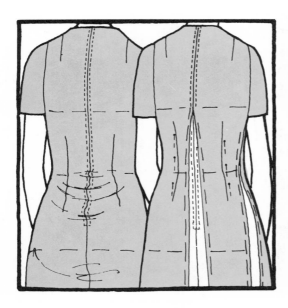
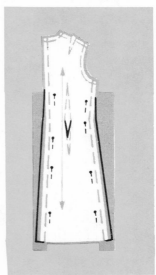

One Large Hip: Remove the stitching from waistline seam and darts of shorter side. Drop the skirt until grainlines and hem are straight, extending sides and top of skirt to cor- rect position. Re-pin darts to fit body contour and baste the skirt to the bodice along new waist seamline. Make a separate pattern piece for left side of garment; alter appropriate half.

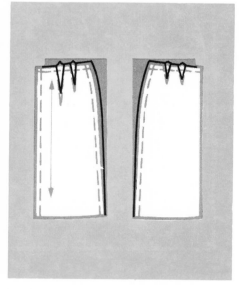

For an A-line style, remove stitching from waist area of shorter side seam and from dart. Spread until grain and hem are straight. Re-pin back darts to fit body contour. Make a separate pattern piece for left side of garment and alter appropriate half of pattern.

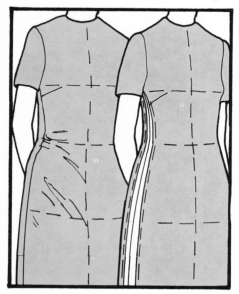

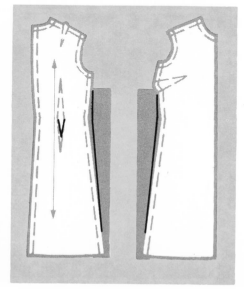

ABDOMEN: Release front waist seam and darts. Drop skirt front until it hangs evenly; extend top edge of skirt with a fabric strip. Re-pin darts to fit body contour; if this makes waist smaller, add the amount needed to side seams. Re-stitch darts and seams.

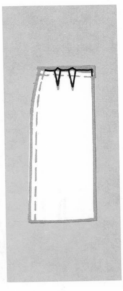

For an A-line garment, slash front section from lower edge to bust area. Spread as needed until the side seams, waistline, and hipline fall into position. When transferring the alteration to pattern, slash through bust dart so pattern edges overlap and lie flat.

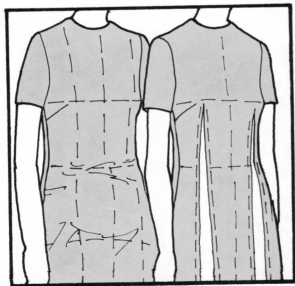

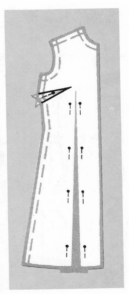

COMBINING SIZES

Sometimes using a pattern in two sizes is easier than making major alterations on either the skirt or the bodice.

Buy your two patterns according to your body measurements. Note the difference in waistline measurements of the two sizes; if your waist measurement agrees with one pattern size, adjust the other to correspond. To adjust both waists to the same measurement, determine the amount to be enlarged on one and reduced on the other; divide this amount among the seams and adjust each pattern piece accordingly.

Always keep center fronts and backs, and grainlines straight. On fitted garments with a waist seam, the waistlines must match when joined; you may have to move either bodice or skirt darts to accomplish this.

To combine two patterns in an A-line style, cut both patterns apart and tape corresponding sections together.

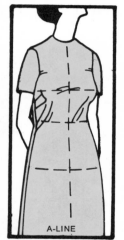
FITTED   A-LINE

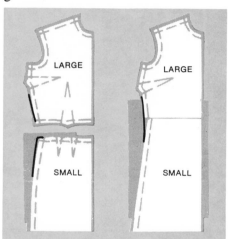
LARGE BUST – SMALL HIPS

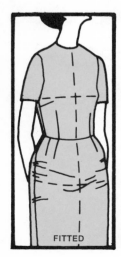

FITTED   A-LINE

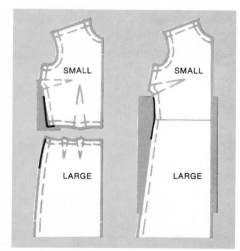
LARGE HIPS – SMALL BUST

PANTS

Comfortable, practical, and great fashion are the bywords of the pants story. The hitch is that they're only true when pants fit perfectly. Choose your pattern size by waist measurement; when your hip measurement is disproportionately larger choose size by hip measurement. If individualized fit is your goal, plan to make a basic pants pattern in muslin. Refer to the Fitting Checklist on page 93 for general information on how to adjust and alter your pants pattern. A pants muslin is an invaluable tool in achieving perfect fit on all your pants, no matter what the style.

5-MINUTE FIT

Your tape measure is your guide to fitting adjustments. In the Pattern section, you'll find which measurements to take, and how to take them. Use your chart of these measurements to make length and circumference adjustments on your pattern.

CROTCH LENGTH: This is the single most important adjustment to be made in fitting pants. Unless the crotch is cut to fit you, it will never conform to your figure. No amount of fitting pants in your fashion fabric can remedy a crotch seam that wasn't cut at the proper depth and angle.

Establish position of crotch on the **back** pattern piece if none is indicated on the pattern. Make a dot on the seamline at widest point of pattern or at lowest point of crotch curve seamline. Place a right-angle triangle along grainline so its base crosses point of crotch; draw a line along edge of triangle across pattern piece from inner seam edge to side edge.

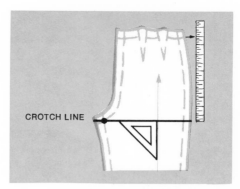

CROTCH LINE

Take your measurements and compare them to those of your pattern. The side measurement from the crotch line to waist seamline should equal the crotch length measurement plus ½″–¾″ sitting ease. Adjust back, then make an equal change on the **front** pattern piece.

Shorten: Subtract amount of change at adjustment line of pattern.

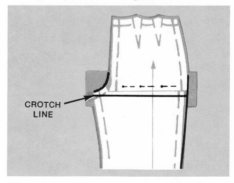

CROTCH LINE

Lengthen: Add amount of change at adjustment line of pattern.

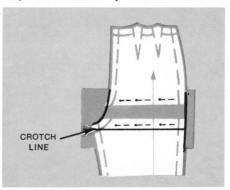

CROTCH LINE

POSITION LINES: Draw lines on the **back** pattern piece that will establish points of your body to use later if the need for alterations is apparent. Extend the grainline to the edges of the pattern. At the side, measure down along side seamline from waist seamline the distance established as your high hip measurement point; mark a location dot. Place a right-angle triangle along grainline so its base crosses this dot; draw a line along edge of triangle from dot across the entire pattern piece. This is your *High Hip* position line. Repeat it on your **front** pattern piece; make sure that position lines on back and front match at the side seamlines.

Use the same procedure to draw position lines at *Full Hip, Thigh, Knee* and *Calf* levels. (Knee and Calf are important guidelines in making shorter length or slim fitting pants.) Make a note of your body measurements at each position line.

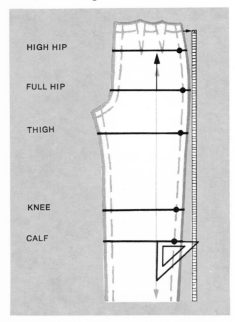

PANTS LENGTH: Check total length of pants along side seamline after making crotch alteration. To lengthen or shorten, add or subtract amount of change (see page 93).

WAIST CIRCUMFERENCE: Note difference between measurements of your waistline and pattern waistline.

To change pattern waistline, add or subtract ⅛ of this amount from each center and side seam of pattern front and back (see page 93). Make corresponding adjustments on waistband or facing pattern pieces.

HIP CIRCUMFERENCE: Purchasing your pants pattern by hip measurement should make adjustments unnecessary in this area. Very slight changes can be made just as you would those of a skirt (page 96-97).

LEG CIRCUMFERENCE: Measure thigh line from seam to seam on front and back pattern pieces; the sum of these measurements should equal your body thigh measurement plus 1″ to 2″ for wearing ease. To make pattern leg **wider** or **narrower** add or subtract ½ the amount of change at inner leg seam on front and back pattern pieces; retain the curve of the crotch seam.

For slim-fitting and tapered pants, you'll have to pay extra attention to lower leg circumference measurements. Pants of these types should fit closely, yet still allow easy movement. Check your knee, calf, and instep body measurements against those of your pattern at each position line. Allow approximately 1″ wearing ease at each point. If any changes are necessary, make the adjustments by adding or subtracting at edges (see page 93).

15-MINUTE FIT

Just like the basic fitted or A-line shell, your basic pants are cut from muslin. Use a tracing wheel and dressmaker's tracing paper to transfer marked position lines to the right side of muslin.

When constructing pants of either muslin or fashion fabric, the crotch seam is usually sewn after leg seams to prevent bunching and binding. To support pants during fitting, and to prevent waistline from being strained, baste a temporary waistband of grosgrain ribbon along waist seamline.

THE LOOK: Put on your pants and stand erect. Side seams should hang straight and be at right angles to the floor. Marked position lines should parallel the floor. Seams or position lines that are pulled or distorted in one way or another should cue you to the fact that alterations are necessary. Tell-tale wrinkles and sags are another sign to look for in analyzing fit. Make your goal smooth, trim pants that move easily with you.

SOLUTIONS: If only a few wrinkles show up on your muslin, the problem may be one of those easy ones to solve. For wrinkles at high hip, release darts; re-pin to fit body contour, shortening or lengthening as needed. Re-stitch.

Inner leg seam can be slightly taken in or let out as needed at crotch point. When waistline is pulled down slightly at center front or back, set the waistband a bit higher at center seam, tapering it to the seamline at sides.

The following pants alterations are made according to the methods discussed in the Fitting Checklist on page 93.

Large Abdomen: Release front waist seam and darts; extend top of pants and add to front inner leg seam until side seams are correctly positioned and pants hang wrinkle-free. If waistline has been reduced, add amount needed to front side seams. Re-pin darts to fit contour.

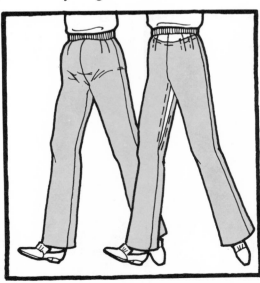
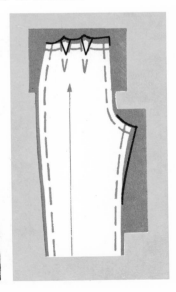

Protruding Hip Bones: Remove stitching from darts and side seams. Re-pin darts to fit contour. Add to front side seams if the waistline was made smaller. Re-stitch darts and seams.

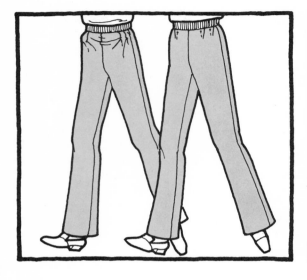 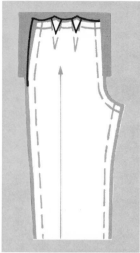

Sway Back: Use the skirt alteration on page 108.

Large Buttocks: Sometimes you'll find that more length is needed at the center back than is allowed for in the pattern. Release darts, and extend top and add to back inner leg seam of pants until side seams are correctly positioned and pants hang smoothly. Re-pin darts to fit contour. If waistline has been reduced, add amount needed to back side seams.

 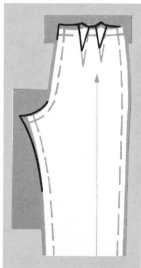

Flat Buttocks: Pin out wrinkles in a horizontal tuck across high hipline or where needed. Eliminate excess fabric along each leg by making perpendicular tucks which taper to nothing at side seams, waist, and knee. Release darts at top of pants, and re-pin to fit body contour. Take out excess waistline measurement at side seams, if necessary.

 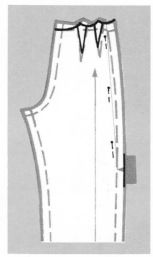

YOUR BASIC PATTERN

Wearing the pants in the family is great fun when fashion's new favorites fit you just perfectly! Compare your basic pattern to any new pattern style, and simply repeat necessary adjustments and alterations.

Depending on style, you may even be able to bypass a few fitting changes. Length measurements can't be ignored, but many circumference problems are eliminated in certain styles. The old waistline-fit story is unheard of in low-slung hipster pants.

The Navy's bell bottoms and those long, lean stovepipes remove lower leg measurements from the scene. A cue on easy-pleated gangster pants in a Thirties mood: adjust or alter, but don't remove the built-in style ease. As always, fashion has an endless list—but then, your basic pattern is a pretty adaptable item!

CONSTRUCTING PANTS

After cutting pants in your fashion fabric, always baste them together for a fitting session. It's your chance to discover any minor changes in fit required by the draping qualities of your fabric. A slight strain here or a ripple of fullness there can be removed by following the hints in the Fitting section on pages 174-176.

Use a small straight or zigzag stitch to stitch the curve of the crotch seam. Reinforce this seam because it's one of those that gets a lot of strain. Clip the seam allowances at the top of the crotch curve on both front and back; press seam allowances open above clips. Make a second line of stitching ¼″ from the first in the seam allowance between clips. Trim and overcast this edge, but do not press seam.

Ahead of the Game

Fabric Perfect

Beautiful endings are based on great beginnings. If you expect to wind up your sewing story with a fashion smash, be prepared to handle your fabric properly from the start. Besides, getting your fabric ready for sewing is a great way to get to know it!

ON GRAIN

Woven fabric has two sets of yarns or threads that are interwoven at right angles to one another. The two long finished edges of the fabric are *selvages. Lengthwise grain* parallels the selvages, while *crosswise grain* runs from one selvage to the other. Lengthwise grain and crosswise grain should be at right angles to each other.

True bias is a diagonal at a 45° angle to any straight edge or grain of a fabric whose lengthwise and crosswise grains are perpendicular. Fabric cut on the bias stretches.

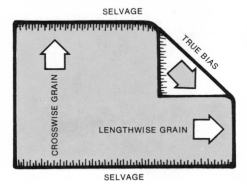

Knits are made in a different manner, and depending on type, can stretch lengthwise, or crosswise, or both. Knits usually have threads that interlock across the width or crosswise grain of the fabric, and ribs

(called wales) that correspond to the lengthwise grain.

STRAIGHTEN ENDS: All garment pieces must be cut from fabric that is on grain. To find out whether your fabric is on grain, you'll first have to straighten the ends. Cut along a crosswise thread if one can be clearly seen. Or, snip through the selvage, and slowly pull a crosswise thread until fabric puckers. Sliding the puckers ahead of your shears, cut along this thread across the width of fabric.

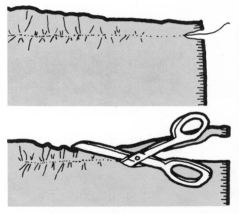

In some fabrics it's difficult or impossible to pull a thread. In cases like this, insert pins along a crosswise thread (or in knits, a loop); cut along the line of pins.

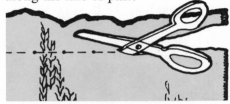

Never tear fabric to straighten ends, because doing so can stretch or pull fabric off grain.

STRAIGHTEN GRAIN: Sometimes the manufacturer has pulled or pressed fabric in an off-grain position during one of the finishing processes. The result is a fabric that has cut ends which are either slanted or curved off grain.

Test fabric for grain perfection by placing it on a cutting board or a table that has right angle corners; align one corner of the fabric with one corner of the table. If the corners and edges of the fabric and cutting board or table don't match, you'll have to straighten the grain of your fabric before laying out and cutting your pattern.

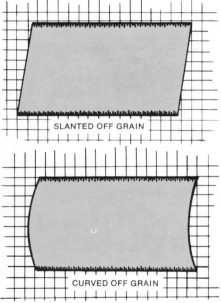

If your fabric is only slightly off grain, make a lengthwise center fold with right sides together. Match the selvages and the ends, then pin the two layers together every 5″. The wrinkles which appear are due to the off-grain state of the fabric. Thoroughly steam press and smooth the fabric with your iron or hands to align grains. Make firm, even strokes

across the fabric from the selvages toward the center fold.

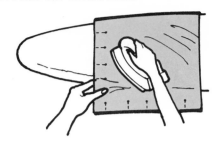

If fabric is severely off grain, pull the edges at a corner in a direction opposite the slant of the ends. Pull firmly, check to see if grain has straightened, then repeat if necessary.

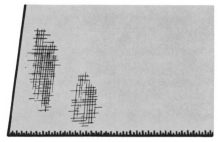

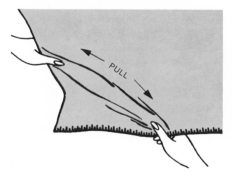

Washable fabrics can be easily straightened during the pre-shrinking process. Use the procedure recommended for pre-shrinking washable fabrics. Hang fabric lengthwise over a taut clothesline. When the fabric is still a bit damp, match the selvages exactly and pull the fabric on grain.

Never dry fabric in a breezy place, and never secure it with clothespins. Either of these procedures can pull your straightened fabric off grain once again. Fabrics that seem to resist straightening may require a repetition of the straightening process, or a combination of several of the techniques that have been discussed.

Some fabrics have been treated in such a way that they can never be straightened. Fabrics with permanent finishes, some knits, and fabrics which have been bonded in an off-grain position are prime examples and must be used as they are. Avoid purchasing fabrics with prints that are off grain.

PRE-SHRINKING

If fabric has been pre-shrunk by the manufacturer, you probably won't have to worry about doing this yourself. When purchasing fabric, take a minute to read the label on the end of the bolt or the attached hang-tag. These will usually tell you whether the fabric is washable or dry cleanable and will give you specifics on shrinkage.

Check the Fabric section for complete definitions of terms which may be pertinent to fabric shrinkage.

WASHABLE FABRICS: Fold fabric evenly and place it in cool water. Let it soak for a while.

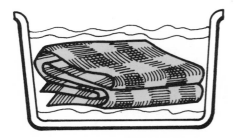

When the entire fabric is wet, gently squeeze the water out; never wring or twist fabric, as this can pull it off grain. Hang the fabric over a bar or a taut clothesline.

When the excess water has dripped from the fabric, either machine- or air-dry it as you plan to dry the finished garment.

Some fabrics, especially knits or those that are loosely woven, should not be allowed to dry completely while hanging. The weight of the water can distort the shape of the fabric.

DRY CLEANABLE FABRICS: Many of these fabrics, especially those with low residual shrinkage, can be pre-shrunk by simply giving them a thorough steam pressing. This is a good precaution to take on any wool fabric because some of these have been treated with a finish that is removed when exposed to steam. Pre-shrinking by steam pressing assures that the finish will be removed uniformly.

Fabrics not labeled pre-shrunk or which have a higher percentage of residual shrinkage should be taken to a professional or a self-service dry cleaner for pre-shrinking or steaming.

121

Layout Wise

Turning yards of flat fabric into pieces of your garment is the object of cutting layouts. Butterick has carefully planned these for you so that every pattern piece fits correctly on the allotted fabric.

PRESSING

Steam press fabric to remove the folds and creases which come from it being wrapped on a bolt. If the lengthwise fold has a crease which won't press out, plan the cutting layout to avoid placing pattern pieces over the crease or to have the crease in an inconspicuous spot on the finished garment. The problem of a permanent crease often occurs in fabrics knitted from natural or man-made yarns and in fabrics treated with finishes which can't be removed.

PREPARING PATTERN AND FABRIC

Select the pattern pieces for the view of the design that you're planning to make; cut apart small ones that have been printed on one tissue. Cut away margins if desired. Press pattern pieces with a warm, dry iron.

Refer to the section on adjustments and alterations (pages 93-117) for guidance in custom fitting your pattern. Approximate the finished length of your garment and the depth of the hem; indicate the new hemline and cutting line on your pattern.

The Cutting Guide section of your instruction sheet is an accurate and clear guide for cutting your fabric. Locate, circle, and study the layout for your pattern size, view, and fabric width. Experts have prepared and tested Butterick's cutting layouts for precision and economy.

Find a large cutting surface on which to work. A table is ideal if it's at a comfortable height. If you're forced to resort to the floor or if you must extend a small table, a commercial cutting board is handy.

Sometimes there will be several ways to arrange your fabric for cutting out one garment; keep all folds on the straight grain.

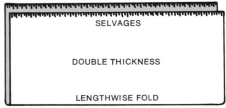

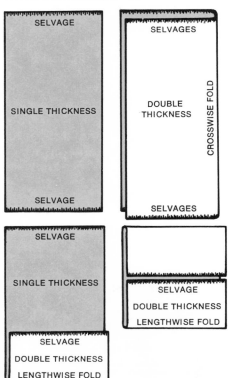

Smooth the folded fabric so that it's grain-perfect. About every 3" or so, pin the layers together where they meet along the fold, ends, and selvages; you may have to clip the selvages every few inches to make the fabric lie flat. Align all ends and selvages with the markings on your cutting board or the edges of your table; this assures you that the grain is straight, and makes pinning your pattern to the fabric a bit easier. Never let fabric ends hang over the edge of the cutting surface. It's likely that this will distort the grain and make accurate cutting impossible.

PINNING PATTERN

Position appropriate pattern pieces on the fabric according to your cutting layout. Pattern pieces are always placed printed side up unless otherwise indicated by diagonal shading on the layout. Complete your cutting layout before beginning to cut out any of the pattern pieces. This enables you to see the relationship of your pattern pieces to one another. It also assures that you followed the cutting layout correctly; after cutting some pieces out, it's usually too late to correct mistakes.

Begin the layout by positioning and pinning pattern pieces that are to be along the fold. Pin pattern to fabric every 6"-8" along the fold, inserting pins at right angles to the edge. Smooth pattern away from the line of pins and insert pins diagonally at corners. Then pin remaining edges of pattern to fabric. Space pins at 3"-4" intervals and insert them perpendicularly to the cutting line. Pins should point toward the edge but, to avoid their interfering with your shears, should never extend beyond the cutting line.

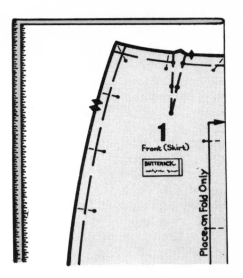

To position all other pattern pieces, follow the printed grainline on each. Every 6"-10", measure the distance from the grainline to the selvage; pin at each measuring point while keeping the distance the same.

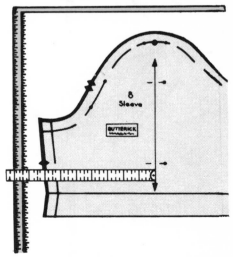

Pin remaining edges of pattern pieces to fabric as before; this time smooth tissue away from the pinned grainline instead of the fold. Margins which overlap will be cut away as you cut out each piece.

HOW TO CUT

Use long, sharp shears to make firm, steady slashes; never close blades completely. Making short, choppy strokes with the shears causes irregular edges. Never use pinking or scalloping shears to cut out a pattern; these were designed for use in finishing seams, and can't withstand the wear and tear of long-distance, heavy cutting. These special shears also distort garment edges in such a way that you won't get the maximum seam allowance that may eventually be needed for fitting.

Cut exactly on the cutting line. For greatest accuracy as you cut, keep one hand flat on the pattern piece to prevent the fabric and pattern from shifting or being lifted from the cutting surface.

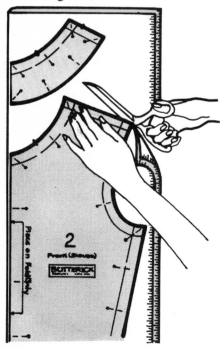

Use the end of your shears to cut notches outward and groups of notches in continuous outward blocks.

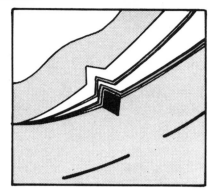

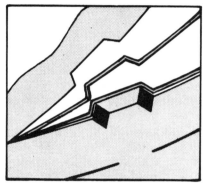

Be sure to cut each pattern piece the required number of times. It may be necessary to remove a pattern piece and re-position it to cut it an additional number of times. If your layout shows a pattern piece that extends beyond the fold of your fabric, include it in the layout, but cut all other pieces first. Then unfold fabric and pin this remaining pattern piece to the right side of the fabric. This is the last piece to be cut.

Softly fold the pieces of your garment as you cut them out and lay them on a flat surface. Never remove the pattern from the fabric until marking has been completed. Save fabric scraps for buttonholes and plackets, and for testing stitching and pressing.

Making Your Mark

The construction symbols and lines so carefully planned and printed on your pattern must be transferred to the wrong side of each garment section. This step in getting a garment together is called marking, and is your guide to quick and accurate sewing. If an underlining is to be used, mark it instead of your fabric.

WHAT TO MARK

Here's a list of all the symbols you'll have to mark on pattern pieces.

 These symbols indicate specific matching points on adjacent garment pieces.

 Button and buttonhole markings indicate exact size of button and length of buttonhole. Mark each on appropriate section.

 Placement lines for details and trims should be marked on wrong side and transferred to right side with thread tracing.

 Darts must be marked so they can be accurately stitched. Mark point to indicate length.

 Points of slashes are marked for precision in slashing.

 Corners where seamlines cross are marked so they can be matched exactly.

 Centers and foldlines are marked and thread traced for quick and accurate identification. These will be major reference points in construction and fitting.

Careful marking of these symbols makes sewing easy. Let the character of your fabric and the symbol to be marked guide you in determining which marking technique should be used.

It's unnecessary to mark straight seamlines, but seams that are curved or otherwise more complicated are easier to stitch when they've been marked.

On the following pages, you'll find specific information on many ways to transfer pattern symbols to your fabric. Each has its advantages.

HOW TO MARK

The nature of your fabric determines the method of marking you should use. Choose a technique which indicates lines and symbols clearly and which will last as long as these markings are needed. Never choose a technique which in any way damages the fabric. Learn to do each of the following methods efficiently because you'll probably need them all eventually.

TRACING PAPER AND WHEEL: Fast, accurate, and easy, this is the ideal method for hard-surfaced fabrics and underlinings. Test the colors of dressmaker's tracing paper on a scrap of your fabric; select a color which will disappear when steam pressed or cleaned. White is best for light colors, including white. Yellow, red, and blue are recommended for medium and dark colors.

Insert a double layer of tracing paper so that the carbon side of each layer is against the wrong side of each layer of fabric.

125

Hold fabric in place with one hand and trace over all markings with the other. Use just enough pressure on the tracing wheel to make light lines; too much pressure might damage your fabric. When tracing straight lines, you'll find it easier if you use a ruler to keep you on the track.

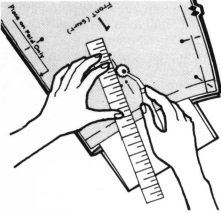

Trace through the center of each symbol on a line of construction. Indicate symbols by making short lines across the line of construction. Work on developing a personal system of shorthand to represent each of the different construction symbols appearing on patterns.

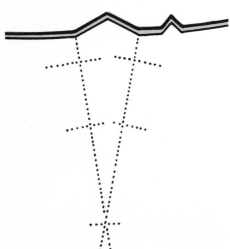

PINS AND CHALK: Use either chalk or a chalk pencil to mark fabrics whose surfaces are either soft or hard (you'll find that a chalk pencil is neater and more accurate).

Push a pin through the pattern and both layers of fabric at each symbol to be marked. Turn the piece over and make a chalk mark on the wrong side of the fabric where each pin comes out.

Turn the piece back to the pattern side and remove the pattern by forcing the pinheads through it.

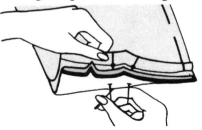

Work from edge toward center of the piece. Make a chalk mark on the wrong side of the fabric at each pin. Remove the pins as each symbol is marked.

TAILOR'S TACKS: This is the preferred method for delicate fabrics that are easily marred or damaged. It's also ideal for fabrics that have a soft, napped surface which won't show markings made by one of the other techniques.

Use a long double strand of thread; don't make a knot in the end. Take a single, short running stitch through the pattern and fabric at a symbol to be marked; leave a 1″-2″ thread end. Take a second stitch across the first and draw the thread up to form a large loop. If the next symbol to be marked is reasonably close, carry the thread loosely to this symbol and repeat the technique.

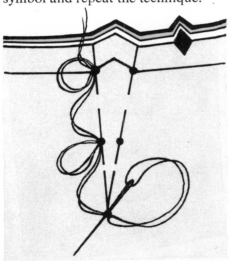

After a group of symbols have been marked, snip the end of the thread 1″-2″ from the last marking. Clip connecting loops and threads. Raise the pattern carefully and force the tacks through it. Gently roll the upper layer of fabric back and cut the threads between the layers so that tufts remain in each layer of fabric. These tufts indicate points to be matched on corresponding garment sections.

THREAD TRACING: This is a quick means of indicating grainlines and center lines. Thread tracing is also used to transfer placement markings to the right side of the fabric. Mark the wrong side of your fabric first, using one of the methods previously explained.

Use a single thread; don't knot the end. Begin with a small backstitch on the wrong side of the fabric. Follow the markings with uneven basting so they will appear on right side of the fabric as well as the wrong side. For napped, pile, and delicate fabrics, use silk thread to avoid permanently imprinting the fabric.

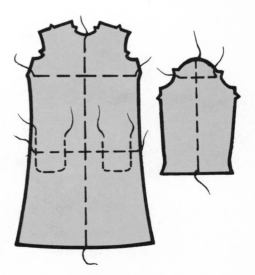

Something Special

Fabrics That Groove

Nature and technology swing together to produce a bevy of fun fabrics. If you've ever dreamed of making that little-nothing pattern in a lush or fantastically wild fabric . . . read on!

PLAIDS

Multiple stripes crossing at right angles form plaids. A four-sided area in which pattern and color of design are complete is called the repeat. Spacing and design of the repeat determine whether plaid is even or uneven.

WHAT TO BUY

The easiest patterns to make are those with few construction lines. Avoid those labeled "Plaid fabrics are not suitable." Patterns stating "No allowance for matching stripes and plaids" can be used for plaid fabrics if you allow extra fabric for matching. To figure the amount of extra fabric needed for matching, consider the size of plaid repeat, your pattern size, and the number of lengths of major pattern pieces required by cutting layout.

When selecting fabric, remember that size and repeat of plaid should be in scale with your pattern and figure. If plaid is printed rather than woven or is on a bonded fabric, be sure plaid design follows the straight grain.

HOW TO MATCH

Lines of plaids should be continuous from front to back and neck to hem in both one- and two-piece garments. After making all fitting adjustments, determine finished length of garment, and mark hemline on pattern before doing layout.

To ensure a perfectly matched design throughout construction, **slip-baste** all seams from the right side before machine stitching on wrong side (see page 156).

EVEN PLAIDS: Stripe arrangement is the same on crosswise and lengthwise grains. When fabric is folded diagonally through the center of any repeat, spaces and colors of plaid will match in both directions.

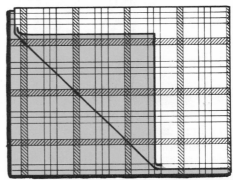

The dominant stripe of the plaid is your major concern in pattern placement. A dominant vertical stripe looks best when it has been placed along the center front. A dominant horizontal stripe can be placed along a straight hemline, but avoid positioning it at the bust, waist, or hip. When the pattern has a curved hemline which can't be aligned with the plaid, place the least dominant feature of plaid at the hemline.

When folding fabric for a cutting layout, be sure that the fold is at the center of a dominant stripe or plaid design. Use a "With Nap" layout if this is required by fabric shading. Pre-determine and mark the hemline as previously directed. To make the matching procedure easier, draw your plaid on the pattern at matching points.

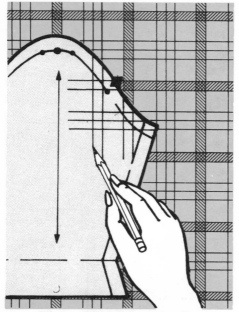

Then match pattern pieces so seamlines at corresponding notches and symbols are on corresponding parts of the plaid.

If your pattern is one which has a straight center seam, place this seamline in the middle of a plaid repeat. For a pattern with a shaped center seam, place the beginning or the most obvious part of the seam in the middle of a repeat.

Place the lengthwise center of a sleeve in the middle of a repeat. Match the plaid at the notch on the front armhole seamline to the plaid at the notch on the front of the sleeve.

The back armhole seamline, darts, shoulder seams, and side seams above the bust dart may not match. Don't be concerned about this because these aren't the garment areas that are most obvious.

Sometimes eye-catching interest can be achieved by cutting fashion details like pockets, yokes, and cuffs on the bias. Using bias binding (pages 280-283) is another way to emphasize the contrast of straight grain and bias plaid design. For a more subtle, but no less intriguing touch, match fashion details to the corresponding part of the garment.

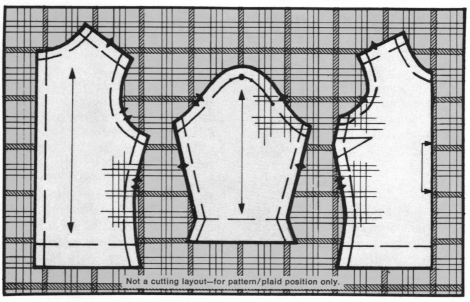

Not a cutting layout—for pattern/plaid position only.

Chevrons: Plaids will form a V and match at the seamline when adjoining pieces are cut on the same angle; this is called a chevron.

It's easy to create a perfect chevron. Simply match an even plaid at corresponding notches and symbols on the seamlines of adjacent pattern pieces. By doing this, you'll form a mirror image of the plaid on adjoining garment sections. Match the plaid on front and back pattern pieces, too. Work from the bottom up to accomplish this. Remember to locate curved hemlines at the least dominant part of the plaid repeat to avoid distortion as much as possible.

Some plaid fabrics have been woven or printed in such a way that the plaid itself looks as though it's on the bias even though it's on the straight grain. If your fabric is one of these, plan your cutting layout as you would for an even plaid. Match the plaid at corresponding notches and symbols of adjoining pattern pieces so that the design will chevron at your garment seams.

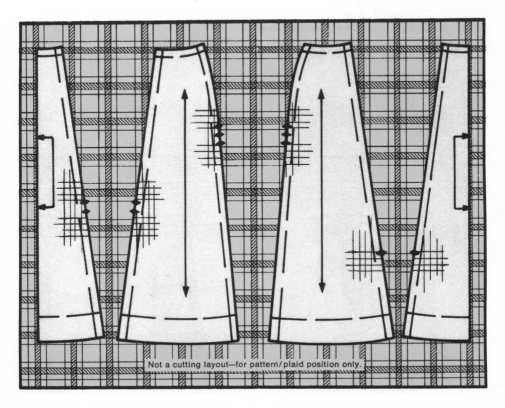

Not a cutting layout—for pattern/plaid position only.

Checks: When larger than ½″, match checks as you would an even plaid. When smaller than ½″, checks need not be matched unless garment lines and broken checks would be too visually disturbing.

UNEVEN PLAIDS: When folded diagonally through the center of any repeat, spaces and colors of plaid will not match in both directions.

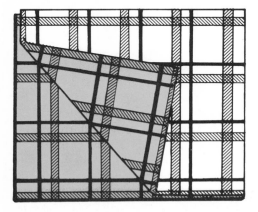

An uneven plaid is positioned and matched much as you would an even plaid. However, the directional character of an uneven plaid makes it necessary to note the following differences between the two. Select and use a "With Nap" cutting layout for your pattern pieces.

Uneven plaids can't be matched in both directions—horizontally and vertically—so don't expect the impossible or be disappointed when it doesn't happen! Determine which of the horizontal and vertical stripes in the plaid you would like to emphasize and plan your cutting layout accordingly.

Pin front and back pattern pieces to the fabric; keep center lines on a dominant vertical stripe. Carefully match the horizontal stripes of the plaid at side seamlines.

You may have to re-fold your fabric or even cut your pattern pieces from a single layer of fabric in order to match an uneven plaid properly. If you find it necessary to do this, be sure that the right and left garment sections cut from one pattern piece are opposites—it's easy to confuse these in cutting layouts of this type.

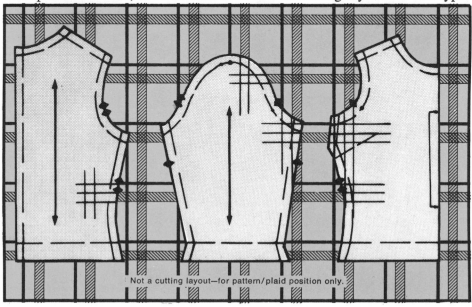

Not a cutting layout—for pattern/plaid position only.

132

STRIPES

Horizontal or vertical, stripes are printed or woven parallel lines; corduroy and other wide ribbed fabrics, whether horizontal or vertical, are considered stripes. As a general rule of construction, stripes should run in one direction throughout the garment. Stripes of different widths and the spacing of stripes determine whether stripes are balanced or unbalanced.

BALANCED STRIPES: When fabric is folded along the dominant stripe and a corner is turned back, stripes on the two layers form a chevron. Balanced stripes are easily matched and chevron attractively on shaped seams.

Vertical: Fold fabric along center of dominant stripe or pin two dominant stripes together. Pin pattern on fabric with lengthwise grainline of pattern parallel to stripes. Plan pattern placement so dominant stripe is at center of front, back, and sleeve.

Horizontal: Fold fabric so that the stripes match along selvages; pin. The lengthwise grainline of the pattern should be perpendicular to the stripes. Position pattern over a dominant stripe of the fabric just as you

would if it were an even plaid (pages 129 to 130). If hemline is curved, place it at the least obvious part of the stripe design.

UNBALANCED STRIPES: When fabric is folded along a dominant stripe and a corner is turned back, the layers will not form a perfectly matched chevron.

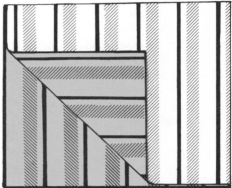

Vertical: Fold fabric along the center of a dominant stripe or match and pin two dominant stripes together. Use a "With Nap" cutting layout so stripes will be consecutive around the garment.

Place center front and center back along the center of a dominant stripe as for a balanced vertical stripe. To accomplish this, it may be necessary to re-fold the fabric or even to cut each pattern piece on a single layer. Shaped or bias seams can't be chevroned or matched on stripes of this type.

Horizontal: Matching stripes carefully at selvages, pin the layers of fabric together. Use a "With Nap" cutting layout and plan pattern placement as you would for balanced horizontal stripes. On shaped or bias seams, stripes can be chevroned most effectively.

DIAGONALS

Fabrics which have an obvious diagonal stripe demand special attention when selecting a pattern. Your best choice is a simple garment with straight seams and darts and set-in sleeves. Don't use patterns stating "Obvious diagonal fabrics are not suitable". Avoid design features which would oppose the diagonal—these include long, curved seams or darts, kimono sleeves, and V-necks. Subtle, inconspicuously diagonal fabrics like denim and gabardine require no special handling.

Try to match stripes at seamlines so they will be continuous. This is impossible in many cases, so don't be too disappointed if your attempt isn't completely successful. Diagonal stripes can't be matched on curved seams.

Fashion details like collars, pockets, and bands can be cut on the same grain as the garment, on the bias, or on an opposite diagonal if the fabric isn't napped. When diagonal fabrics are cut on the bias, the result is a stripe that is horizontal or vertical. Experiment to discover the various effects obtainable from diagonals.

BORDER PRINTS

An expanded version of a horizontal stripe, these fabrics have a printed border along one selvage and are usually cut so the print is at a garment edge. Patterns illustrated in border prints are most suitable and include special cutting layouts. Other patterns must have a straight hemline and will require extra yardage.

Lay pattern out on the crosswise grain; garment piece can be only as long as fabric is wide. Determine hemline of finished garment

and place it along border. Center a dominant motif at front and back of garment. Match border at side seams. Eliminate seams if possible.

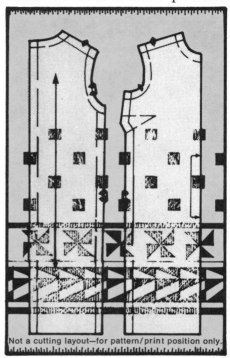

Not a cutting layout—for pattern/print position only.

LARGE-SCALE PRINTS

Careful placement of fabric motifs on pattern pieces, and concurrently on your figure, is your key to successful sewing with large prints. Choose a pattern style which has few design lines, as these tend to disrupt the print. Long evening or lounge clothes are a good choice because of the tremendous yardage involved.

Use a "With Nap" layout if the fabric has a one-way print. Try to avoid placing large flowers or designs over major body curves like bust or hips. Plan your layout so the print will be centered vertically on the finished garment.

NAPPED FABRICS

Whether woven or knitted, napped fabrics have been brushed on one side to produce a slightly fluffy directional surface. Melton and fleece are prime examples.

Determine the direction of nap by stroking the fabric with your hand. If it feels smooth, the nap is running down; if it feels rough, the nap is running up. Nap affects color and texture of fabric: when nap runs down, fabric is lighter, shinier, and more durable; when nap runs up, the color is deeper and richer, and the textured surface more apparent.

Choose a pattern recommended for one-way designs or napped fabrics and purchase yardage accordingly.

When laying out pattern pieces, be sure that they are all placed in the same direction.

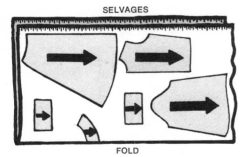

SELVAGES

FOLD

Following a cutting layout for fabrics "With Nap" should ensure this. If, however, you have any doubts about the correct placement of pattern pieces, make this quick test. Hold each pattern piece against your body in the appropriate finished position. Draw an arrow that points toward the floor on each pattern piece. This simple procedure enables you to see at a glance the directional relationship of the pattern pieces to one another.

Then put the pattern on your fabric so that the arrow points in the direction you'd like the nap to run.

PILE FABRICS

A built-in textured surface made by adding loops or cut yarns to a woven or knitted base is how these differ from napped fabrics. Familiar pile fabrics include velvet, velveteen, corduroy, terry cloth, and velour.

Pile fabrics are usually cut so the nap runs up on the finished garment; this causes the color to appear richer and enhances the plushness of the fabric.

If pile is very thick, it may be necessary to cut a single thickness of fabric at a time. Cut facings from lining fabric to reduce bulk.

Mark fabric with tailor's tacks and baste seams closely with silk thread. Decrease machine pressure and stitch with the nap while holding fabric taut. Use a fine needle and 10-12 stitches per inch.

If cut edges have a tendency to fray, finish seams with machine zig-zagging, edgestitching and overcasting, or binding. The easiest ways to insert zippers are the hand and the invisible applications.

Test pressing techniques on a fabric scrap, because pile is quick to squash and impossible to raise. Use a needleboard or its substitute, and a self-fabric press cloth. See the Pressing section for more information.

Wrinkles that come from folding or wearing a garment of a pile fabric can be effectively removed by shower steamings.

FUZZYS

Extra-deep pile on a woven or knitted backing gives us plushy fabrics that are pretty close to nature's furs. These fabrics have fast become the darling of the fashion scene. When selecting a pattern, let yourself be guided by texture, color and/or print, and pattern envelope recommendations. It's usually wisest to stick to simple designs without a lot of seams and details. Purchase yardage required for napped fabrics.

Plan layouts and handle like napped fabric. Cut one layer of fabric at a time, using very sharp shears. If pile is extra-long, use a razor blade to cut pattern as from real fur (see page 279).

Baste seams closely, pushing hairs back from the seam as you work. Set machine for about 8-10

stitches per inch and use a coarse needle and heavy-duty thread. Decrease machine pressure if hair is thick. Use a needle point to work caught hairs out of a finished seam.

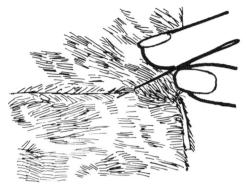

Shear pile from seam allowances to reduce bulk. Slash darts and open them, then shear the pile here, too.

Test the temperature of your iron carefully, because some of these fabrics are easily melted. Press seam and darts open with a dry iron, as steam will mat the fabric surface. On short-haired fabrics, use a needleboard or its substitute as your pressing surface (see Pressing, page 173). Press on wrong side; never touch iron to fabric face.

The type of closure that would be best to use depends on the depth of the pile. Use hooks and eyes, snaps, frogs, loops, nylon tape fasteners, or leather closures on any type of fuzzy fabric. Make worked buttonholes only on short-haired fabrics; never attempt to make bound buttonholes in any fuzzy fabric. Avoid using zipper closures.

SOFT SHEERS

Chiffon is one of the best known fabrics in this family. Choose a pattern recommended for soft, sheer fabrics; gathers and billowy sleeves will make the most of your fabric. Styles with fewer seams present fewer problems.

Lining isn't necessary, but a coordinating slip made about 1" shorter than the garment is often the perfect finishing touch. Or, try wearing a body-stocking under sheers for great fashion, great comfort, and great sheerness!

Fit your pattern lightly. The fragility of soft sheers demands plenty of ease for movement. Tightness will result in pulled seams after the first wearing.

Straighten fabric ends, snip selvages, and check grain. Cover your cutting surface with a taut sheet; pin fabric to sheet with sharp, fine pins to prevent slippage.

Cut with sharp shears; hold fabric in place with your free hand as you work. Cut as many layers at a time as you want for each pattern piece; "quilt" them together along the straight grain with silk thread. Use extra-long basting stitches.

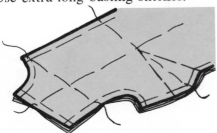

Mark carefully, as soft sheer fabrics are easily picked and stretched. Tailor's tacks are perfect for the job.

SEAMS: Slippage of your fabric will be the major thing to watch. Baste seams carefully, then stitch with the layers of fabric between sheets of tissue paper. Use a fine, sharp needle and silk thread. Special seams which combine seam and seam finish are ideal for sheers.

French Seam: Use this for straight seams. Pin wrong sides of fabric together; stitch ¼" from seamline in seam allowance. Trim close to stitching. Turn so right sides are together and crease along stitched seam; press. Stitch along seamline, encasing raw edges.

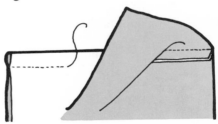

French Whipped Seam: Use this for straight or curved seams. Stitch a plain seam, then stitch ⅛" from the first line of stitching in the seam allowance. Trim seam allowances to within ⅛" of second line of stitching. Overcast or use a fine zigzag to finish raw edges.

PRESSING: This is primarily a testing story because some sheers will pucker or stretch when exposed to heat and steam. Press very lightly with tip of iron.

DARTS: Stitch along dart lines and finish as you would a French whipped seam.

CLOSURES: Hand or machine worked buttonholes can be made; loops and buttons also work well as closures. Metal zippers may be too heavy, but polyester zippers can be used quite satisfactorily.

HEMS: Plan either a very narrow rolled hem or a very deep hem. For the rolled hem, see page 242.

A deep hem makes sheer gathered skirts hang gracefully. The hem allowance can be as much as 12"; experiment to find the best-looking depth. Turn up desired hem allowance; baste close to fold. Turn raw edge in ¼" and sew invisibly to garment.

CRISP SHEERS

Voile and organdy are ever-popular examples of this easy-to-handle group of fabrics. Use the recommendations and techniques explained in soft sheers; this time you won't have to worry about fabric slippage and fragility. Neatness is the only word of caution: all interior construction can be seen from the outside.

LACES

Differences in width, weight, and fiber content provide an amazing variety of lace fabrics. Select a pattern that is suitable for the elaborate nature of lace. Usually your best choice is a simple design with few seams. Fancy seaming is often wasted on intricate lace.

PREPARATION: Plan your cutting layout so the best features of the lace will be prominent in the finished garment. Because net forms the background of most lace designs, there is usually no grain to worry about unless the design of the lace itself is vertical or horizontal. On right side of lace, a cord often outlines motifs.

Sometimes you can take advantage of lace motifs by placing them along garment edges or by using them as a trim. Laces made with decorative edges instead of selvages are ideal for this. To form a decorative edge on laces with a repeat design, cut around motifs along the intended edge. You can also use this technique to form trimming bands or to separate lace motifs for use as a trim. Apply either of these to the garment as explained in Lace, pages 275-278.

When planning to use lace motifs along garment edges, arrange pattern pieces for the cutting layout so that finished edges of garment are along decorative edges of the lace.

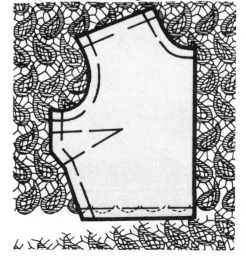

138

To add body to lace, underline it with marquisette, organdy, or organza. Use these fabrics for facings, too. Transfer pattern markings with tailor's tacks.

CONSTRUCTION: Baste seams, then stitch with medium length stitches. When stitching lace which hasn't been underlined, handle seams, darts, and closures as you would those in soft sheers. Keep the lace between layers of tissue paper as you stitch to prevent it from catching on the machine. Work neatly, because the sheerness of some laces makes interior construction visible from the outside. Underlined garments don't require special seams and darts, but are best finished with the hand zipper application.

PRESSING: Always test on scraps first. Regular steam settings are usually satisfactory. To avoid flattening raised designs, press lace from the wrong side with a Turkish towel as your pressing surface (see Pressing). If lace is easily snagged, always use a press cloth when pressing.

HEMS: Finish hem edges with either horsehair braid (see Hems, page 243) or net.

For a net finish that is 1″ wide when completed, cut net strips about 2½″ wide. Fold strip in half lengthwise and pin to right side of lace, with raw edges extending ¼″ beyond hemline.

Stitch along hemline; make a second row of stitching ⅛″ from the first in the hem allowance. Trim close to second line of stitching. Turn net to inside, favoring garment edge. Slipstitch folded edge of net to garment.

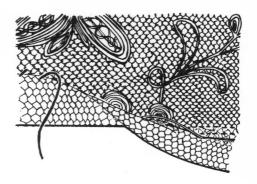

LEATHERS AND VINYLS

A whole new way of living, leather and its man-made relatives appear in countless colors and textures. The surface of leather has many personalities—it can appear as almost anything from the familiar smooth to fashion suede. Slick or mat, smooth or rough, vinyls are either all plastic or are plastic fused to a knitted or woven fabric backing.

Leather and vinyl crease easily —keep them rolled until you're ready to use them. Every mark you make is permanent, so choose an uncomplicated design—fewer seams and darts mean less marking and matching symbols.

Avoid styles which require easing. Set-in sleeves can be used in leather or in vinyls with a knitted cotton backing. It may be necessary to remove some of the ease from the sleeve cap (see page 102). Always test pattern in muslin and make alterations first; letting out seams in leather or vinyl can cause disaster.

For leather and heavy vinyls, plan a cutting layout on a single layer. Always check surface of leather for irregularities. Never pin pattern to leather or vinyl; for a cutting layout, hold pattern in place with tape or weights.

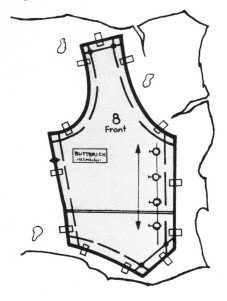

Mark the wrong side with chalk or a smooth-edged tracing wheel and dressmaker's tracing paper. Use grease pencil to mark the right side of vinyl; these markings can be easily wiped off with a soft cloth when no longer needed.

SEAMS: Layers to be stitched can be held together with paper clips or tape.

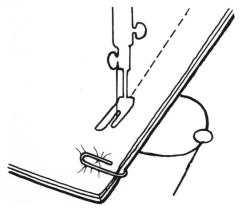

Use a size 11 or 14 regular or a leather needle with mercerized thread; set your machine at 8-10 stitches per inch and test pressure. Tissue paper between presser foot and leather or vinyl helps to feed it through the machine.

You can make regular seams in either leather or vinyl. As you stitch, stay seams with ribbon seam binding to prevent stretching (see page 166). Tie knots at the ends of seams; never backstitch, as this will weaken the leather or vinyl.

To press, use a warm, dry iron and a brown paper press cloth. Topstitch seams, use rubber cement, or pound them to flatten.

Use a mallet or a hammer wrapped in cloth to press open seam allowances. Apply rubber cement under the stay and each seam allowance; pound.

Let the rubber cement dry, then lift the seam allowances and peel away the rubber cement. Seams are now open, flat, and make no impression in the garment itself.

For leathers and those vinyls with backings that don't fray, try this extra easy technique: eliminate one seam allowance, then lap sections, matching seamlines. Use rubber cement to hold the layers in place. Topstitch close to one edge; make a second row of topstitching ¼"-½" away.

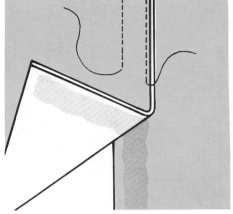

On facings or details like collars and flaps, eliminate seam allowances from both layers. Match cut edges, wrong sides together, then topstitch close to the edges; make a second row of topstitching ¼"-½" from the first.

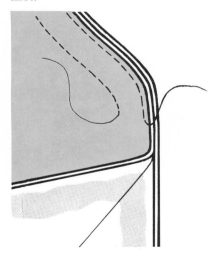

DARTS: Stitch, then trim dart to ⅜". Press dart open; flatten dart as you would a seam, pounding with a mallet or a padded hammer and applying rubber cement if necessary.

BUTTONHOLES: Make a test buttonhole. On some vinyls you can use a regular bound buttonhole method.

On leather or on vinyl which doesn't fray, cut a rectangular opening the length and width of buttonhole at each buttonhole marking.

For each buttonhole, cut two strips 1½" wide and ½" longer than the buttonhole. Fold strips lengthwise, wrong sides together, and grade edges so that one layer is wider. Flatten with mallet and rubber cement as you would a seam.

With folded edges meeting, center strips over buttonhole opening on wrong side of garment; use rubber cement to hold the strips in place.

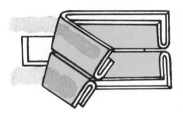

Also use rubber cement to hold the facing in place on the inside over the buttonhole area. From the outside, edgestitch the buttonhole rectangle through all thicknesses. Trim away the facing just inside the stitching. The buttonhole is then exposed.

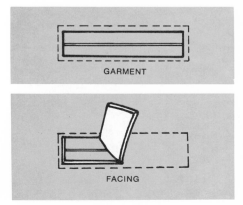

GARMENT

FACING

HEMS: Trim hem allowance to 1"- 2". Apply rubber cement to hem allowance. Fold hem up. Then either pound it in place with a mallet or padded hammer, or press it in place with an iron, using a brown paper press cloth. **Notch** curved hems so they'll lie flat (see page 164).

WEAR AND CARE: Vinyl doesn't breathe; for greater comfort, insert metal eyelets in areas of a garment which need ventilation.

Since vinyl can't always be dry cleaned, remove soil with a damp, soapy sponge. Make linings of drip-dry fabrics to guard against water-spotting.

Avoid steaming or getting leather wet. Send soiled leathers and suedes to professional dry cleaner for special processing.

BONDED FABRICS

Fusing two or more layers of fabric together in such a way that they act as one results in what is commonly referred to as a bonded or a laminated fabric.

The outer layer of a fabric of this type can be almost any fabric—wools, knits, laces, and denims, however different they seem, can all be bonded. The inner layer is usually either acetate tricot or a loosely woven cotton.

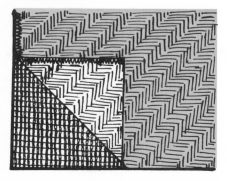

Sometimes a piece of chemical foam no more than 1/16" thick has been sandwiched between the other two, or forms an exposed backing layer.

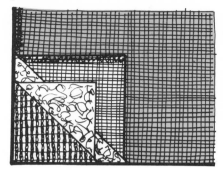

Bonding serves many purposes —it changes the hand of the outer layer, stabilizes an open weave, reinforces a stretchy or pliable surface, and pre-lines a garment.

When a foam layer is included in the bonding process, the end product is a fabric which has a lot of body and which is an excellent insulator.

When buying a bonded fabric, be sure that the lengthwise edges of all layers are evenly bonded, and that the bonding is firm throughout. Avoid fabrics which look flimsy or have weak areas, and look for trademarks that guarantee quality bonding.

Check to see that the outer fabric is on grain and that the backing is bonded to it in such a way that it too is on the same grain. The lengthwise grain of most bonded fabrics is quite stable. Tricot-backed fabrics sometimes have a bit of give on the cross-wise grain.

When using a bonded fabric which includes a layer of foam, adjust your pattern to allow for the slight additional ease which may be taken up by the foam.

Sometimes it's a good idea to underline bonded fabrics in areas which will get heavy wear—like pockets and buttonholes. This serves to strengthen the fabric. Interfacing is rarely needed, because bonded fabrics by nature have considerable body.

Tailor's tacks are the best means of marking bonded fabrics because the inner layer is sometimes delicate and easily torn, and the spongy texture may not accept marks from a tracing wheel.

If the fabric has a foam layer, stitch seams between layers of tissue paper, using a fine needle. The seams that are used in men's shirts are recommended for fabrics with a foam layer because they're very flat (see page 251). Never fit garments of foam-backed fabrics tightly, because foam weakens under stress.

Stay seams that may stretch or be subjected to strain; use ribbon seam binding or stretched bias tape for this (see page 166).

Slash darts and press them open. **Grade** the seam allowances of enclosed seams. These measures are essential to reduce bulkiness in dart and seam areas (see pages 166-167).

Edges needn't be securely finished, because bonding usually prevents raveling. Just stitch ¼″ from raw edges of facings, hems, and seam allowances.

Press bonded fabrics from the wrong side with a warm steam iron; test the temperature of the iron so that you won't damage any of the layers. In fabrics which have an exposed layer of foam, always press from the right side with a warm steam iron. Never touch the iron to the foam side, as heat may cause the foam to melt.

Sew the hem of a garment of bonded fabric through the backing fabric only; this makes a hem that won't show at all on the outside. When fabric is bonded only to a layer of foam, you'll have to sew the hem to the garment through all layers; the foam alone won't hold the stitches.

Linings are an optional matter unless the foam layer is exposed. If this is the case, a lining must be used to protect the foam side from wear.

PERMANENT PRESS

No-iron fabrics have been specially treated to resist wrinkling. The same treatment is also used by manufacturers to permanently set pleats or tucks in fabric.

Read the information on the hangtag or the end of the bolt when purchasing permanent press fabric. Soil-release properties are desirable because grease spots are difficult to remove from these fabrics.

Buy notions, trims, and interfacing which have the same easy-care qualities as your fabric.

Make all necessary pattern adjustments and alterations before cutting your fabric. Creases can't be removed from garment seams which have been changed to fit.

Some permanent press fabrics can't be straightened—don't buy them if either the fabric or the print is off grain. If the center fold won't press out, either avoid it when laying out pattern pieces or place it in an inconspicuous area of the garment.

When stitching seams, puckering is a problem. Hold fabric fairly taut when feeding it through the machine. Straight seams require greater care than slightly bias ones.

Sleeve caps may be difficult to ease as permanent press fabrics do not shrink well. Use the alteration on page 102 to remove some of the ease.

Pre-shrink even polyester zippers in hot water. Air-dry before inserting them to prevent puckers from forming over the zipper. The lapped application is preferable. Ease the zipper tape to the fabric as you baste.

Leave soiled garments on the hanger until ready to launder. Keep washing loads small to avoid unnecessary wrinkling. Pre-soak spots and launder frequently to prevent a build-up of soil.

KNITS

Looped rather than interwoven yarns give stretchability to most knitted fabrics. In some knits, this stretch has been either prevented or controlled by stabilizing the fabric during the knitting or finishing process. This stabilization is accomplished by bonding or interlocking the loops.

The most familiar types of knits —double knit, jersey or plain knit, and tricot—have many variations.

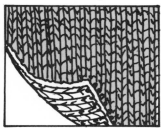

DOUBLE KNIT

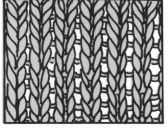

JERSEY OR PLAIN KNIT

TRICOT

The surfaces of these can be lacy, shiny, nubby, tweedy, napped, or even furry.

Knits are available in many weights—from the lightest of lingerie tricots to the heavy bonded raschel or rib knits. Don't confuse weight with stretchability when choosing either your fabric or your pattern; knits of any weight can be stable or stretchable.

STABILITY VS. STRETCHABILITY: Knits are either stable or stretchable. Stable knits have a limited amount of stretch. They can be used to make any garment that is suitable for woven fabrics. Stretchable knits have considerable elasticity; they stretch to fit the body.

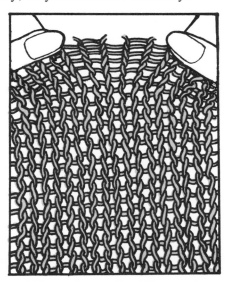

For these knits, use patterns designated "For Knits Only." Much of the wearing ease has been removed from such patterns to make the most of body-hugging knits. The flexibility of the fabric rather than the use of seams and darts make your garment conform to your figure.

Garment areas that need stabilization should be interfaced. Lining or underlining knits reduces their tendency to cling. Refer to Shaping, pages 177-181.

NOTIONS: Most knits act so differently from wovens that they demand at least some of the following made-for-knits notions.

Select thread that has a bit of give in a weight appropriate for your fabric. Thread that consists of a polyester core wrapped in cotton fills the bill.

If they're available to you, purchase ball point sewing machine needles in a size that's right for your fabric. Use a new needle for each knit garment you make. Have very sharp, fine needles for hand sewing, too. Ball point pins or sharp silk pins are another essential. If your knit is delicate, you might even use fine needles instead of pins. Any rough spots on either needles or pins can pick your fabric.

In the closures category, match the weight of buttons and zippers to the weight of your fabric. Polyester coil zippers are usually your best choice, especially for lightweight knits like jersey or a Ban-Lon® fabric. Keep in mind that buttons and zippers that are too heavy will distort your fabric.

Any interfacing, lining, underlining, or trims required for your garment should share the properties of

your knit. Choose flexible trims and shaping fabrics which correspond to the care required by the knit itself.

PREPARATION: Cut tubular knits along a lengthwise row of loops near one fold. If this lengthwise rib is difficult to see, mark it with pins or thread tracing.

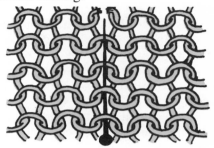

Knit fabrics can be off grain; to determine the condition of yours, thread trace across the width of the fabric and cut along one row of loops.

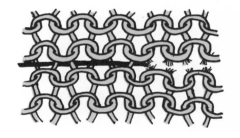

If necessary, straighten fabric (see pages 119-121). Pre-shrink a washable knit exactly as you plan to care for your finished garment.

FIT YOUR PATTERN: Length and circumference adjustments and personal alterations on your pattern are as necessary for knits as they are for wovens. Don't expect the qualities of your fabric to eliminate fitting—in fact, perfect fit is even more important here because of the tendency of knits to cling.

LAYOUTS AND CUTTING: Most knits have a shaded effect when seen from different angles. For this reason, a "With Nap" layout is recommended.

Press any creases or folds from your fabric. If they won't press out, avoid them or locate them inconspicuously on your garment when laying out pattern pieces.

Refer to the section on cutting layouts (pages 122-124) for a complete explanation of this procedure. Keep in mind the following special points concerning the handling of knits.

- Take great care to avoid stretching the fabric or distorting its grain. Working on a surface large enough to hold your entire piece of fabric is especially important.
- Pin pattern pieces to wrong side of knit fabrics because cut edges will tend to curl toward the right side of the fabric.
- In some knits, it's difficult to see the lengthwise rib. Mark the lengthwise grain with pins or thread tracing for speedy placement of pattern pieces.
- Use very sharp shears to cut out knits. This prevents the raw edge from being distorted.
- When you need strips of fabric for binding, cut these on the crosswise grain rather than on the bias. Knits have a maximum amount of stretch on the crosswise grain.
- If you're making a stretchable knit for the first time, cut seam allowances about 1" wide on major vertical seams. This leaves you some room for experimentation in fitting your fabric to your figure.

MARKING: Any of the procedures explained on pages 125-127 can be used. Take extra care when marking lightweight knits, because dressmaker's tracing paper marks are sometimes difficult to remove.

SEWING: Test pressure, tension, and stitch length on fabric scraps (see pages 159-160). Usually pressure and tension should be light; 12-15 stitches per inch are preferred.

Make a test seam to determine whether a little give will be needed to make a smooth, flexible seam. If so, either use a small zigzag stitch or stretch your fabric very slightly as you stitch. Avoid stretching fabric too much, as this will result in a wobbly seamline.

Trim, grade, and clip and/or notch seams as you would normally do to reduce bulk in garments of woven fabrics. Slash and press darts open (see page 183).

Little or no seam finishing is needed on most knit fabrics. The raw edges of knits rarely ravel and so can be left as is. Finish seams in unlined jackets, vests, or coats with double-fold bias tape (see page 169). Or, zigzag stretchable lace to the seam allowances.

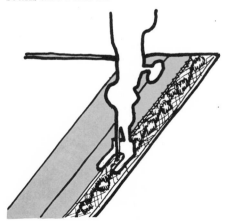

Use stretched bias tape (see pages 166 and 281) to stay shoulder, neckline, waistline, and other curved seams which may be subjected to strain. Knits often require this additional support in these areas.

To save time, fuse interfacings in place. Apply and turn facings in the usual manner, then secure them to the garment by using a fusible adhesive.

The most attractive zippers in knits are those inserted by either the hand or the invisible application.

Fit your garment as you sew. Don't expect the elasticity of knits to eliminate fitting your fabric to your figure.

Decide whether yours will be a classic or a natural looking knit. Nonstatic lingerie makes possible the classic goal of sleek, smooth fit. If you're going natural, make a bodystocking or bodysuit your basis for fitting.

CLASSIC   NATURAL

Follow the fitting guidelines on pages 174-176. The slightest change in a seam can make a world of difference in the overall appearance of a garment. Prints and textures in knits are easily distorted by bad fit.

An important step toward perfect fit is wearing proper garments under knits. Avoid undergarments with lumpy seams or tight elastic which might show through your garment.

Let knit garments hang for 24 hours before marking the hem. Finish the hem edge by staystitching ¼" from the raw edge; this will stabilize your hem stitches. Or, finish with a stretchable lace seam binding.

Prevent bulk and stitches from being pulled in hems on heavy knits. Mark and pin hem up along hemline; finish hem edge. Pin baste along the middle of hem allowance. Turn finished hem edge down over pins and catchstitch along fold. Then blind catchstitch the free edge in the usual manner.

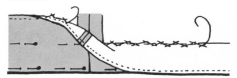

PRESSING: Give knits the same careful attention in pressing that you'd give wovens. Protect your fabric with a self-fabric press cloth; use a Turkish towel as your pressing surface for textured knits.

Creasing edges and shrinking excess ease from polyester knits is almost impossible. Use the alteration on page 102 to reduce the ease in sleeve caps. Topstitching will hold the crease in edges of collars and necklines; use regular thread and stitch ¼" from finished edge.

LINGERIE FABRICS

Create your own especially-for-you lingerie. Butterick has patterns for everything you could possibly need — bodysuits, bras, slips, briefs, and sleep-wear. Lingerie is surprisingly easy to make and takes an absolute minimum amount of fabric. Besides, think of the money you'll save while still enjoying a drawer full of custom-made goodies!

Suggested fabrics are primarily the stable woven types—satin, surah, taffeta, or batiste—and stretchable knits like tricot.

Stable fabrics include those with little or no stretch on either the lengthwise or crosswise grain. Undergarments are cut on the bias, or as indicated on pattern cutting layouts so they'll have the give needed for free, unrestricted movement.

Since tricot has the most crosswise stretch, convert your pattern pieces by drawing a lengthwise grainline at a 45° angle to the bias grainline.

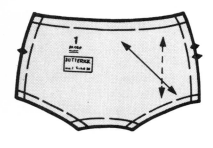

Place pattern pieces so fabric will stretch horizontally on the garment. When you sit, the fabric gives.

Since tricot neither ravels nor frays, you can save time and fabric by pre-trimming the pattern seam allowances to ¼".

Wet your fabric thoroughly, then allow it to dry. This process relaxes the fabric if it had been stretched during finishing and removes any excess finish.

Find the right side of tricot fabrics by pulling them in direction they stretch the most. Tricot will usually curl toward the right side.

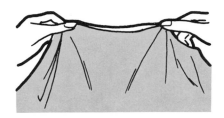

Pin fabric to your cutting board or a sheet to prevent it from creeping. Pin pattern pieces to fabric in seam allowances. *Don't let your fabric hang off the cutting surface.* Use fine pins or needles.

To mark fabric, use a colored pencil which will wash out. Dressmaker's tracing paper can be difficult to remove. Indicate the wrong side of your fabric with a piece of transparent tape or pins.

SEWING: Ball point needles are best, but standard needles in size 9 or 11 can be used, too. Be careful when stitching that you don't bend the needle, and check to see that the throat plate is free of rough edges. Adjust tension and pressure. Make a test seam, adjusting stitch length to 10-12 stitches per inch.

To begin stitching, hold needle and bobbin thread taut behind the machine; lower needle into fabric. Then lower the presser foot. Stitch for a short distance while holding the threads; this prevents jamming the thread and fabric into the needle hole in the throat plate.

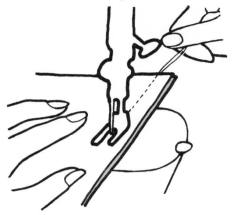

Continue stitching, holding fabric taut and stretching it slightly as you stitch.

To stitch seams with a straight stitch machine, make two close rows of stitching. With a zigzag machine, use a close, medium width zigzag stitch.

Casings allow you to replace elastic easily. Tricot adapts easily to narrow cut-in-one casings (see pages 232-235). To apply elastic without a casing, cut ½" wide elastic 3"-4" shorter than waist measurement; cut ¼" wide elastic 2" shorter than leg measurement. Join ends of each strip securely.

Divide the edge to be finished in quarters; mark both the garment and the elastic with pins at these points.

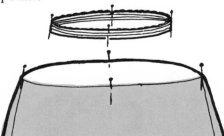

Place elastic right side up on the wrong side of the garment. Pin elastic to garment, matching all four pins on each. *Never* stitch over pins. Use a straight stitch to stitch between pins; stretch elastic and fabric as you stitch so you'll be able to get in and out of the garment easily.

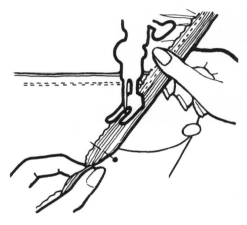

Trim fabric to ¼" if necessary. Turn elastic to the outside, enclosing seam allowance; smooth the garment along stitching. Sew the elastic to the garment, stretching both as you stitch. Use two rows of straight stitches or one row of zigzag stitches.

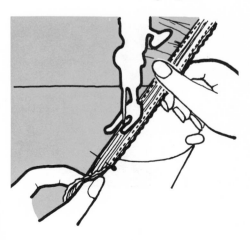

To finish neck and armhole edges with double binding, turn to page 282. For hem edges, apply stretch lace like the regular lace on page 276. Or, use a self-finish as explained on page 275 for a double ruffle.

Shell edging is a decorative yet sturdy hem finish. Make a narrow hem (page 242), then hand sew two tight overhand stitches over hem allowance at ½″ intervals.

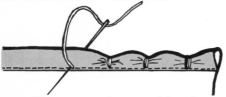

If your sewing machine has a blindstitch setting, use it; refer to your machine manual for details.

METALLICS

From sleek lamés to shimmery brocades, all fabrics woven or knitted with some metal threads are called metallics. It's the metal that demands special care when making garments of these fabrics.

Metal threads are permanently damaged by pin marks, ripping, and creasing. To minimize these dangers, sew with a fine needle and synthetic thread; it may even be necessary to substitute fine needle for pins throughout layout and construction. Use your finger protected by a thimble to open seams without snagging.

Steam tends to tarnish or discolor metal, and excessive heat can cause considerable damage, so thoroughly test pressing techniques on fabric scraps.

Some metallics fray badly and must not be over-handled. In this case, don't select a pattern with small details like buttonholes. Overcast all seams as they are stitched.

Metal threads can be uncomfortable, like tiny, scratchy needles. To prevent the wearing of your new dress or suit from becoming a painful experience, line the garment with a soft, dense fabric. Use this lining fabric for facings, too.

CREPE

Drapeable, supple crepe looks best in designs which reflect its essentially fluid character. Don't attempt to force a pattern whose design is architectural on crepe. If you plan to underline crepe, select an underlining fabric with a soft finish that is similar to that of the crepe itself. Use a lightweight interfacing in garment areas which require additional shaping or stability. Sewing techniques and words of caution are the same as for soft sheers, except that now sheerness isn't a problem.

SATIN-LIKE FABRICS

Satin, ciré, and similar fabrics create clothes with a well-polished sheen. Often the finish or weave produces a shaded effect when held in different directions.

A precaution is to handle shiny fabrics as little as possible because they soil and rumple very readily. Plan to use a cutting layout for fabrics with nap.

It's wise to underline some shiny fabrics—like satin, for instance—to prevent all stitches and construction from showing on the outside of the garment. In cases like this, using an underlining is actually easier than not using one. Silk organza is an excellent fabric to use for this purpose.

Watch for pin-marks—once made they're a permanent feature of a garment. Pin pattern to fabric in seam allowances only so marks won't show on the finished garment.

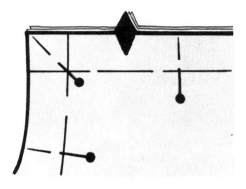

Cut with very sharp shears. Use tailor's tacks of silk thread. Place mark next to the stitching line in the seam allowance.

Set machine at about 12-16 stitches per inch and use a fine sharp needle and silk thread. Hold fabric taut as you stitch to prevent slippage.

Test pressing techniques on scraps. Press seams and darts lightly so they'll look soft when finished.

Apply zippers by hand, but do not machine baste the seam in the process; the needle marks will never disappear.

BROCADES

Supreme luxury—brocades are rich, opulent, fascinating. They're completely covered by raised interwoven designs that can play many surfaces or colors against one another. When metal threads make up a part of the design, adopt the techniques for metallic fabrics.

Brocades are reversible—you can use either side of the fabric for your garment. However, once you've chosen your side, stick to it! Chances are pretty good that there is some difference between the two.

Always use a "With Nap" layout. The elaborate surface of brocades makes them directional fabrics.

Brocades with large designs look best when the pattern chosen for them has uncomplicated lines. Turn to the section on large-scale prints for further information (page 134).

Check to see whether your brocade is one which won't ease well; this is often the case when brocades are stiff or are made of a synthetic fiber like rayon. To make a garment with a set-in sleeve in such a fabric, it may be necessary to remove some of the ease from the sleeve cap (see page 102).

If brocade tends to ravel, finish seams with machine zigzagging or overcasting. Avoid patterns with design details like buttonholes, because the fabric may not be able to support these securely.

The surface of some brocades is easily damaged; handle these as you would a satin-like fabric (beginning on page 150). When pressing, use a Turkish towel as your pressing surface to prevent the brocade from being flattened. An iron that's too hot can destroy certain synthetic fibers in brocades, so test-press on scraps of fabric first.

For Velvets, refer to **Pile Fabrics** on pages 135-136.

Sew

You're on the home stretch . . . ready to SEW! And we're right with you to show you all the stitchery . . . all the put-together tricks to make the most of your sewing projects for yourself, your family, your friends.

Everything's beautifully organized in your sewing corner of the world: lots of light on the subject . . . scissors, thread, and bobbins handy . . . pressboard just a step away to shape and smooth the way as you sew.

And on the following pages—all the helpful hints and "how-to" details to aid and abet your creativity. We've taken the mystery out of making facings, collars, sleeves. Put in tailoring tips to do you proud!

We'll show you how to zip it up . . . button it down . . . make it an open and closed case for fashion. And finish it off with terrific trims!

Butterick methods make it easy. Make it fun! So now let's go . . . let's sew!

152

Nitty Gritty

Making Shape Waves

The Big Three

Closures That Make It

Pulling It All Together

Something For Everyone

Trims And Trifles

Tailor It Yourself

The Basics And Then Some

Dear Reader,

Sewing should be fun, easy, fast and creative. We've set out to make sure it's that way. **The Basics And Then Some** is a master plan of getting your garment together like a pro. Here's the key to tactical sewing:

From first stitch to last, chapters and sections are arranged in sewing order.

Sewing instructions take you step-by-step toward great fashion.

Illustrations are from **your** point of view. They're big, easy-to-understand, and come right after the instructions they're picturing.

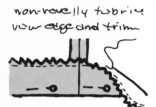

A glimmer of yellow in a drawing is an instant indication of the right side of fabric.

Cross reference in each section and an index in the back tell you where to look for more information.

SEW AND GO . . . extra easy are methods specially selected to highlight flat construction. They're simple, fast, and fool-proof—what a way to sew!

Best wishes,
THE EDITOR

Nitty Gritty

If you plan to make a garment that you'll enjoy wearing, you'll need to learn a few techniques before you begin. Basting, hand and machine sewing, seams, pressing, fitting, and shaping are the means you'll use to put all your creations together. When you're learning to sew, mastering these basics will mean that you can master anything, make anything that catches your eye. For those of you with a little experience, these methods will be a time-saving professional goal toward which you should strive.

HAND SEWING

Needle and thread in hand has one advantage over the sewing machine: even a beginner can control the fabric easily while sewing at her own speed. Hand sewing includes basting, a fast temporary kind of sewing, and a wide range of permanent stitches. Here are some procedures that make hand sewing a breeze. For a starter, needle and thread must be appropriate to fabric weight; sizes and types recommended for specific fabrics are charted in the equipment section. Use a single strand of thread 18″–24″ long. Cut thread end at an angle, pass it through the needle's eye, and knot the same end. Use a thimble on your second finger to prevent casualties.

BASTING

Basting is meant to help hold the garment together for fittings, match plaids, secure seams for stitching, mark, and other tricky things. To make it speedy, work on a flat surface and pin layers together. Begin with a single backstitch for easy removal without snagging your fabric. Baste next to the stitching line in the seam allowance. Gear stitch length to suit your fabric and probable strain. Backstitch every few inches for stronger basting.

Never machine stitch directly on basting and always remove it before pressing permanent stitching. Use silk thread if your fabric is fragile and easily marred, such as satin or velvet. Silk thread is ideal for holding edges in place for pressing, as in collars or pleats.

EVEN BASTING joins seams that are subject to strain or areas that need close control. Keep eased, bias, or curved edges on top when joining them to straight areas. Take even stitches about ¼″ long and ¼″ apart.

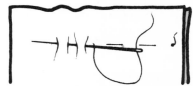

UNEVEN BASTING attaches interfacing and underlining edges to fabric, holds seams and edges not subject to strain, and marks. Take a long stitch on top and a short stitch through the fabric. Develop your own combo of long and short stitches to make this basting a simple routine.

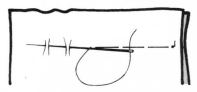

DIAGONAL BASTING holds facings, interfacings, and linings in place during fittings. With silk thread, this stitch helps control hard-to-handle fabrics as you press. Make short straight stitches through the fabric at right angles to the edge; diagonal stitches will form on top. Space stitches evenly.

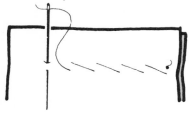

SLIP BASTING helps match plaids, stripes, and prints; holds intricate curved sections together; and secures fitting adjustments made from the outside. Turn under and crease one edge along the seamline and lap over the other piece. Match fabric design at the seamline; pin. Slip needle through the upper fold, then through the lower garment section. Make stitches about ¼″ long; they'll look like even basting on the wrong side.

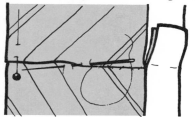

PERMANENT STITCHES

Hand sewing goes where the machine can't or where you want the quality touch that only fine hand sewing affords. It anchors or finishes parts of your garment invisibly. Use thread the same color or one shade darker than your fabric. For permanent stitches, you need a tangle-free thread coated with beeswax. Relax, and don't pull those stitches too tight!

Specific knots begin and end your work. Here is the quickest for beginning. With the threaded needle in one hand, put the long thread end over the needle and hold as shown. Wind thread around needle a few times above thread end.

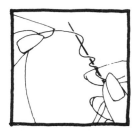

Hold the coiled thread and pull needle through it to draw thread up taut and form a knot.

For an ending knot, take a small stitch on wrong side, pulling thread until only a loop remains. Pass needle through loop to form second loop. Run needle through second loop and pull thread taut.

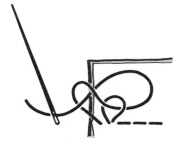

Substitute several small back-stitches for knots, if you prefer.

RUNNING STITCH is used for easing, gathering, tucking, mending, and sewing seams which will not be strained. It's also used to sew facings and hems in place when a garment is lined. Take several small stitches, evenly weaving the needle in and out of the fabric. For easing and gathering, stitches can be up to ¼″ long; for seams, use stitches no more than ⅛″ long.

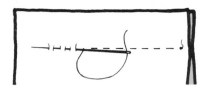

For a lined garment, take long stitches on top and short stitches through fabric, catching only a thread of the bottom layer.

BACKSTITCH is for sturdy repair of hard-to-reach seams. It looks like machine stitching on the upper layer, but on the under layer stitches overlap. Bring the needle through to upper side of fabric. Take a stitch back no more than ⅛″ and bring needle out ⅛″ ahead of the first stitch. Pull thread taut, but don't pucker fabric. Insert needle at end of last stitch to repeat.

Three variations of backstitching have specific applications:

Half-backstitch is used most commonly for understitching facings and linings. The needle is carried back only half of the length of the last stitch, but is still brought out one full stitch ahead.

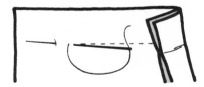

Pickstitch is used mainly for a decorative effect. It is done much like the prickstitch, except that the bottom layer of fabric is not caught when backstitching. Take care not to pull the thread too tightly, because it should form a small bead on the surface of your fabric.

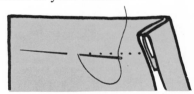

Prickstitch is used for inserting zippers with a custom touch. Carry the needle back only one or two threads, making the surface stitch very small and barely visible.

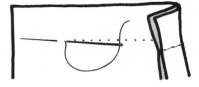

SLIPSTITCH provides an almost invisible finish. It is used in hemming and in attaching linings, pockets, and trims to your garment. Slide the needle in one folded edge and out, picking up a thread of the under layer at this spot. Take even stitches no more than ¼" apart.

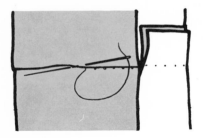

OVERCAST STITCH prevents raw edges from raveling and is one of the best seam finishes. Working from either direction, take slanted stitches over the edge. Stitches should be evenly spaced and uniformly deep.

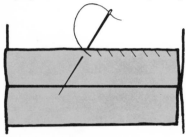

OVERHAND STITCH holds two finished edges together. Often it's used in attaching lace edging or ribbon to a garment. Insert needle diagonally through fabric from back edge to front edge; pick up only one or two threads.

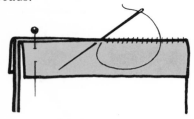

Whipstitch is a variation of overhand stitch, and can serve the same purpose or can *tack* a raw edge in place. Insert needle at a right angle to the edge, forming slanted stitches.

HEMMING STITCH is for hems, especially those finished with seam binding. Take a tiny stitch in the garment, then bring needle diagonally through seam binding or hem edge. Take all stitches in this manner, spacing them about ¼" apart.

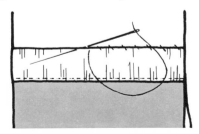

CATCHSTITCH holds two layers of fabric in place flexibly. Use it to attach facings and interfacings to garment and to hem stretchy fabrics. Work from *left* to *right,* taking a small horizontal stitch from right to left in the upper layer of fabric. Just beyond the edge of the upper layer, take an identical stitch diagonally from the first in the under layer. Sew in a loose zigzag manner.

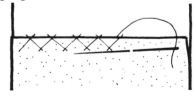

BLINDSTITCH will hem and secure facings inconspicuously. It makes a blind hem—one in which stitches can't be seen from either side of garment. Finish raw edge and roll it back ¼"; take a small horizontal stitch through one thread of garment. Then pick up a thread of hem or facing diagonally above previous stitch. Work in a zigzag manner. Don't pull stitches too tight; every 4 or 5 inches, stretch the blindstitched area and tack for a more durable stitch.

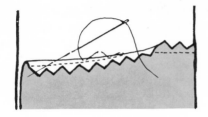

BUTTONHOLE STITCH: Refer to
Buttonholes.
PADSTITCH: See **Tailoring.**
CHAINSTITCH: Refer to **Belts.**

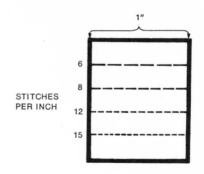

MACHINE SEWING

You've probably always thought that the sewing machine has it all over hand sewing as far as making clothing is concerned. Because the sewing machine is so important, learn to use it to its best advantage. Get to know your machine by carefully reading the manufacturer's booklet. This will tell you about the various machine parts and what they do, as well as how to thread your machine and bobbin and solve common problems. Then read our suggestions for doing machine stitching the easy way.

Check your machine before stitching. Frequently lift the throat plate and brush dust and threads from the feed dog and bobbin. Oil your machine after 8 hours use, or at least once a month.

The chart in the equipment section can help you select needle and thread sizes best suited to your fabric.

STITCH LENGTHS depend on your fabric and the stitching function; use 6–8 stitches per inch for basting, 8–10 stitches per inch for gathering and easing, 12–15 stitches per inch for normal stitching, and 15–20 stitches per inch for reinforcing.

Consult charts in equipment and special fabric sections for specific recommendations.

PRESSURE is the force of the presser foot on fabric. When the pressure is right, fabric feeds smoothly. Texture affects pressure required; thick, soft, or fluffy fabrics require less pressure than thin, crisp, or flat fabrics.

Test for correct pressure by pinning the ends of two fabric scraps together on lengthwise grain; stitch without thread. Fabric should feed through machine without strain, slack, or feed dog imprint. If it doesn't, adjust pressure mechanism. The illustration shows pressure that is too great, causing one layer of the fabric to bubble.

TENSION controls looseness or tightness of threads that form a stitch. Upper tension controls needle thread; lower tension, bobbin thread. Balanced tensions form perfect stitches locked in the center of the fabric; use the same thread for both needle and bobbin. Loose upper tension causes bobbin thread to lie flat on fabric surface. Tight upper tension causes needle thread to lie flat.

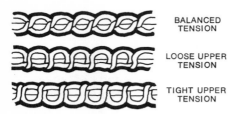

BALANCED TENSION

LOOSE UPPER TENSION

TIGHT UPPER TENSION

Test the tension by cutting a fabric square on straight grain; fold diagonally and cut along fold. Pin and stitch together on the bias, using the appropriate needle for your fabric and cotton thread (silk and synthetic threads won't break). Fabric shouldn't pucker and stitches should look the same on both sides. Grasp fabric at both ends of stitching and pull suddenly to break threads.

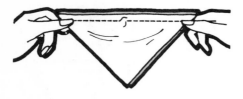

If both the bobbin and needle threads break at the same point, it means that the tensions are balanced. If only one thread breaks, the upper tension needs to be changed. Adjust the tension and test again.

STRAIGHT STITCHING is started with the needle at its highest point.

Put thread ends under pressure foot and pull them away from you. Place fabric under presser foot with seam allowance edge to the right.

Holding thread ends and fabric, lower needle into fabric; then lower presser foot. Stitch at a constant speed. Guide fabric through machine with your fingers; do not pull or stretch it. Keep enough fabric on machine to feed evenly.

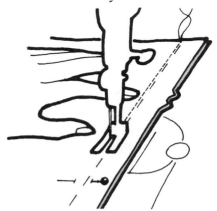

At seam end, raise needle to highest point and lift presser foot. Pull fabric away and cut threads.

Guidelines on throat plate, or a seam guide set the desired distance from the needle, will help you stitch a straight line. Guidelines are usually spaced at ⅛" intervals and begin ⅜" from the needle. Keep fabric edge even with one of these marks to stitch ⅜", ½", ⅝", and ¾" seams (⅝" is standard).

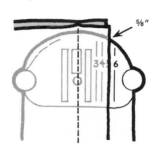

Use the presser foot edge as a guide for distances smaller than ⅜". If your machine doesn't have guidelines or a seam guide, stick a piece of tape on the throat plate; mark the appropriate distances from the needle on the tape.

CURVES are stitched like straight seams, but require more control on your part.

Seam guides are great for straight stitching and essential for curves. Set seam guide desired distance from needle. For inward curves, angle seam guide to align one corner with needle; stitch with cut edge against corner only. For outward curves, set the seam guide parallel to presser foot with upper corner even with needle; stitch with cut edge against flat part.

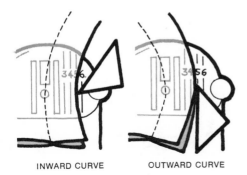

INWARD CURVE   OUTWARD CURVE

MACHINE BASTING is a fast alternative to hand basting and is excellent on simple seams in firm fabrics. Avoid using it on fabrics which slip or show needle marks.

Loosen the upper tension to ensure easy removal and use the longest stitch on your machine. Remove basting by clipping needle thread at 2" intervals and pulling out bobbin thread. If you have a machine that does the chain stitch, use it for basting, as chain stitching pulls out very quickly.

Pin basting keeps layers of fabric from shifting while being machine basted or permanently stitched. With a hinged presser foot, seams can be permanently stitched over pin basting. Place pins every 1½"-2" at right angles to seamline, with heads toward fabric edge.

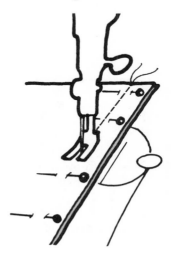

SECURE stitching by backstitching or knotting.
Backstitch only when it won't show. Position needle on seamline ½" from edge of fabric; reverse stitch to edge, change stitch direction, and stitch forward *exactly over* previous stitching. To end seam, stitch to edge of fabric and reverse stitch for ½".

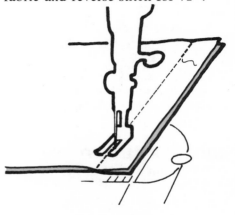

Knot end of seam with a *tailor's knot* or *square knot;* trim threads to ½".

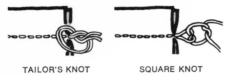

TAILOR'S KNOT   SQUARE KNOT

At other locations, pull one thread until a small loop appears at its base. Pull this loop with a pin until thread comes through and tie.

PIVOTING is turning a corner without breaking the line of stitching. Stitch slowly and stop at pivot point with needle in fabric; lift presser foot. Rotate fabric on needle to change position for stitching.

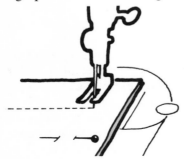

Lower presser foot and continue.

EASING is a long stitch used to join a long edge to a short edge by controlling fullness in the long one. It is described in Seams.

DIRECTIONAL STITCHING prevents garment seam areas from stretching as you work because stitching is done as much as possible with the fabric grain. Run your finger along the cut edge to find the grain direction. If threads lie smoothly, you're going with the grain; if they fray, you're going against the grain.

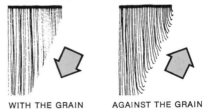

WITH THE GRAIN   AGAINST THE GRAIN

Generally, stitch from widest to narrowest part of each garment piece.

STAYSTITCHING is done directionally ½" from bias or curved edges immediately after removing the pattern tissue. It serves the same purpose as directional stitching and also provides a guide for clipping and joining edges. Staystitch zipper openings ¼" from the edge.

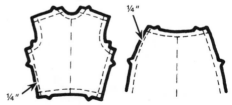

ZIGZAGGING is a miracle-worker. With a zigzag machine or attachment, you can make buttonholes, stitch seams with give in stretchy fabrics, and overcast raw edges. Refer to your machine manual for other uses.

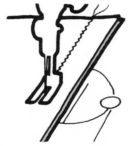

REINFORCING adds strength and is usually done on curves, corners, and points which will be clipped into or trimmed very closely. Using 15 - 20 stitches per inch, stitch for about 1″ on either side of the point or curve. (See curves and corners in Seams for specific applications.)

REMOVING STITCHES requires care so no damage is done to fabric. Cut stitches at 1″ - 2″ intervals on one side of seamline with small scissors or seam ripper—never a razor blade. Pull out thread on opposite side.

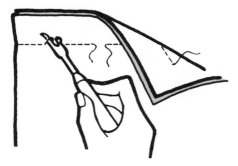

Never pull seam edges apart, as this may tear or stretch fabric.

For descriptions and functions of available machine attachments, see the **Equipment** section or your sewing machine manual.

SEAMS

Well-made seams make garments you can be proud to wear. Seams to strive for are smooth—never puckered, stretched, or shaky; they are neatly finished—never a mass of ravelings and threads. Remedy seam goofs early by ripping them out and re-stitching. Postponing corrections until later makes them difficult or impossible.

STRUCTURAL SEAMS

Technique is the word for construction seaming. These seams hold a garment together and are the fastest part of getting your fashion idea into form.

PLAIN SEAMS are the simplest. Match notches and markings; pin or baste, then stitch along the seamline. Press layers together directionally to blend the stitches into the fabric.

Then press open. If fabric tends to mar, press over seam roll or with brown paper under seam allowances.

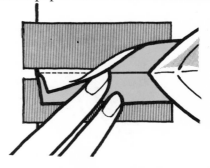

INTERSECTING SEAMS are joined after stitching and pressing open two seams. Pin the seamed sections together, matching seams. Put a needle through stitching of seams at new seamline; stitch. Trim corners of seam allowances to reduce bulk.

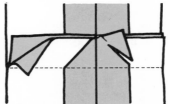

EASED SEAMS are used to join a larger section to a smaller one. Stitch larger section between markings, 8-10 stitches per inch, close to seamline in the seam allowance. With easestitched side up, match markings and pin sections together. Pull up ease thread until larger section fits smaller one. Knot ends of ease thread and distribute fullness evenly as you pin or baste; stitch.

Press the two layers together to shrink out fullness, then press seam open. For handling ease in sleeve caps, see Sleeves.

CURVED SEAMS require special techniques. There are two types of curves—*outward* and *inward* (see diagram).

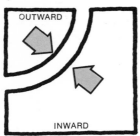

Like Curves: A seam with two like curved edges is usually a long vertical seam in a princess silhouette. Pin or baste the two sections together, matching seamlines and markings, and stitch.

An outward curve is *notched* by cutting small wedges or notches from seam allowances at evenly spaced intervals. Turn seam allowances to their finished position. The amount of excess fabric to be removed forms ripples in the seam allowance. Crease ripples as shown and cut away.

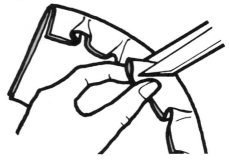

When pressed open over a tailor's ham, a correctly notched seam is smooth and edges of notches meet. On very lightweight fabrics, overlapping clipped edges can substitute for notching.

An inward curve is *clipped*. Make small cuts or clips in the seam allowances at even intervals; distance between clips depends on sharpness of curve.

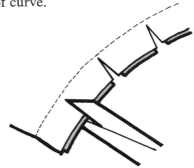

After pressing, a correctly clipped seam is smooth and the clips are spread open.

Opposing Curves: This seam joins an inward curve to an outward curve.

Staystitch inward curve. Pin or baste sections together; clip seam allowance of inward curve just to line of staystitching so it fits the corresponding section. Stitch, keeping clipped section uppermost.

Press seam over a tailor's ham in one of three directions: (1) open, notching excess from seam allowance of outward curve; (2) toward outward curve, notching excess from underneath seam allowance; and (3) toward inward curve, making additional clips in underneath seam allowance if necessary.

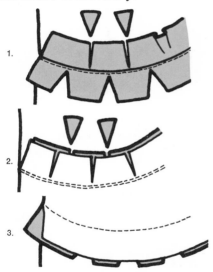

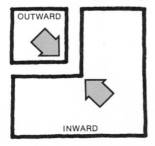

CORNER SEAMS need some preliminary steps. All corners are either *outward* or *inward* (see diagram).

Reinforce inward corner for 1″ on both sides of point, using small stitches next to seamline and pivoting at corner point. Clip to point, but not into stitches.

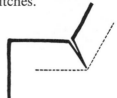

Pin or baste sections together with clipped section uppermost. Stitch, pivoting at point.

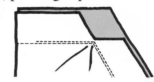

These seams can be pressed in one of three ways: (1) open, trimming excess fabric from outward corner and catchstitching edges together; (2) toward outward corner, trimming excess from outward corner and catchstitching all trimmed edges together; (3) toward reinforced inward corner.

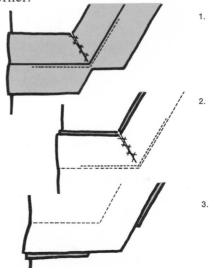

TAPED SEAMS are stronger and less likely to stretch. Use preshrunk twill tape or ribbon seam binding for straight seams. Use bias tape with slack pressed out (refer to Preshaping Bindings) for curved areas. Extend tape edge ⅛" over seamline of one garment section. Pin or baste in place. Tape is permanently sewn as seam is stitched.

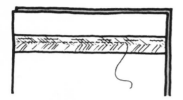

STRETCHY SEAMS will not shift if you pin strips of tissue paper to fabric, stitch through both, then carefully tear paper away. When a little extra give in the seam is needed to prevent splitting, use a small narrow zigzag or straight stitch (12-15 stitches per inch), being careful not to stretch fabric.

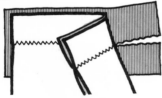

SEAMS IN NAPPED FABRICS should be pinned and basted closely, then stitched in the direction of the nap. Keep any garment sections without nap on top as you stitch.

BIAS SEAMS will not stretch if you cut a strip of tissue paper the length of the seam on your paper pattern and pin to fabric same as for Stretchy Seams. Pin or baste edges together. If one matching section is on the straight grain, it can act as a stay. Stitch with bias layer of fabric up, smoothing any wrinkles away from seamline.

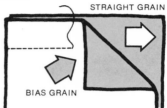

STRAIGHT GRAIN

BIAS GRAIN

ENCLOSED SEAMS

Seams that form a finished edge, such as a collar or cuff, require different techniques than structural seams because the seam allowances are turned in one direction and are enclosed by both sides of the garment.

PLAIN SEAMS are stitched like Plain Structural Seams. The difference is that seam allowances turned together in one direction must be trimmed and graded to eliminate excess bulk. Otherwise, they may form an undesirable ridge on the outside of your garment.

Trim by cutting away part of the seam allowances to make them narrower. When you are dealing with bulky fabrics or more than two seam allowances going in the same direction, *grade* as you trim by cutting each seam allowance ⅛" narrower than the one to the outside of it. Trim interfacing close to stitching and the facing seam allowances to about ¼", leaving the garment seam allowance the widest.

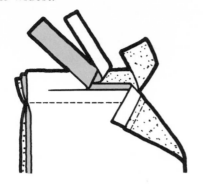

Press all enclosed seams to set stitches, then press open over a point presser (see Pressing). For edges like those of a collar, press seam allowances toward underside of garment area. For facings, press seam allowances toward facing and understitch.

Understitch to prevent the underside of the garment or facing from rolling to the outside. Pull facing away from garment section; machine stitch or half-backstitch close to the seam through facing and all seam allowances.

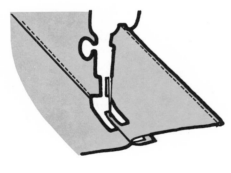

Turn facing to inside, enclosing seam allowances. Press, using a press cloth and *favoring* garment edge by rolling seam just slightly to inside so facing won't show on outside. Press again from outside, using a press cloth.

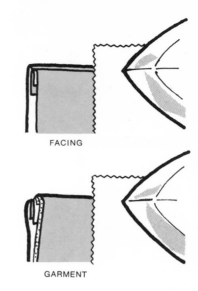

FACING

GARMENT

For hard-to-handle fabrics, baste along edges with diagonal basting and silk thread before pressing.

CORNER SEAMS or points are stitched nearly the same as a Plain Enclosed Seam. Stitch to within 1" of corner. Use reinforcement stitches to corner and take a diagonal stitch across point. Continue for 1" more, then readjust stitches to normal length.

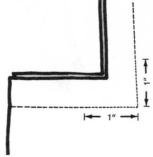

Handle inward corners, often found in necklines, by clipping them to the corner without cutting into stitching. Outward corners, like those in collars, are trimmed to remove bulk. Fold corner seam allowances over stitching line to the position they will take when turned. The overlapping seam allowance fabric must be trimmed.

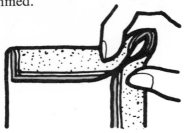

Cut seam allowances diagonally across tip of corner; avoid cutting into stitching. If corner is very pointed, taper seam allowances with an additional diagonal cut on each side of point.

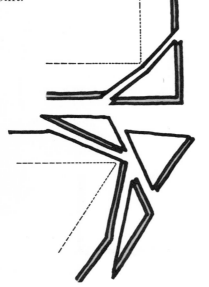

Now trim and grade remainder of seam. Press, turn, and favor same as Plain Enclosed Seam, understitching where necessary. Use only a point turner or dull object to push out corner; scissors might tear fabric.

CURVED SEAMS are stitched the same as a Plain Enclosed Seam.

Those which will receive strain, such as necklines and halter armholes, should be reinforced. Use stretched bias tape, pressing it into the shape of the curve as you take out slack. Apply as in a Taped Seam.

Trim and grade seam allowances. Clip inward curves and notch outward curves before turning; *do not* clip tape. Space a few clips or notches at even intervals, then turn seam allowances to underside of garment section to see if they will lie flat without straining or excess fullness. Sharper curves need more clips and notches to achieve a flat, smoothly finished edge.

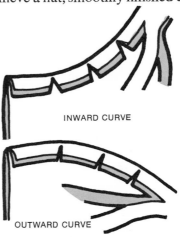

INWARD CURVE

OUTWARD CURVE

Press, turn, and favor same as a Plain Enclosed Seam, understitching where necessary.

SEAM FINISHES

All's well that ends well—this is especially true of seams which may ravel away to nothing unless given a finishing touch.

EDGESTITCHING is done by machine stitching ¼″ from cut edge of each seam allowance. An edgestitched seam can be left as is or treated in one of two ways: (1) cut along edges with pinking or scalloping shears for fabrics which ravel very little or (2) trim ⅛″ from edge and overcast by hand for fabrics which ravel quite a bit.

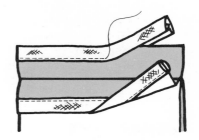

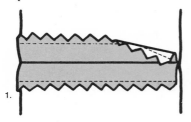

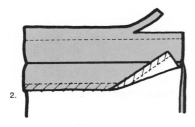

MACHINE ZIGZAGGING is good for fabrics which ravel easily. Zigzag near each raw edge, using a narrower stitch for lightweight fabrics and a wider stitch for heavy, bulky fabrics.

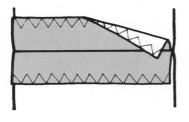

BOUND EDGES are ideal for seams in loosely woven or easily frayed fabrics and in unlined jackets and coats. Encase each raw edge in double-fold bias tape. Place the slightly narrower folded edge of tape on top and edge-stitch through all layers.

TURNED-UNDER EDGES are for plain weave, lightweight, or sheer fabrics. Stitch ¼″ from raw edge. Turn edge in along stitched line, stitching again from the right side of the seam allowance along the folded edge as you turn. This method is good on curved seam allowances **OR...**

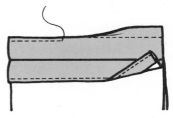

SEW AND GO . . . extra easy: On relatively straight edges, stitch close to folded edge from wrong side as you turn under raw edges of seam allowances.

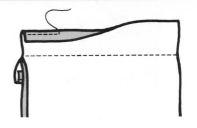

DECORATIVE SEAMS

Accent a design line, flatter your most attractive feature, or add that special something to a plain-Jane dress by stealing from our collection of decorative seams.

LAPPED SEAM is started by turning in the edge of overlapping fabric section along seamline; press. Working from the outside, pin or baste folded section to other section with seamlines matching and raw edges even; edgestitch.

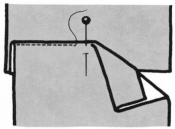

Tucked seam is made in the same manner. Form the tuck by stitching the desired depth from the fold through all thicknesses. Don't stitch closer than ¼ " to raw edges.

WELT SEAM begins as a plain seam with seam allowances pressed to one side. Trim the seam allowances closest to garment to ¼ " and stitch through untrimmed seam allowance and garment close to trimmed edge, encasing trimmed seam allowance.

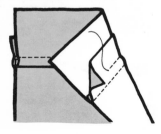

SLOT SEAM starts with a basted plain seam that is pressed open. Cut a strip of fabric the length of the seam and slightly wider than both seam allowances. Center strip under seam and baste. On outside, topstitch same distance on each side of basted seam.

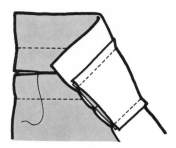

CORDED SEAM is stitched with a cording or zipper foot. First encase cording in a bias strip and stitch close to cording. Machine baste cording to right side of one section. Pin second section to corded one. With corded layer on top, stitch alongside machine-basted seamline through all layers.

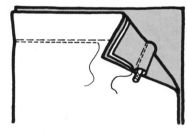

Piped seam is made like the corded seam, except commercial piping or folded bias strips are substituted for bias-covered cord.

SELF-BOUND SEAM: See **Sewing for Children.**

See the **Men's** section for seams used in man-tailored garments—these include the flat-fell seam, simulated flat-fell seam, and double welt seam. Seams for **Special Fabrics** are discussed in that section. Decorative additions to seams, such as topstitching and saddle stitching, are listed under **Trims.**

PRESSING

Have iron, will press—that should be your sewing motto. Pressing is one of those essential things that has to be done right. Everyone knows about using steam irons and ironing boards on the weekly wash, but pressing as you sew is a little more particular than just ironing.

CONSTRUCTION PRESSING

Pressing is *not* ironing. Pressing is lifting and setting down, not pushing your iron from one spot to another in a long, unbroken motion.

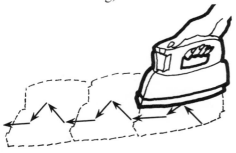

Pressing techniques are different than ironing, too.

- Pressing is continual, from the first darts to the final hem. All darts and seams are pressed *before* they are crossed with other seams.
- Use steam to ease, to flatten seams, and to mold curves. Heat and moisture, not weight, press shape into your garment.
- Use the specific tool for each part of your garment to create the desired effect and protect surrounding fabric from being accidentally wrinkled.
- Above all, take care of your fabric. Test the effects of steam, pressure, and temperature before you begin.

Do most pressing on the wrong side. Just touch up garment on the right side, using a press cloth. Press with the grain and in the direction you stitched.

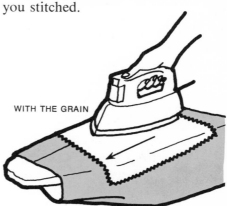

WITH THE GRAIN

Never press sharp creases until you've *thoroughly checked the fit* of your garment, and *never* press over pins or over basting unless you used silk thread.

PRESSURE should be light. Never rest the full weight of the iron on your fabric. Much pressing is done with just the tip. However, some wools may require greater pressure; with a pounding block or clapper in hand, make quick pounding motions over the area.

HEAT which is excessive can deteriorate fabrics or cause shine. Set

iron to the correct temperature, and
test on a self-fabric scrap.

MOISTURE is needed for pressing
most fabrics, but should be used with
care since it can spot, change texture,
or give an over-pressed look. On
some fabrics, a steam iron alone provides enough moisture. For other
fabrics, a damp press cloth will be
needed; test on a scrap of your fabric
first to determine the amount of wet-
ness required.

A dry press cloth protects the
right side from shine or imprints.
Many types can be used: cheesecloth, drill cloth, a special non-
woven cloth for steam irons, see-
through press cloths, or self-fabric.

Press *as you sew,* not after your
project is completed. Use the following equipment to press specific
shapes and textures.

FLAT AREAS of your garment are
pressed directly on the ironing board.

Sleeve boards are miniature
ironing boards for pressing narrow
garment sections. Press garment area
along middle of board to avoid creasing fabric along edge.

If you don't have a seam roll,
use brown paper between seam allowances and garment.

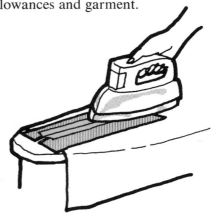

CONTOUR AREAS, such as curved
seams, darts, and eased areas, should
be pressed on rounded surfaces. A
tailor's ham is used for big curves.

For fabric that imprints easily,
a seam roll will allow you to flatten
seams without pushing the seam allowances into your garment.

Press mitts fit over your hand or the end of the sleeve board and are used for smaller curves.

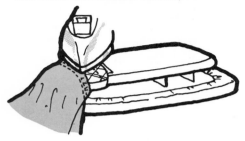

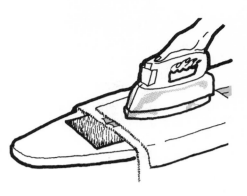

CORNERS or points can be pressed many ways. If the corner is at a finished edge, lay section wrong side up over a point presser; the narrow end should fit into the corner or point. Open the seam with the tip of the iron. This makes it easier to crease edges along the seam when turning.

TEXTURED FABRICS require special treatment to protect their surface. Pressing face down on a towel or piece of self-fabric is sufficient for most fabrics.

For pile fabrics such as velvet, however, use a needleboard; placing the pile side down on the bed of tiny needles keeps it from being flattened. If the pile is exposed on both sides, use a self-fabric press cloth for one side and needleboard for the other.

If you do not have the pieces of pressing equipment suggested, see the chart below for some substitutes.

Tailor's Ham	Hard pillow; press mitt; rolled-up Turkish towel
Seam Roll	Rolled magazine, covered with a towel to prevent ink smears on fabric
Point Presser	Cardboard cut to shape of your pattern piece; pointed, dowel-like object; small point turner
Sleeve Board	Fold section flat, keeping seam at middle, and press seam at edge of ironing board without creasing folds on either side of seam; rolled magazine covered with towel
Needle-board	Thick Turkish towel; self-fabric scrap
Pounding Block	Rolled magazine covered with towel; ruler

173

FINAL PRESSING

When you've completed your garment, give it a touch-up pressing. Put your garment on dress form or padded hanger. Pad curves like sleeves and collars with tissue paper. Steam and pat garment into position, never touching fabric with iron. Let garment dry completely.

For pressing unusual fabrics and specific garment areas during construction, or a guide to buying good pressing equipment, see the chart on **Fibers and Fabrics, Special Fabrics,** the articles devoted to garment areas, and **Equipment.**

FITTING

Try on your creation at least once before everything is permanently stitched. Even the best seamstress sometimes finds that a little touch here and there is in order before her garment fits. Well-fitting clothes will increase your comfort and self-confidence and give you plenty of room for movement. Smoothly hanging garments are always more flattering than ones with wrinkles and tell-tale bulges.

Don't expect miracles, though. Fitting only takes care of the little details that make your fabric conform to your figure as the garment is put together. Make major changes in fit on the pattern tissue before cutting into your fashion fabric.

We have included the list of hints below to make fitting a simple process for every garment you sew.

- Lap centers or seamlines and fasten openings by pinning horizontally.

- Increase or decrease circumference by dividing the needed amount among all seams and darts; never make adjustments in closure areas.
- Position fabric correctly by smoothing it perpendicular to wrinkles. Shift basted seams when wrinkles indicate the need for relocation. Increase one seam allowance and decrease the other; retain a 1/4″ seam allowance. Stitch seam binding to narrow seam allowances if fabric ravels.
- When adjusting garment length, also adjust corresponding facing and lining pieces. Relocate waistline by adjusting bodice seamline.
- Adjust darts to conform to bust position and shape.
- Redistribute sleeve cap ease when you see diagonal ripples. Remove basting in cap area and slide fullness until wrinkles are gone.
- For slightly wider or narrower shoulders, move cap on shoulder. Make slight circumference adjustments on garment underarm seam in the same manner.
- Move sleeve darts or ease until they hit bent elbow at correct spot.

STAGE 1: Prepare garment and try on

Thread trace center front and center back before removing pattern, then staystitch neck and armhole curves. Baste darts and major sections of garment together; do not include collar, cuffs, facings, sleeves, or pockets. Clip neckline and armhole to staystitching in a few spots;

this enables you to test-fit without the unfinished seam allowance causing tightness.

Try on garment *right side out* with appropriate undergarments, shoes, and belt. This way you can fit each side of the garment to the corresponding side of your body; perfectly symmetrical figures are very rare. Pin openings for zippers, plackets, or buttons together along centers or seamlines. Stand before a full-length mirror in a well-lighted room.

STAGE 2: Check grainlines, seamlines, and center markings

Are side seams and center seams or markings perpendicular to floor? Do they divide figure roughly in half? Are hem edges parallel to floor? Is crosswise grain at bust and hips at right angles to lengthwise grain at center markings or seams?

Is the waist seam located as shown on the pattern envelope? And is it snug enough to hold garment in position? Are shoulder seams straight across the middle of shoulder from base of neck to top of shoulder?

STAGE 3: Check darts, neckline, armhole, and details

Do both sides of the garment look the same? Lopsidedness is a result of fitting one side more closely than the other. Wrinkles are signs of stress, strain, or improper distribution of fullness.

Darts should end about ½″ from fullest part of bust. Does neckline encircle base of neck smoothly and comfortably? Do armholes curve smoothly over end of shoulder bone? Is the lowest point of armhole seamline 1″ below armpit? Is placement of pockets, buttonholes, and other details correct and practical?

Remove garment for making any necessary changes. Stitch major seams and darts and apply facings.

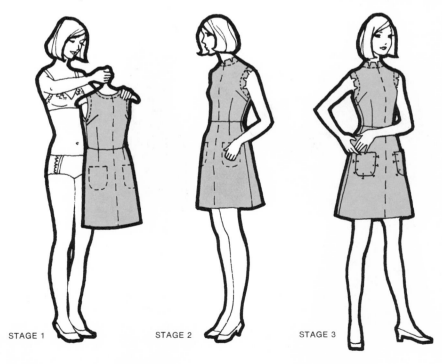

STAGE 1   STAGE 2   STAGE 3

STAGE 4: Check sleeves

Baste sleeve in armhole and try on garment. Sleeve should fall smoothly from points about halfway down front and back curves of armhole seam. Are cap and body of sleeve smooth and evenly rounded? Watch for distortion of grain in the sleeve cap. Does sleeve join bodice at the shoulder bone?

Are elbow darts or ease centered over elbow when arm is bent? Place one dart at elbow, two darts on either side of elbow, or middle dart in a group of three at elbow.

STAGE 5: Check hem length

Let flared or bias garments hang for 24 hours before marking hem. Wear appropriate undergarments, shoes, and belt. Try on skirt with vest, top, jacket, or tunic to get the effect of proportion. Have a friend mark your hem as you stand in front of the mirror. Stand still with arms at your side as *she* moves around you and inserts pins along hemline; place pins every 3″ on straight skirts and every 2″ on flared skirts.

Turn up hem, putting pins at right angles to hem so it can hang freely. Hem must appear even, in spite of what measurements sometimes say. When hem looks crooked because hemline doesn't follow fabric design, as in a plaid or stripe, change hemline to adapt to optical illusion.

Turn to the **Tailoring** section for fitting outerwear. Problems in fitting pleated garments are discussed in **Pleats.**

STAGE 4

STAGE 5

SHAPING

Shape is what fashion is all about, and shaping fabrics or techniques can do for your garment what the girdle, bra, and body stocking do for your figure.

INTERFACING

Collars, cuffs, necklines, bands, hems, and opening edges are often interfaced for the extra body that will enable them to support the rest of the garment. Garments not interfaced will sag after one cleaning. Use the chart on pages 63-65 in making an appropriate selection.

Your pattern usually indicates interfacing areas or pattern pieces; if not, use facing pieces. For garments with foldlines, cut interfacing from facing area of the garment pattern, extending foldline edge 5/8".

Methods for attaching interfacing will depend on fabric weight. For lightweight to medium weight fabrics, use techniques described below. For bulky or heavy fashion fabric, and medium to heavyweight interfacing, see Tailoring.

PREPARATION: Trim interfacing corners diagonally and all edges without seamlines 5/8" to avoid extra bulk.

Interfacing pieces are often stitched together before being attached to garment. Lap and pin interfacing sections, matching seamlines. Stitch; trim seam allowances closely.

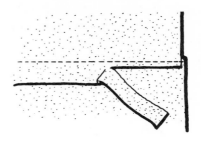

Slash darts through center to tip; lap, matching stitching lines. Stitch, securing point with extra stitches.

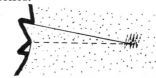

ATTACHING: Interfacing is attached to garment foundation, such as opening and shoulder edges, undercollar, and the part of cuff sewn to sleeve. Baste or pin interfacing to wrong side of garment, matching seamlines and foldlines.

Interfacing will be caught in seams when garment is sewn and should be trimmed close to stitching.

At *foldlines,* place interfacing with extension 5/8" past foldline and invisibly sew to fabric at foldline with long, loose blindstitches.

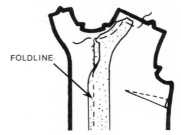

FOLDLINE

If interfacing was cut without ⅝″ extension, sew edge to garment invisibly along foldline. Take a small stitch through interfacing, catching one thread of fashion fabric. Repeat ½″ to 1″ below, forming diagonal stitches along the edge. **OR . . .**

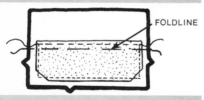

FOLDLINE

For fabrics that don't mar, use press-on interfacing or adhesive to bond interfacing fabrics in place. Trim ¾″ from all seamline edges, then apply by manufacturer's instructions.

UNDERLINING

Form a framework for construction by underlining your fashion fabric. Construction details and hand sewing will never show on outside since all edges are sewn to underlining, not fashion fabric. Choose an underlining from the chart on pages 63 to 65 to complement, not overwhelm, fashion fabric.

After cutting garment, mark center front and back along lengthwise grain. Use same pattern pieces to cut and mark underlining; for marking use tracing wheel and carbon paper.

ATTACHING: Working on a flat surface, center underlining over fashion fabric. Baste together along lengthwise center lines; pin along remaining lines and edges.

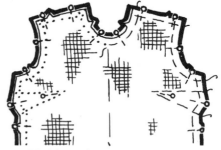

Hold each pinned section over appropriate body area. If the layers don't mold smoothly together, remove pins and fold, underlining side in, along center line. Insert folded towel or sheet into center fold and smooth fabric. Underlining will extend beyond fabric edge. Pin layers together as they lie along markings and edges.

Baste through both layers along all underlining markings. For easy removal, don't baste directly on stitching lines. Handle the two layers as one during construction. **OR . . .**

LINING

Besides being pretty, lining covers inside construction and increases durability. Use the chart on pages 63-65 for help in choosing the best one for your garment.

Skirts and pants are lined before waistline and hem are finished; dresses can be lined before facings or sleeves are applied.

FULL LINING: If pattern doesn't include lining pieces, cut lining from major garment pieces, excluding facings, pockets, etc. Repeat garment fitting adjustments in lining.

Classic: These general instructions for lining skirts or pants can be modified to suit any style.

Stitch lining darts and major seams, ending seam for zipper opening ½″ below marking. Press darts and seams. Clip crotch seams in pants and press open.

Pin lining to garment, wrong sides together, at waist. Follow Zipper Finish directions on page 181 to attach lining at zipper area, then baste waist edges together.

Attach facing or waistband. Finish hem as described on page 181.

Lined to Edge: This method is used for sleeveless garments — dresses, vests, and jumpers. It eliminates facings, so it's ideal for garments made of bulky fabrics; garments must have center front or center back seams.

For a sleeveless garment with *shoulders less than 2″ wide,* assemble garment and lining separately, leaving shoulders and center closure seam open. Attach lining to garment and finish shoulder seams as for a one-piece neck and armhole facing with shoulders narrower than 2″.

Complete closure. For zippers and hems, see page 181.

For garments with *shoulders wider than 2″,* assemble garment and lining separately. Stitch shoulder seams, but not side seams. Use the one-piece neck and armhole facing method for shoulders wider than 2″ to attach lining to garment; also stitch appropriate closure edges. Turn and press, following same method.

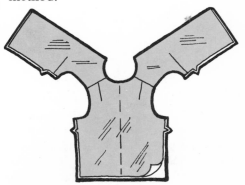

179

Open out lining at sides. Stitch front to back in a continuous side seam from lining edge to garment edge, matching armhole seams; press open.

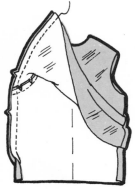

Fit garment or make hem adjustments. Establish and mark hemline on garment. Turn garment wrong side out; pin right sides together with lining edge extending ¼″ beyond garment edge. Stitch along garment hemline, leaving opening for turning; trim and grade.

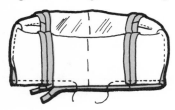

Turn garment and press hem, favoring garment edge. Sew opening edges together; complete closure if necessary. **OR . . .**

SEW AND GO . . . extra easy: Assemble garment and lining, stitching shoulder seams and leaving side seams open. Pin a narrow tuck across each garment shoulder and a horizontal one across each front and back section, tapering to seamlines

on opening edges. Following lining seamlines, stitch lining to garments at all edges but side seams.

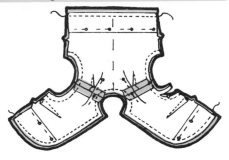

Release tucks; trim and grade seams. Turn as for one-piece neck and armhole facing with shoulders wider than 2″; press, favoring garment edge.

Stitch garment and lining at sides, matching seams; begin and end on lining 1″ from hem edge, leaving an opening.

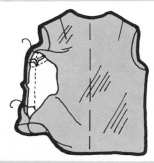

Press side seam open. Sew opening edges together.

PARTIAL LINING: To prevent skirt seats from stretching or pant knees from bagging, use a partial lining, especially when fabric is medium weight to heavyweight wool or a knit.

Skirt: Cut lining from skirt back, transferring pattern markings. Treat the two layers as one throughout construction.

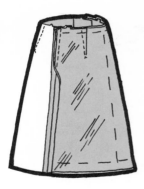

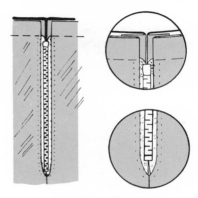

If you prefer a half lining, end it just below skirt seat and insert the same as the skirt lining above.

Pants: Cut two lining sections, each 10″ long and as wide as knee area of front pants piece. Try on pants and mark center of knee cap. Remove pants. Center a lining section over the marked knee of each pants leg; stitch sides to pants seam allowances. Loosely blindstitch the remaining upper and lower edges invisibly to the pants.

HEM FINISHES: Lining hems can be attached to garment or hang freely. Free-hanging hems are suggested for pleated or very full garments; attached hems cover interior construction.

Attached: Hem garment, trim lining even with lower edge. For wearing ease, pin a ¼″ tuck in lining 5″ to 6″ above lower edge. Easestitch ¼″ from lower edge, if needed. Turn lower lining edge in ¼″ and pin to garment hem where it falls, matching seams. Adjust fullness when needed and slipstitch; release tuck.

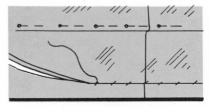

ZIPPER FINISH: Apply zipper to your garment without catching the lining in your stitches. Lining closure seam should end ½″ below bottom zipper stop. Turn lining seam allowances in ⅛″ from zipper teeth; pin. Slipstitch lining to zipper tape. To prevent catching the lining in the teeth of the zipper, make a row of prickstitches ⅛″ from slipstitched lining edge through lining and zipper tape.

Free-hanging: Finish hems of garment and lining separately, making lining ½″ shorter than garment. Anchor lining hem to garment at seams with French tacks.

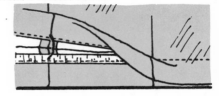

To line a garment with sleeves, refer to **Tailoring.**

Making Shape Waves

If you didn't have a pattern, turning a piece of fabric into something you could wear would be an awe-inspiring job. Fortunately our designers know what to do to make fabric take on contour and shape. They use darts, gathers, and pleats to make fabric conform to the human body. All that you have to do is follow directions and sew in the shape!

DARTS

Tapered folds which shape fabric to fit people are called darts. They are usually formed on the wrong side, and provide carefully shaped fullness. Darts should point toward, but not quite reach, the fullest part of the curve they are covering. If you are taller or shorter than average, you may have to adjust your darts slightly. If you move vertical bodice darts, always shift skirt darts, too. Refer to the alterations and fitting sections for standards on size and placement of darts.

Although darts are often *straight,* they can be curved to create a certain contour. *Concave* darts are used to flatten fabric at the base and give curve at the dart tip. *Convex* darts cause fabric to curve at both base and tip.

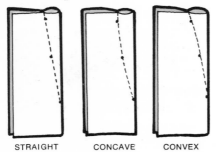

STRAIGHT   CONCAVE   CONVEX

STITCHING darts is done after matching markings and pin basting. Stitch most darts from wide base to end. Taper stitches very gradually near point so end won't pucker; your last 2-3 stitches should be directly on the fold. Secure wide end by backstitching, but tie tailor's knot at the tip for accuracy.

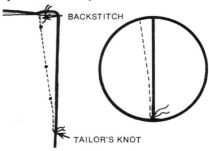

BACKSTITCH

TAILOR'S KNOT

Double-pointed or contour dart consists of two darts meeting at the wide ends. Stitch, beginning at one tapered point and stopping at the other. Knot both ends.

French dart is a diagonal seam with a dart at the end. Match markings and baste to distribute ease properly.

PRESSING darts is a matter of when and where. Use a tailor's ham or a press mitt; add brown paper for fabrics that mar. Press darts before intersecting by seams. Working from the wide end and following stitching, press fold flat to blend stitches; do not press beyond tapered end.

Spread garment over curved surface and press dart into position.

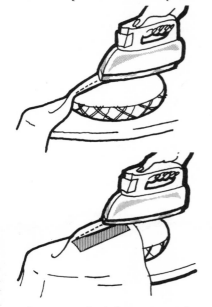

Press vertical darts toward center of garment and horizontal and diagonal darts downward.

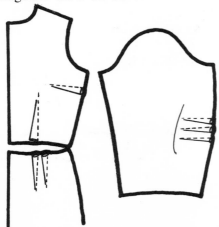

REDUCING BULK is done in four ways: (1) trim wide darts to a depth of ⅝" and grade cut edges; (2) slash darts in heavy fabrics along foldline to ½"-1" from point and press open; (3) clip double-pointed darts along the fold; (4) trim bases of darts diagonally after they are intersected by seams.

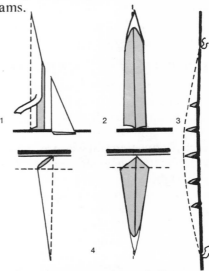

DART TUCK releases fullness at one or both ends and can be made on the outside or inside of the garment. Matching markings, pin baste; stitch between markings.

For outside dart tucks, work thread ends to inside and tie.

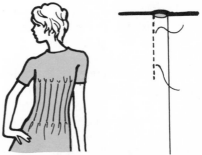

See **Shaping** for darts in interfacing and the **Special Fabrics** section for other methods of handling darts.

GATHERS

Draw up some fabric on a line of stitching, and you've got gathers! Most often found in full skirts and ruffles, they can be used as design features in many ways. Soft, lightweight to medium weight fabrics are best, since heavier fabrics require special attention. Gathers fall more attractively if their folds follow the lengthwise grain.

GATHERING STITCHES

Let the fabric type and weight determine the method to use. For machine gathering, loosen the upper tension and use 6-12 stitches per inch; lightweight fabrics need smaller stitches than heavier weights. From the right side, make two lines of stitching, one on the seamline and another ¼″ away in the seam allowance. Leave 3″ long thread ends at both ends for pulling.

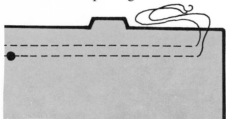

Divide large amounts of fabric into sections and make separate rows of stitching for each section. Don't catch the seam allowances in your stitching unless fabric is lightweight. On very heavy fabric, use buttonhole twist for a stronger bobbin thread.

For hand gathering, make two even lines of gathering stitches, using a small running stitch about ¼″ long.

Gathering foot attachments are available for most sewing machines. Read your machine manual for full details.

SEAMS WITH GATHERS

Two common design features are gathers on one side of a finished seam and gathers on both sides of the seam.

ONE SIDE: Make rows of gathering stitches in the larger section. Pin garment pieces together, matching seams, notches, and markings. Pin the sections together at their centers. Divide the remaining areas and pin at 6″ intervals.

Ease your fabric into gathers by gently pulling the bobbin threads of both rows of stitches. Work from both ends and gather only half a section at a time. Wind the thread ends in a figure eight around a pin at the ends of the gathering line and distribute the fullness evenly throughout the gathered area.

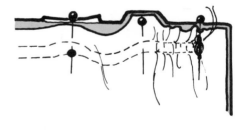

Baste; then, using the long edge of the iron, press the seam allowances together to flatten gathers. *Don't press beyond the seamline.*

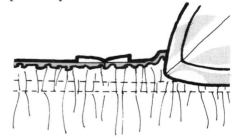

With regulation stitch length and the gathered section uppermost, stitch the seam. Make your stitching line just inside the gathering line on the garment side to prevent it from showing on the outside when the seam is finished. Smooth gathered fabric as you stitch so folds won't be caught in stitching.

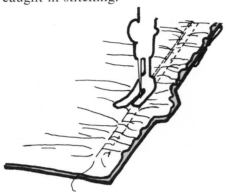

Stabilize all seams subject to strain with a stay. Place the seam binding on the seam allowance, keeping one edge next to the seam line; baste. Edgestitch seam binding stay to seam allowances; avoid catching the garment in your stitching.

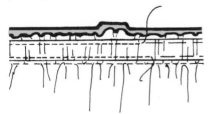

Press the seam allowances together as stitched and then upward, or as directed by your pattern instructions. On the outside, press the adjacent ungathered section flat, using a press cloth and placing brown paper strips between the pressed area and underlying seam allowances.

From inside, touch up gathered area with tip of iron.

BOTH SIDES: Put gathering stitches in both sections. Prepare a stay by cutting seam binding to length of included pattern guide or desired measurement. Transfer centers and markings to seam binding. On inside of one garment section, place seam binding over seamline with one edge ⅛" above it. Pin in place, matching centers and markings. Adjust gathers; baste.

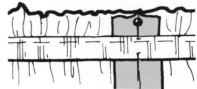

Pin to remaining garment section, matching centers, notches, and markings. Adjust gathers, baste and press as instructed previously for gathers on one side; stitch.

Press seam allowances together. With tip of dry iron, press them up, or as pattern specifies. Never rest iron on fabric.

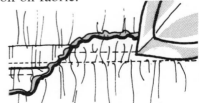

From outside, touch up area over seam allowances with tip of dry iron.

FINAL PRESSING: Never press gathers flat. From the inside whenever possible, glide tip of iron into and out of folds, holding adjacent section or top of gathers.

If needed, repeat above procedure on outside, using a press cloth.

PLEATS

The aim of pleating is to add closely controlled fullness to a garment. Pleats are fabric folds of a definite and regulated width, made by doubling cloth and securing it with pressing and/or stitches. Pleats can be pressed or unpressed, depending on the desired silhouette.

To make successful pleats, start with the right materials. Choose your pattern by hip measurement, since pleats must hang straight from your hips. Buy fabric that can take pleating—your best bets are firm, bouncy fabrics like synthetics (except rayon), blends, wools, linens, and heavy silks.

Types of pleats are the results of different ways of folding your fabric. There are four major types: *knife* or *side pleats,* with all folds turned to one side; *box pleats,* with

two folds turned away from each other; *inverted pleats,* the opposite of box pleats, with folds meeting one another; and *accordion pleats,* made with special commercial equipment.

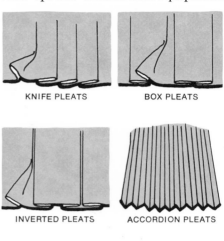

KNIFE PLEATS   BOX PLEATS

INVERTED PLEATS   ACCORDION PLEATS

MARKING

There are two lines in pleats which need marking. The first is the *foldline,* which shows where the outside crease will be; the term *roll line* is used instead for unpressed pleats, where there is no sharp crease. The second is the *placement line;* the creased or rolled edge is brought to this line. Mark carefully on wrong side. If fabric doesn't mark easily or traced lines will show, use tailor's tacks. Identify lines by using two different colors for marking.

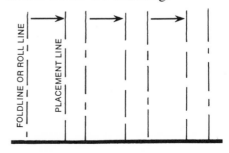

MAKING

Pleat construction is a simple process of folding and pressing along markings. Pressed or unpressed pleats are made the same but pressed differently. Join all vertical seams in section to be pleated, except the one for placket if an opening is needed. This seam will become an inside pleat fold so the pleat progression won't be disturbed.

FROM THE OUTSIDE: Transfer markings to outside with thread tracing. Crease along foldline or roll line. Bring this creased edge to placement line and pin. Continue until all pleats are pinned. Secure each pleat by basting through all layers; begin 6"-8" from lower edge or at finished hem and work to waist.

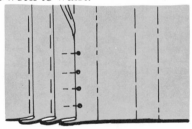

Pin pleats to ironing board at waist seamline and hem edges; steam just enough to set. Machine baste along waist edge and fit pleats.

FROM THE INSIDE: Bring foldline or roll line markings to each placement line; baste through both lines.

Turn pleats in direction indicated; press and continue as if made from outside. **OR...**

SEW AND GO... extra easy: If garment has all-around pleats on straight grain, determine skirt length before cutting fabric; use longest measurement (often the side seam) and allow desired hem depth. Finish hem as instructed on pages 188 and 189, then form pleats. Stitch last seam from bottom up, reinforcing through hem and leaving opening for placket; do not press open. Whipstitch raw edges together across hem; trim ends so they don't show on outside. Fit pleats before finishing placket.

PLEAT WITH AN UNDERLAY: This is made by stitching a separate underlay to the back of an inverted pleat. Mark foldlines or roll lines; pin and baste with right sides together along marked lines. Open pleat extensions and press just enough to set pleat. Center underlay over extension edges and stitch together, keeping garment free; do not press seams open.

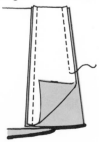

Machine baste pleat and underlay in place across upper edge before fitting.

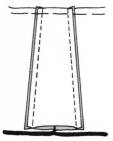

FITTING

Stitch remaining seam, leaving an opening for placket; do not press open. Remove hand basting from pleats and try on. Pleats should be smooth from waist to hip and fall straight from hip to hem. Look for excessive ease or overlapping pleats and strained or opened pleats.

Make any necessary changes at waistline. Do not distort grainline on outside fold and keep ½"-1" ease at waist seamline. Adjust by making either (1) a tiny tapered adjustment on placement line of each free-hanging pleat without changing foldline or roll line, or (2) move stitching line on shaped pleats.

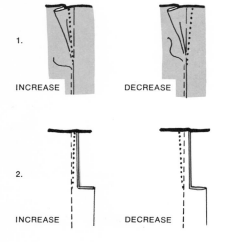

1.

INCREASE   DECREASE

2.

INCREASE   DECREASE

Pleats with underlays should not be adjusted. See the fitting section for circumference· fitting hints.

To straighten an uneven hem, drop or raise pleats at waist where needed until hem is even. Waistline seam allowance may be narrower or wider than ⅝"; mark any changes.

PLACKET OPENINGS

Finish plackets with snap tape, hooks and eyes, or zippers.

Insert zipper as in Zippers for knife or side pleats. For box or inverted pleats and those with an underlay, stitch last seam and place zipper at left side or center back seam where pleat folds meet; use slot or invisible zipper application. **OR ...**

SEW AND GO ... extra easy: Stitch socket part of snap tape to underlying pleat layer and ball part to inner side of overlapping pleat.

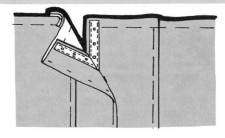

HEMS

Press seams open within hem area. Mark hem; baste and check as in Fitting, page 176. Finish raw edge; on all seams, clip at top of hem as shown; complete hem.

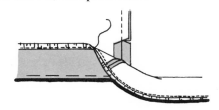

For a very curved hem, remove excess hem fabric before finishing so pleats lie smoothly. Re-stitch seam below hemline at a slant opposite that of garment above hemline.

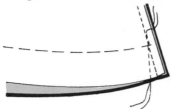

Remove previous stitching below hemline. Complete hem; if desired, edgestitch fold.

To permanently crease pleat edge, edgestitch inside fold through all thicknesses of hem.

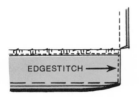

EDGESTITCH ⟶

EDGESTITCHING

This finishing touch ensures a permanent crease at foldlines and can create three very attractive looks: (1) for straight pleats, stitch on outside and/or inside folded edge of pleat; (2) for pleats topstitched from the hip to the waist or shaped pleats, stitch through all layers along the pleat fold above the hipline; and (3) to edgestitch entire pleat, edgestitch from hem to hipline through outside fold of pleat. Then edgestitch from hip to waist through all layers. For shaped pleats, release stitching in the hip area for 1″, then edgestitch as above.

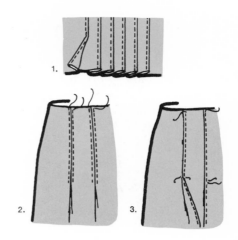

1.

2.   3.

PRESSING

After double-checking fit, pin pleats right side out to ironing board along waistline and hem. *Never set iron on pins.*

Unpressed pleats should be steamed just enough to set shape and fall as intended. Do not rest iron on fabric.

Steam pressed pleats. Insert brown paper under each fold. Press with press cloth to set permanently.

For a sharp, lasting crease, especially at hem, turn pleats wrong side out and repeat entire procedure.

The Big Three

Facings, collars, and sleeves are just about the most crucial points of garment construction. Any of these can make or break what started out to be a great look. A facing which shows, an off-center collar with the underside sticking out, or a puckered sleeve announce loudly that your masterpiece is homemade, and worse yet, that you haven't quite mastered your skill. Accuracy and perseverance will pay off highly in terms of better results.

FACINGS

No one wants to wear clothes with raw edges showing! Facings were invented to conceal those edges. Working behind-the-scenes wonders, facings support the lines of the garment and create smooth, flat edges. Although there are endless variations, all facings fall into three basic categories — shaped, extended, and bias. Learning how to make some of the most familiar examples is a good way to get to know how to make any facing.

If you know from experience that fitting faced areas — armhole, neckline, or closing edge — means trouble, change the tissue before cutting fabric. You can find aids in solving these problems in the pattern alterations and fitting areas.

SHAPED FACINGS

One of the most common facings for necklines and armholes is the shaped or fitted type. It's easy to apply and gives good results. For a zipper closing, check zipper section for appropriate facing and zipper techniques.

Stabilize garment edge to be faced with a suitable interfacing (see Shaping). Stay edges with seam binding; for stretchy fabric or bias edges, use bias tape (see Seams).

Stitch and press major garment seams.

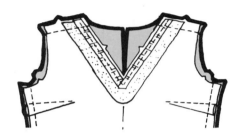

Join facing sections and trim facing seam allowances to ¼″; press open. Use a seam finish appropriate for fabric weight on long unnotched facing edge; sketches in this section show the turned-under and stitched method. Facing edges of lined garments don't require a finish.

Pin or baste facing to garment; match seams, notches, and markings. Stitch, reinforcing corners of a square or V-neck with smaller stitches as you sew.

Trim and grade seam allowances, then clip curves. Clip to corners, but avoid clipping tape.

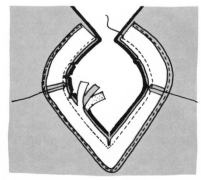

Press seam flat as it was stitched and then open, using a point presser (see Pressing). Press facing and garment seam allowances toward facing with tip of iron.

Understitch facing to seam allowances as far as possible. Turn facing to inside. Press with press cloth, favoring the garment edge.

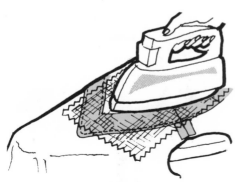

Sew facing to garment seam allowances and complete closure. **OR** . . .

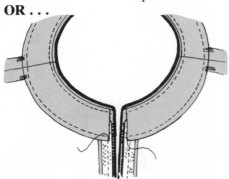

SEW AND GO . . . extra easy: A faster and easier way to anchor facings is by machine. Pin facing in place, matching seams. On outside, stitch in seam of garment through all layers, stopping at facing edge and backstitching at both ends. Stitches will be embedded in the seam and practically invisible.

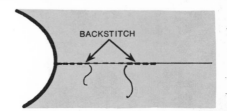

BACKSTITCH

EXTENDED FACING

Facings cut in one with the garment and folded inside to form straight finished edges are called extended facings. They are usually combined with a shaped neck facing.

Stabilize garment edge; stitch seams in garment that are necessary to apply facing; assemble facing and finish edge as instructed in Shaped Facing on the opposite page.

Turn facing to outside along foldline. Pin and stitch neck edges together; match seams, notches, and markings. Trim and grade seam allowances; clip curve as needed.

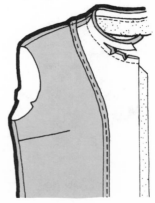

191

Press, understitch, turn facing to inside, and complete as instructed for a Shaped Facing, page 191.

Complete closure according to sewing guide or as desired.

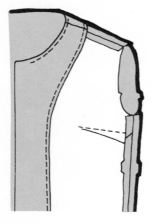

BIAS FACING

Simple to handle and excellent for sheers and heavy or bulky fabrics, the bias facing is a convenient substitute for shaped or fitted facings. Use commercial single-fold wide or narrow bias tape in place of a self-fabric facing.

Stitch and press garment seams as necessary to apply facing. Cut tape the length of edge to be faced plus 2″ for shaping. Open out one folded edge of bias tape and press; shape it into a curve which corresponds to the garment edge by stretching the folded edge as you work.

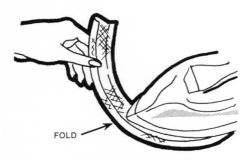

FOLD

Pin tape to garment with crease of opened edge along seamline. Turn in and trim ends to ½″. Stitch; trim seam allowances and clip as needed.

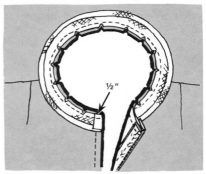

½″

Press seam as for a Shaped Facing, page 191; do not understitch. Turn bias inside along seam, favoring garment edge; pin and sew folded edges to garment, making stitches invisible on the outside. Attach hook and eye if needed.

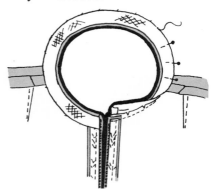

When facing ends meet, as on an armhole, sew them together.

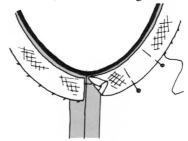

SLASHED FACING

A neckline with a short center front or back opening is often finished by a slashed facing, which is usually a variation of the shaped facing. Proper handling of the slashed area is your key to success.

Stabilize garment edge and stitch garment seams necessary to apply facing; assemble facing and finish edge as instructed for a Shaped Facing, page 190.

Pin baste facing to garment along neck and opening edges, matching seams, notches, and markings. Stitch, reinforcing point as you sew and taking one stitch across point. Slash opening all the way into point; avoid cutting stitches. Trim and grade opening edges and neck seams; trim corners and clip curves.

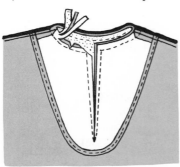

Press, turn facing to inside, understitch, and complete as for a Shaped Facing, page 191. Fasten edges together if desired.

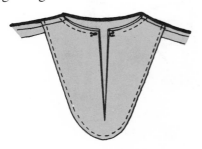

ONE-PIECE NECK AND ARMHOLE FACING

When neck and armhole edges are finished by one continuous facing, it's called a one-piece neck and armhole, all-in-one, or combination facing. Names aside, this is a variation of the familiar shaped facing. For bulky fabric, cut facing pieces from a lining fabric.

Use the technique below only when garment has *shoulders wider than 2"*. Interface and stabilize garment neck edges as for Shaped Facing, page 190. Stitch garment and facing shoulder seams separately and press open. Don't stitch side or closure seams. Finish long unnotched facing edges by appropriate method. Pin a tiny temporary tuck in garment shoulders.

Pin facing to garment, matching seams, notches, and markings. Stitch neck and armhole seams, following the facing seamline. Trim and grade seam allowances, clipping as needed.

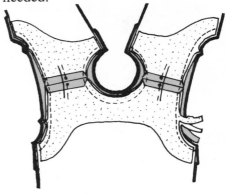

Release pinned tucks from garment shoulders. Press as for a Shaped Facing, page 191. Turn the facing and garment right side out by inserting hand from front between facing and garment, and pulling each back section through shoulder.

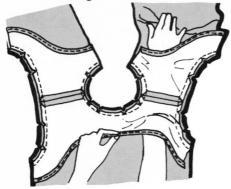

Understitch facing to armhole and neck seam allowances as far into shoulder as possible, breaking stitching and continuing on other side of shoulder to complete.

Pin side seams together, matching armhole seams. Stitch continuously from garment edge to finished facing edges; press seams open.

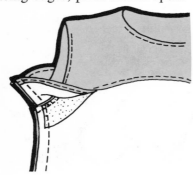

Position facing, press again, and attach side edges of facing as for a Shaped Facing, page 191.

Use this method for garments with *shoulders narrower than 2″*. Interface garment and, if needed, stay seamline as for a Shaped Facing, page 190. Assemble garment and facing separately as you normally would, but *do not* stitch shoulder seams. Finish long unnotched facing edges. Pin a tiny temporary tuck in all garment shoulders, as shown, so facing won't show when garment is completed.

Pin the facing to the garment. Following the facing seamlines, stitch neck and armhole edges, beginning and ending ⅝″ from the shoulder edges. Trim and grade seam allowances and clip curves or trim corners diagonally.

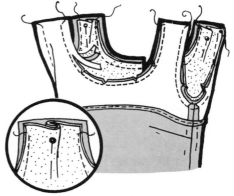

Release tucks in garment shoulders. Press as for Shaped Facings, page 191. Understitch facing to seam allowances as far into shoulder area as possible.

Fold facing shoulder seam allowances back and stitch garment shoulder seams, being careful not to catch facing in stitching; pull thread ends to one side and tie. Trim facing seam allowances to ¼″.

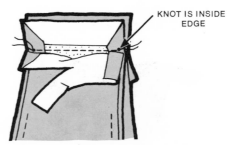

KNOT IS INSIDE EDGE

Press garment seams open; turn in facing shoulder edges and sew together.

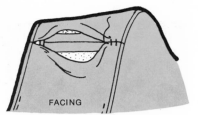

Press and complete as for Shaped Facings, page 191.

COLLARS

Designers love collars, and you will too if your collar is beautifully made and pressed to flatteringly frame your face.

Get into the swing of things with some collar-oriented words. *Flat collars* curve at the neckline like the garment neckline and lie against the garment; *rolled collars,* including the *notched collar,* can curve at the neckline opposite the garment neckline curve or have a straight neckline to make them rise from the garment neckline seam and turn down; and *standing collars* have a straight or slightly curved neckline edge to keep them erect.

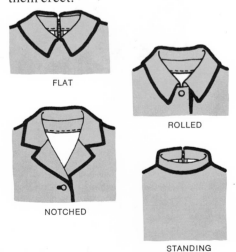

FLAT

ROLLED

NOTCHED

STANDING

The "line" along which the collar turns down is called the *roll line,* or *roll* for short. The *stand* of a collar is the erect area between the neck seam and roll line. The *fall* is the area from the roll line to the finished edge that turns down; a standing collar does not have a fall. The part that shows is called the *upper collar,* the underneath part, the *undercollar.*

Suit or coat patterns usually include separate pieces for upper collar and undercollar. Others will have one piece marked with the number to be cut.

Before proceeding, stitch garment seams comprising neck area. Refer to Shaping for applying interfacing to collar and closure edges. Assemble facing units necessary to complete the neck edge. Staystitch neck edge of garment and facing. Prepare zipper and closure areas.

ENCLOSED COLLARS

A collar with its neck seam allowances turned down and sandwiched between the garment and the facing is an enclosed collar.

FLAT: This collar can be made in one or two sections. It works best with the interfacing attached to the upper collar sections; all other collars have interfacing attached to undercollar. Interface one half of sections. Pin and stitch interfaced sections to remaining ones; reinforce corners. Trim and grade seams; notch curves and trim corners diagonally.

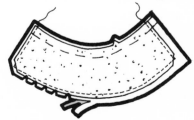

Use a point presser (see Pressing) to press seam open. Then press toward undercollar.

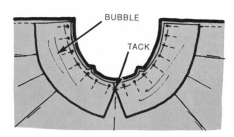

Finish raw edges with a suitable facing, encasing collar neck edge.

Turn and press collar; favor upper collar edge so undercollar won't show. If fabric is hard to handle, use diagonal basting and silk thread along finished edges.

Shape collar before attaching it to garment. With upper collar on top, roll neck edges as shown; pin along roll, just above neck seam. Baste neck edges together as they fall along seamline of undercollar.

ROLLED: What sets the rolled collar apart is a carefully shaped stand. Use this construction for light to medium weight fabrics. (For heavy or bulky fabric, use the Notched Collar method, page 197, disregarding reference to lapels, or the method used for Tailoring.) Prepare collar same as a Flat Collar, pages 195 and 196, using interfaced side for undercollar.

Establish the roll by shaping the collar like your pattern illustration; favor upper collar edge over the seam. Use a tailor's ham for easier shaping. Pin along the roll line. Steam.

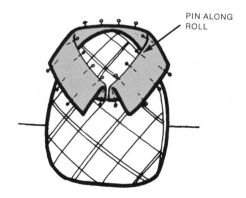

Baste the two halves of a two-piece collar together where they meet at the neck seamline; this will prevent leaving a gap between them after they are stitched to the garment. Pin the collar to the garment neck edge with the undercollar down. The upper collar will bubble slightly because of the roll you have built into it.

Baste neck edges together as they fall, following seamline of undercollar. Attach to garment same as the Flat Collar, page 196; finish neck edges with a facing.

COLLAR AND LAPELS

When the garment has lapels, the collar is finished with a facing, but the seams at the neck edge are pressed open, not enclosed, to avoid bulk.

NOTCHED: This collar resembles the rolled type, but always has a front opening with lapels. The following method is recommended for medium weight, heavy, or bulky fabrics. For lightweight fabrics, use the Sew and Go Notched Collar construction, page 198.

Stitch undercollar sections together and interface. Pin undercollar to garment neck edge, matching markings; clip garment neck edge where necessary. Stitch between markings. Trim seam to ¼"; press open.

If fabric mars easily, underline upper collar and facings before joining to prevent seam imprints from showing. Pin upper collar to neck edge of facing, matching markings, and clip facing neck edge as needed; stitch. Do not trim seam; press it open, clipping where necessary.

Finish unnotched edges.

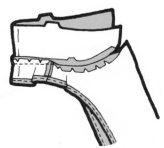

With right sides together, pin upper collar and facing to undercollar and garment at neck seams only; leave outer edges unpinned. Match centers and seams carefully. Baste neck seams together. Try on garment *wrong side out,* with upper collar and facing on top, to check roll of collar. Shape collar like the pattern illustration.

When collar is rolled correctly, undercollar and garment seam allowances extend beyond those of upper collar and facing. Pin outer edges of collar in place as they fall.

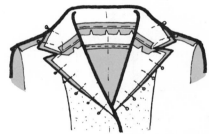

Stitch collar sections together along undercollar seamline at outer edge between markings, easing or stretching to fit. Stitch facing to garment from markings to lower edge; follow garment seamlines, pivoting at corners. Trim and grade seams, clipping and notching as necessary.

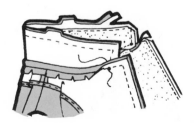

Press all seams open, then in direction they will be turned. Favor garment edge below where lapel begins. Turn collar right side out. Press finished edges, favoring upper collar and facing above point where lapel begins. Lift facing and sew neck seams together with loose blind-stitches. Turn the facing down and anchor the free edge at the garment seams. **OR . . .**

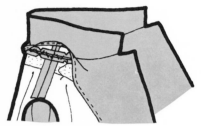

SEW AND GO . . . extra easy: For lightweight fabrics, use this extra-quick way to attach a collar with lapels.

Prepare and shape collar unit same as the Rolled Collar, page 196. After shaping, baste neck edges of collar as they fall.

Pin or baste collar to neck edge of garment with interfaced side down. Match markings and clip garment as needed.

Assemble facing unit. Pin facing to garment over collar; match markings and clip facing where necessary. Stitch, pivoting at corners. Trim and grade seams, clipping and notching as needed; press open.

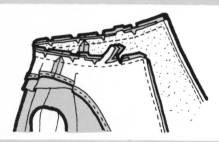

Turn the facing to the inside of the garment. Press, being sure to favor the garment edge below the point where the lapel begins. Anchor the free edge of the facing at garment seams.

SELF-FINISHED COLLARS

Not all collars are finished with neck facings. Standing collars are often applied so the collar itself finishes the garment neck edges.

SHAPED BAND: Interface one collar section. Stitch sections together, to ⅝″ from neck edge. Trim and grade seam and corners; clip curve.

Turn and press collar, favoring interfaced side. Pin or baste interfaced side to garment neck edge; match markings and clip garment as needed. Stitch, trim, grade, and notch seam.

Press seam open, then toward collar.

To finish neck edge, turn in remaining collar edge where it falls over seam; baste or pin. Slipstitch.

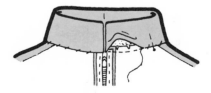

Fasten ends of collar with hooks and eyes. **OR . . .**

SEW AND GO . . . extra easy: Finish neck edges by machine; zigzag or overcast remaining collar edge, then lap and pin over neck seam. From the outside, pin or baste alongside seam and machine stitch in neck seam through all thicknesses.

Fasten with hooks and eyes.

BIAS TURNOVER: Better known as a turtleneck, this collar is a bias variation of the standing collar, rolled down to cover the neck seam.

Attach lightweight interfacing cut on the bias to one half of collar; extend interfacing 5⁄8″ beyond foldline. Fold collar lengthwise, right sides together. Stitch ends to 5⁄8″ from neck edge; trim seams.

Turn and press ends only; avoid creasing foldline. Stitch collar to garment as for Shaped Band Collar.

Shape collar and establish roll by turning and gently stretching folded edge of collar to cover neck seam. Pin along roll and again above neck seam.

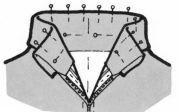

Finish neck seam with remaining collar edge as in the Shaped Band Collar, page 198 or 199. Secure ends of collar with hooks and eyes.

SHIRT COLLAR: See section on **Sewing for Men.**
DETACHABLE COLLAR: Listed under **Trims.**

SLEEVES

From classic to costumey, sleeve styles seem to be the key to the grooviest fashions. Most sleeves are very simply made from one or two pattern pieces; others are cut in one with the bodice. The up-to-the-minute look comes from variations in fullness, length, and finish.

Three sleeves are the foundations of all sleeve styles. The *set-in sleeve* is joined to the garment in a seam that encircles the arm over the shoulder. The *raglan sleeve* joins the garment in a diagonal seam from underarm to neckline. A shaped dart or seam provides shoulder contour. Cut in one with the garment, the *kimono sleeve* has an underarm seam and a long shaped shoulder seam.

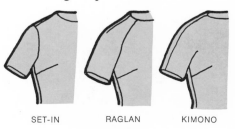

SET-IN   RAGLAN   KIMONO

Accuracy in transferring pattern markings is important since sleeve and armhole symbols and notches are guides for easing the sleeve into a comfortable position on the arm.

Bodice and shoulder fit should be well-established before you work with the sleeve. For a long sleeve, pay special attention to the elbow area. Use the fitting section to evaluate sleeve appearance. If you've had trouble with sleeve fit, see about pattern adjustments before cutting the garment.

A sleeve board allows the sleeve seam to be pressed open without putting creases in the sleeve.

It is easiest to complete the sleeve finish or hem before permanently inserting the sleeve in the garment; make certain the sleeve is the desired length.

SET-IN SLEEVE

The most common, and traditionally the most fearsome, of the group, the set-in sleeve's bark is lots worse than its non-existent bite.

From the right side of the sleeve, easestitch between the markings on the sleeve cap; place your stitching in a line next to the seamline in the seam allowance; then make a second row of easestitching in the seam allowance, ¼″ from the first

row. Stitch the sleeve seam and press the seam allowances open.

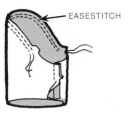

EASESTITCH

Working with the garment wrong side out and the sleeve right side out, pin the sleeve into the armhole; match underarm seams, notches, and markings. Also pin the sleeve shoulder marking to the garment shoulder seam. With sleeve facing you, pull ease threads until sleeve fits armhole; wind threads around pin in a figure eight to hold them in place. Distribute fullness evenly, pinning every ½″. Leave about 1″ of sleeve cap over the shoulder seam flat; Butterick patterns are already marked this way.

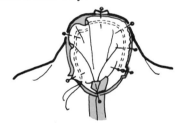

Baste along seamline. For preshaping the sleeve, see Tailoring.

Try on garment; check sleeve length and fit. Cap ease should be where *you* need it—remember that everyone's upper arm and shoulder are different in shape and curve. When your arm is down, the sleeve should hang evenly, in a smooth, relaxed curve which corresponds to that of your arm. Make any necessary changes in fit. Complete sleeve finish.

Re-pin sleeve in armhole and stitch around armhole from sleeve side, beginning at underarm; control fullness as you work.

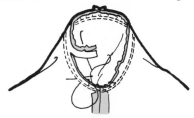

Finish seam by making a second row of stitching ¼" from first in seam allowance. Trim close to second row and overcast or zigzag.

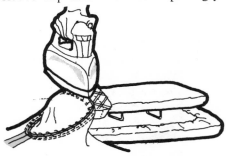

Press along seam over curved surface. Avoid extending iron into sleeve cap and use steam sparingly.

Turn seam allowances toward sleeve along cap. The underarm seam area will stand up. **OR . . .**

SEW & GO . . . extra easy: This set-in sleeve uses extra-quick flat construction techniques.

Stitch shoulder seam of garment, but leave garment side seam and sleeve underarm seam open. Easestitch sleeve cap as on opposite page. Finish lower raw edge for a hem when used. Pin sleeve to armhole; match notches and markings, placing shoulder marking at shoulder seam. Adjust ease and secure threads; distribute evenly and pin every ½". Stitch.

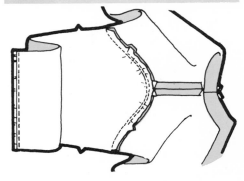

Press sleeve seam allowances; do not extend iron into sleeve cap. Turn seam toward sleeve. If desired, add stitching ¼" away from first in seam allowance. Trim close to stitching and zigzag or overcast edges.

Pin garment side seams and sleeve seams together, matching intersecting armhole seam. Stitch sleeve and side seams; backstitch and break stitching on either side of armhole seam. Press seam open.

Complete hem.

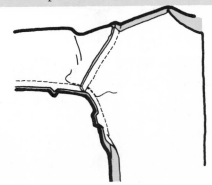

RAGLAN SLEEVE

Stitch shoulder dart or seam and underarm seam; press open (1).

Pin sleeve into armhole, matching seams, markings, and notches. Baste, easing sleeve to fit (2).

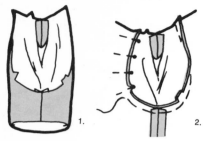

1.   2.

Try on garment. Dart or seam should conform to your shape, with sharpest curve covering end of shoulder. Move arms to be sure there is enough ease. Make any fitting adjustments. Complete sleeve hem.

Stitch sleeve to garment; make second row of stitches ¼″ away from first in seam allowance between notches. Clip at ends of notches. Trim close to stitching and overcast or zigzag. Press seam open above clips; underarm area stands up. **OR . .**

SEW AND GO . . . extra easy: Leave garment side seam and sleeve underarm seam open. Stitch sleeve dart or seam. Pin sleeve to garment front and back, matching markings and notches; stitch. Press seams open, clipping so seams will lie flat. Finish lower raw edge.

If desired, reinforce underarm curves to notches with a second row of stitches and overcasting.

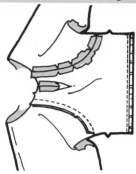

Pin and stitch underarm and side seams, matching armhole seams. Clip curve and press seam open.

Complete sleeve hem.

KIMONO SLEEVE

Pin back to front. Reinforce by centering a piece of stretched bias tape over seamline at underarm curve; pin. Baste shoulder and side seams. Make short clips into underarm curve without cutting tape. Try on garment to be sure there is enough room for movement. Stitch seams, reinforcing curves. Press seams open, clipping underarm curve without cutting tape.

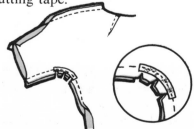

Complete sleeve finish.

Closures That Make It

Recognizing the right closure for the job is usually quite simple.

Learning to make the unseen closure truly invisible and the visible fastening really smashing takes a little more effort. We aim to show you that it's not so hard, even for the most timid seamstress.

ZIPPERS

Super-fast and practical, the zipper is easy to apply. All zippers are made up of the parts shown in the diagram.

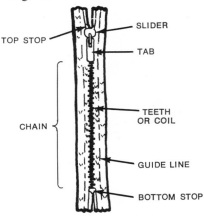

In addition to regular zippers, you can get *invisible zippers* which look like a seam from the outside, or *separating zippers* which come apart at the bottom. You will find zippers made of all kinds of materials—metal with light and heavyweight teeth, nylon and polyester with coils instead of teeth.

PRELIMINARIES

Zippers can be inserted by machine or hand. Machine application is quicker and requires a zipper foot attachment, while hand application allows for greater control.

SHORTENING ZIPPERS: Recommended zipper length is given on the pattern envelope. Some styles require a length that is not available and zipper may need to be shortened.

From bottom, choose application and baste zipper to garment. Take several whipstitches over teeth ¼″ below end of opening.

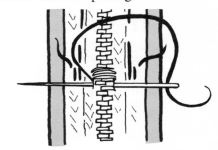

Sew a large straight metal eye above whipstitches to form new bottom stop. Cut off excess ½″ below eye; complete application.

From top (as for a separating zipper), baste zipper to within 1″ of where teeth should end. Open, and remove extra teeth. Make new stops by bending two straight metal eyes in half and slipping one over each zipper tape above teeth; sew securely. Close zipper, turn tape ends down, trim away excess, and anchor ends; complete application (see next page).

APPLICATIONS

Inserting a zipper is easy if you follow these suggestions:

- Press zipper to remove folds. Never rest iron on coil or teeth.
- Pre-shrink it for washable garments.
- Placket opening should be length of coil or teeth plus ¼" from upper seamline to marking; allow additional ⅜" for hook and eye.
- Staystitch opening ¼" from edges.
- Stay bias or stretchy fabric with seam binding cut the opening length.
- Extend seam allowances by lapping and stitching edge of ribbon seam binding over seam allowance.
- Match fabric design at opening —for regular zipper, slip-baste seam allowances together; for invisible zipper, draw lines corresponding to fabric design on zipper tape and match as you insert zipper.
- To stitch past slider, lower needle in fabric, raise zipper foot, and move slider to stitched area; lower foot and continue.
- Close before washing or cleaning.

SLOT OR CENTERED: Zipper is centered under opening edges with a line of stitching on either side.

Attach facing before inserting zipper (see Shaped Facings); waistbands are attached after zipper is applied. Open facings out and machine baste opening edges together along seamlines; press open. Center closed zipper face down over seam allowances with pull tab ⅜" below neckline seam; turn tape ends down to clear upper seamline. Pin or baste.

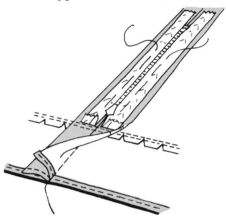

Stitch across lower end and along one side, ¼" from basted seam; repeat for remaining side.

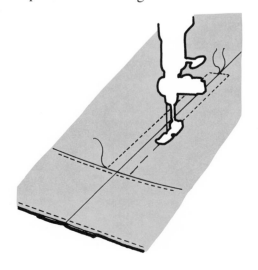

204

Remove basting. Complete facing by turning it inside and folding ends in to clear teeth. Sew ends to zipper tape; fasten with hook and eye. **OR . . .**

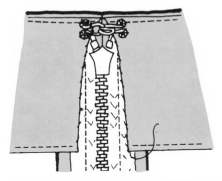

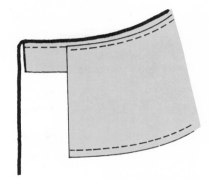

Open facing. Turn in underlap edge ½″; pin, forming tiny fold at lower end. Turn in ⅝″ on overlap edge; pin. Baste and press edges.

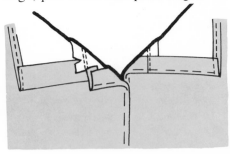

SEW AND GO . . . extra easy: Insert zipper in opening section *before* seaming it to another. Follow slot application, disregarding facing. Remove basting; complete neck edge and apply facing. Then finish ends.

LAPPED: Zipper is concealed in a lapped seam with only one line of stitching visible; the lap usually opens to the right.

Apply facing *before* inserting zipper, turning back 1″ on end of overlap side; trim this end to ⅝″. Stitch, trim, and grade seam.

With zipper face up, pin baste underlap edge over zipper tape so bottom stop is at end of opening and top stop is ⅜″ below neckline seam. Making sure you can move slider, stitch close to folded edge.

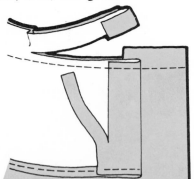

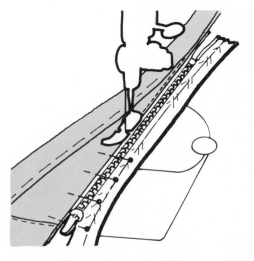

Press and understitch as for a shaped facing. Waistbands are applied after zipper.

Pin or baste overlap edge to zipper tape, covering stitching on underlap. Stitch across lower end and up overlap a scant ½″ from edge.

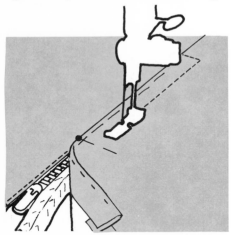

Turn in zipper tape ends. Turn facing to inside, folding in raw end to clear teeth; sew to zipper tape. Sew a hook on inside of overlap, a straight eye on outside of underlap.

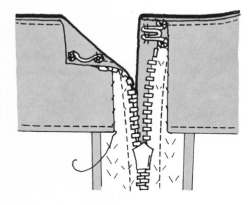

INVISIBLE: Fast, neat, and seamlike from the outside, invisible zippers are good for most designs and fabrics, especially when you can't match colors. They require a special zipper foot; buy it when you buy the zipper if you don't have one.

Apply invisible zipper to opening edges before stitching seam and attaching facing. If you prefer to stitch seam first, end seam 2″ below marking. Insert as follows.

Reinforce neck seamline for 2″ on both sides of opening; 1″ from opening edge, clip seam allowances to stitching. Turn down clipped edge and press.

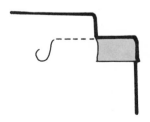

Pin baste opened zipper face down on right side of fabric. Teeth should be on seamline, tape in seam allowance parallel to fabric edge, and top stop ⅛″ below upper seamline.

Line up notch at center of hole on zipper foot with needle. Lower foot over teeth, and stitch close to teeth from upper edge to pull tab; for polyester zipper, open out fold in zipper as you stitch.

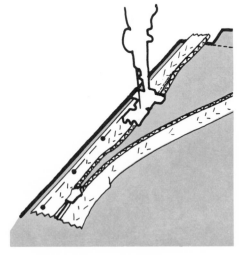

Close zipper to position it on remaining opening edge; pin baste. Open zipper and stitch as before.

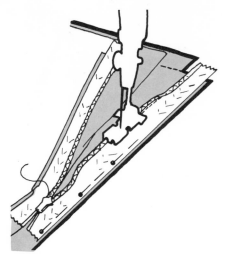

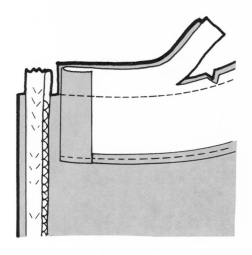

To finish seam below closed zipper, slide zipper foot to left and align its edge with needle or use a regular zipper foot. Keep tape ends free and lower needle, then presser foot, on seamline. Stitch from opening to bottom of garment.

Press and understitch as for a shaped facing. Fold in zipper tape ends; sew facing ends to zipper tape.

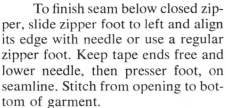

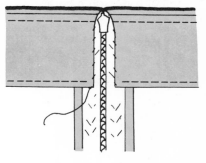

Application shown courtesy of Unique Zippers

Stitch lower tape ends to seam allowances, keeping garment free.

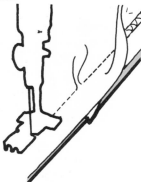

SEPARATING: Separating zippers can be used anywhere—on jackets, coats, skirts, or dresses.

Apply facing. Turn in opening edges of facing 1″; trim to ⅝″. Pin baste, stitch, trim, and grade seam. Press and understitch same as a shaped facing. Complete garment hem.

Machine baste opening edges together along seamline, keeping facing free. Press seam open.

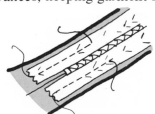

Apply facings, turning ends back 1″ from opening edges; trim to ⅝″. Stitch, trim, and grade seam.

Center closed zipper face down on seam allowances; place bottom stop at hemline or marking and top

stop ⅛″ from top seamline. Turn
tape ends in, tack securely, then baste
zipper in place.

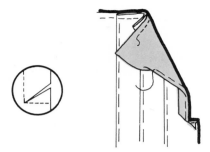

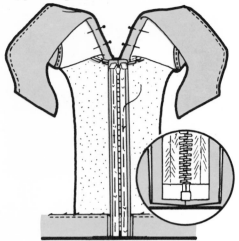

On outside, stitch both sides ¼″
from basted seam; backstitch at ends.

On inside, turn in facing at
lower edge and sew to tape and hem.

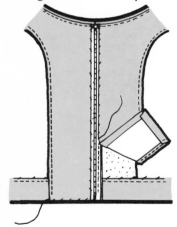

KNIFE PLEATS: Use a regular zipper. Be sure overlapping pleat is deep
enough to cover zipper. *Do not stitch
closure seam.*

Mark a ⅞″ seam allowance on
underlap the desired placket length.
Reinforce seamline at bottom of
opening as shown. Clip diagonally to
point; fold in long edge ⅞″ and the
corner along stitching. Baste.

On outside, lap underlap over
zipper (face up) with reinforced corner below bottom stop; pin baste.
Using a zipper foot, edgestitch fold
to zipper tape, pivoting at corner.
Place overlapping pleat section over
zipper so pleat progression will be
undisturbed; pin.

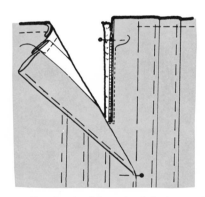

On the inside, pin fabric to zipper tape and seam below zipper together. Stitch seam, beginning at hem
and continuing up through zipper
tape to top of skirt.

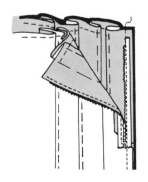

Attach waistband, making sure pleat lies smoothly over zipper.

DRESS PLACKET OR SIDE SEAM: Zipper is in a seam which is closed above and below zipper. Use a regulation dress zipper with top stop, or make one as previously directed.

Insert zipper by slot, lapped, or invisible application. For slot or lapped method, stitch across both ends on outside. For invisible zipper, secure tape ends to seam allowance at top and bottom.

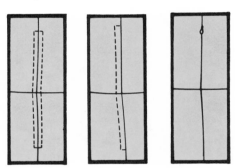

BY HAND: This custom technique is used by couturiers for a fine finish, especially on pile, delicate, or stretchy fabrics.

Position zipper. Secure with prickstitch, using a fine needle and double strand of regular or silk thread or single strand of buttonhole twist.

To hand sew invisible zipper, follow placement instructions, inserting with backstitches close to teeth.

UNDERLAY: To protect your skin or undergarments from rough zipper edges, cut a piece of 1″ wide ribbon at least 1″ longer than zipper. Hem upper edge of ribbon and pin even with top of slider, centering it over zipper chain. Backstitch long edge to facing and seam allowance on one side of opening. Sew lower end to seam allowances only. Fasten top of underlap with small snap.

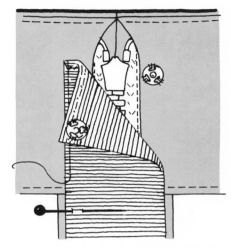

PRESSING: After inserting zipper, press placket area from inside, using a press cloth. On outside, use press cloth and place brown paper between placket lap and garment.

SNAPS

One of the easiest closures to apply and use is the snap, once you know the right way to sew it to the garment. Attach the ball section, which has a small protruding knob, to the overlapping garment section; the socket section, which has a corresponding indentation, is applied to the underlapping section.

Snaps are used to fasten edges subjected to little strain, because they will open under stress.

ATTACHING: Mark overlap for snap placement; anchor thread and position ball section over marking. Sew snap to garment with small close overhand stitches through one hole, picking up a garment thread with each stitch; then carry the thread under the snap to the next hole and repeat. Secure thread alongside snap. To position socket section, rub some tailor's chalk on the ball of attached snap section. Lap the edges, transferring the chalk to underlap. Then sew the socket section at marking in the same manner.

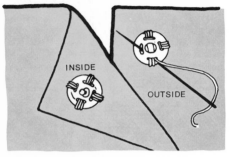

EXTENDED SNAPS: Collars or stand-up necklines can be fastened with extended snaps. Sew the ball section to the inside of one edge as directed above. Then sew the socket section to the opposite edge through one hole.

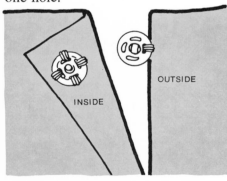

COVERED SNAPS: Do as the couturiers do, and cover your snaps to match your fabric, using lining or underlining fabric.

Cut two circles, each twice the diameter of the snap. Make a small running stitch around the edge, leaving the thread ends free. Place both sections face down on the wrong side of the circles. Draw up the thread, but do not fasten it.

Snap the sections together a few times to spread fabric apart and work ball of snap through fabric.

Draw up thread and fasten securely.

Attach to garment as you would regular snaps.

HOOKS

A quick closure is the hook and eye combination. It will withstand the strain of body movement and give you a smooth finish.

ON LAPPED EDGES: On waistbands and other edges that lap, sew hook slightly inside the overlap edge; this conceals hook. Fasten a straight eye in a corresponding position on underlap.

To attach, anchor thread and sew hook on with overhand stitches worked around the circular holes; pick up a garment thread with each stitch. Slip needle under fabric to bill end of hook and fasten bill to garment with stitches to hold it flat; secure thread.

Straight eyes are positioned as shown below and are fastened with overhand stitches around the circular holes. Nearly invisible thread eyes or loops may be used instead of metal ones; they are described in Loops.

Heavy-duty fasteners are also used on waistbands; position and sew the same as standard hooks and eyes.

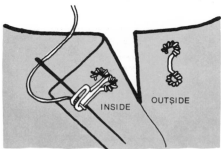

ON MEETING EDGES: Sew hook to garment as explained for Lapped Edges previously, positioning it $\frac{1}{16}''$ inside one garment edge. Use a curved eye for other section, and extend it slightly beyond edge; fasten with overhand stitches around the circular holes, and small stitches holding sides of eye flat to garment.

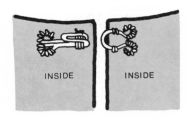

COVERED: For a super-fine finish, cover hooks and eyes with thread color-matched to garment. Use a double strand of thread coated with beeswax or a single strand of button-hole twist for uniform coverage. First sew hook and eye in place as instructed above, then cover them completely with close blanket stitches.

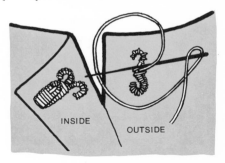

TAPE FASTENER

Pull it open, press it shut. What is it? The nylon tape fastener, that's what! This is a handy device that's solved the problem of making collars and trims removable and closures adjustable and easy to sew. However, avoid using nylon tape fasteners on tight-fitting clothes and lightweight fabrics, or as a zipper substitute.

One strip is covered with tiny nylon hooks, and the other with soft fluffy loops. For flexibility, the pile strip is applied to the overlap and the hook tape to the underlap. Machine stitch strip to the garment underlap. Hand sew top layer, or machine stitch to facing only before anchoring it.

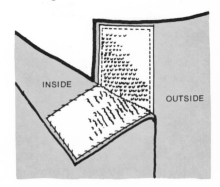

LOOPS

Finish that newest wardrobe addition by lassoing your buttons with loops! Fabric or thread, loops are great fun on any garment.

FABRIC LOOPS

First make tubing for loops, then place them on your garment.

TUBING: Self-fabric loops blend into garment. Fill tubing with its own seam allowances or cording.

Self-filled: Cut bias the desired length and four times the finished width. Lighter weight fabrics require wider seam allowances, heavier weights, narrower ones; experiment to find the best width.

Fold bias in half lengthwise. Stretching bias slightly, stitch halfway between fold and edges; leave both ends open, but slant stitching at one end for turning. To turn, attach needle and heavy thread or bodkin securely to slanted end and pass through bias, eye first, to work raw edges to inside.

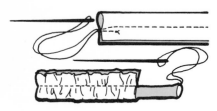

Corded: Cut bias desired length and wide enough to encircle cord plus 1". Cut cord twice finished length. Fold bias around cord with edges even and one end ½" beyond center of cord. With zipper foot, stitch across end and next to cording without catching it, stretching bias slightly. Trim seam, then turn by drawing out enclosed cord.

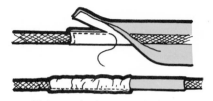

Trim stitched end and excess cording. **OR . . .**

SEW AND GO . . . extra easy: Cut bias desired length and four times finished width. Fold edges to center of strip, then together; edgestitch.

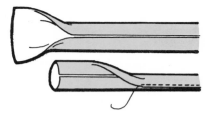

PLACEMENT: Loops are sewn to center line of closure. When adding loops to patterns with centered overlapping closings, change *right* front so center line becomes seamline and cutting line is ⅝" from it. Left front needs no adjustment.

Loop Length: Pin cording to an edge, forming a loop just large enough for button to pass through.

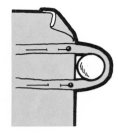

Make a guide by marking a line the length of closure seamline on a strip of lightweight paper. Then draw lines for spread and depth of finished loops, spacing them as needed (see next page). Flat buttons require more spread, less depth than ball buttons.

Single Loops: Cut each loop the correct length plus two seam allowances.

Form loops on paper guide markings, keeping their seams on top and to inside of curve; hold with masking tape. Machine baste loops to paper alongside seamline in seam allowance.

Pin guide to right half of garment, matching seamlines; remove masking tape and baste next to previous basting.

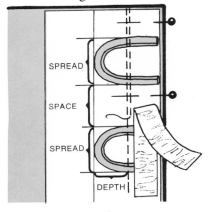

Tear paper away. Attach facing, stitching from garment side.

Continuous Loops: Make small, close loops on paper guide like Single Loops above, but with continuous tubing, extending small curved ends into seam allowance. Trim ends.

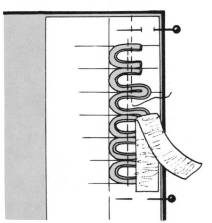

THREAD LOOPS

For thread loops, use a double strand of thread or a single strand of buttonhole twist color-matched to garment. Secure thread on inside, bring to outside; take several stitches the desired length to form core and enclose it with tight blanket stitches. Secure end.

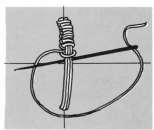

THREAD CHAIN: Substitute a thread chain for any thread loops, using same thread suggestions.

Secure thread on inside; bring to outside. Take a small stitch, drawing thread up to form a loop. With needle thread in right hand, place forefinger and thumb of left hand through the loop.

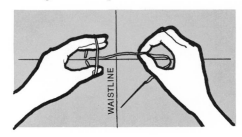

Use the second finger of left hand to grasp needle thread and draw another loop through the first.

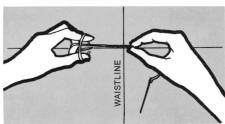

Repeat, tightening each loop, until chain is desired length.

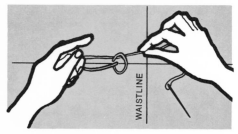

Draw needle through last loop. Tighten loop to form knot and secure chain end to garment.

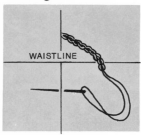

THREAD EYE: Inconspicuous thread eyes are used with metal hooks. Straight thread eyes are taut. Curved thread eyes extend slightly beyond garment edge.

OUTSIDE   INSIDE

THREAD LOOP: Use these to fasten tiny buttons. Make loop long enough for button to pass through.

BELT CARRIER: To prevent a belt from wandering, make thread loops as long as belt is wide, plus ¼".

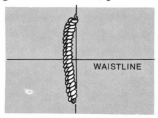

BAR TACK: Reinforce buttonhole ends or slits with a taut ⅛"-¼" long thread loop.

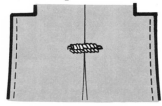

FRENCH TACK: Use a 1" thread loop to hold linings to garment; vary length to form link buttons, or to fasten flaps or tabs in place.

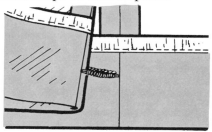

LINGERIE STRAP GUARDS: Sew snap socket to shoulder seam or facing near neck edge. Begin thread loop near armhole edge, and attach end to one hole of ball section of snap.

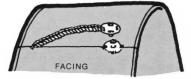

Fasten guard around straps when wearing garment.

BUTTONS

Button, button—be sure you've got it before you make the buttonhole. It's wise to buy the size and number of buttons the pattern recommends. Instructions for measuring buttons are in Buttonholes. Refer to the button chart in Notions for an explanation of available sizes. Buying buttons to fit finished buttonholes is a hazardous procedure, but if you must, measure carefully.

Buttons and buttonholes should be located at points of stress—over fullest part of bust and at a fitted waistline. Secure large gaps between buttons with covered snaps in a matching color.

If garment length was adjusted, re-space buttonholes and buttons evenly between top and bottom buttons. If a belt will be worn, position buttons far enough above and below so they won't interfere. Mark new buttonhole markings on pattern before transferring to fabric.

Since thread for sewing buttons has to withstand wear, use buttonhole twist, button and carpet thread, heavy-duty thread, or a double strand of cotton thread coated with beeswax. Use an 18″ length to avoid tangles. Securely fasten thread on outside of garment at marking.

The names of buttons correspond to the way they are attached to garment—sew-through and shank.

SEW-THROUGH BUTTONS, unless used for trims, should have a thread *shank* to prevent the fabric around closure from being distorted. It should be as long as garment is thick at buttonhole, plus a scant ⅛″ for movement. Form shank by putting a toothpick or bobby pin over button between holes; sew over object when attaching button.

When button is secure, remove object, and wind thread tightly under button to form shank; securely fasten thread to shank.

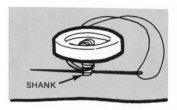

SHANK

SHANK BUTTONS are attached with small stitches sewn through the built-in shank.

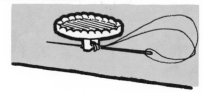

Align shank with buttonhole so threads will be parallel to opening edge.

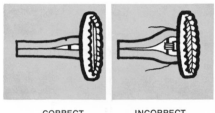

CORRECT   INCORRECT

An additional thread shank may be needed for very thick fabric. For detachable shank buttons, insert metal shanks through eyelets made at button position in garment; fasten on inside with toggles.

REINFORCED BUTTONS are used for coats, suits, or delicate fabrics. For coats, place a small flat button on inside of garment directly under outer button and sew from one to the other, making thread shanks as needed.

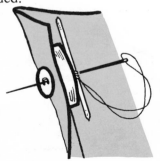

On delicate fabrics, substitute a small folded square of ribbon seam binding; at openings, place it between garment and facing.

LINK BUTTONS are used like cuff links. Make a French tack between two buttons; it should be long enough to pass through two garment edges.

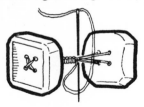

JEWELED BUTTONS often have prongs or rough edges that snag fabric and wear buttonholes. Sew these buttons directly to buttonhole. Use covered snaps underneath on unfinished buttonhole back to secure opening.

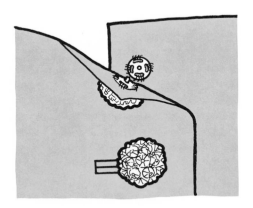

Commercially prepared kits for covering buttons are easy to use and available in many shapes and sizes.

Chinese ball buttons and frog closings are explained in **Trims.**

BUTTONHOLES
Beautiful buttonholes aren't computer-made. Careful planning and testing guarantee success.

BUTTONHOLE SIZE: For flat buttons, buttonhole length equals button diameter plus thickness plus ⅛".

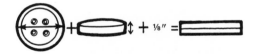

For dome or ball buttons, pin a paper strip around biggest part of button. Remove button and fold paper; distance from pin to fold plus ⅛″ equals buttonhole length.

Usually buttonholes are ¼″ wide—each lip is ⅛″ wide. Make them narrower in lightweight fabrics and wider in heavyweight fabrics.

PLACEMENT: Machine baste or thread trace centers on overlap and underlap sections. Buttonholes are usually no closer than ⅝″ from edge. Mark buttonhole placement on the overlap section only. Never put buttonholes in hem area; on a dress, make bottom buttonhole 4″-5″ from hemline.

Horizontal buttonholes are perpendicular to edge and are marked with placement and length lines. Begin buttonhole ⅛″ beyond center toward edge.

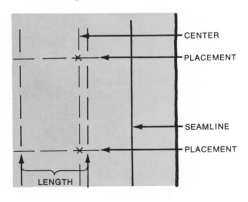

Vertical buttonholes are on center line and parallel to edge; indicate length with short horizontal lines.

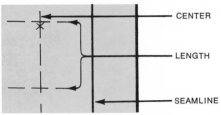

To position and sew buttons on underlap, match center lines of underlap and overlap. For a center closing, sew buttons on center line. For a double-breasted closing, space buttons equally from center line and extend buttonholes in one direction. For an asymmetrical closing, follow pattern carefully.

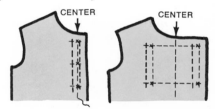

INTERFACING: Reinforce and support buttonholes with interfacing. Make worked buttonholes through interfacing after completing facing. Make bound buttonholes before attaching interfacing unless it is lightweight. Attach interfacing, then cut openings slightly larger than buttonholes. Pull buttonholes through, and sew edges to interfacing.

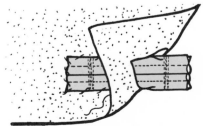

BOUND BUTTONHOLES

Attractive on all garments and common on coats and suits, bound buttonholes are bias strips of self-fabric inserted in a rectangular opening.

TWO-PIECE METHOD: Ideal for firm fabrics, begin with a long, 1″ wide bias strip of self-fabric. Fold strip in half lengthwise; press. Machine baste ⅛″ from fold. Cut strip into sections 1″ longer than buttonhole; trim raw edge to within ⅛″ of stitching. Each buttonhole requires two strips.

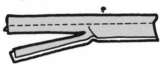

Center one strip over markings, keeping cut edge along position line; pin. Beginning and ending at length markings, stitch directly over stitching on strip. Repeat for other strip. Pull all thread ends to inside and tie.

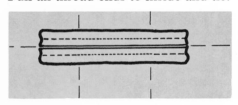

Cut opening from inside with small sharp scissors. Slash through garment only between lines of stitching; use either method shown.

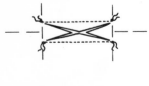

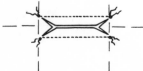

Turn strips to inside and baste edges of lips together.

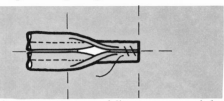

Secure ends by holding garment right side up and folding it back at each end of buttonhole to expose strip ends. Using 20 stitches per inch, stitch across base of each fabric triangle several times.

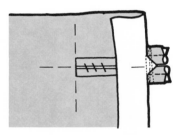

Finish underside after pressing buttonhole. Pin facing to garment through all thicknesses. Push a pin from outside through each end of buttonhole; align pins with facing grain. Slash facing between pins and turn raw edges in. Hem around buttonhole, reinforcing corners.

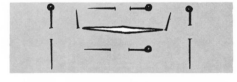

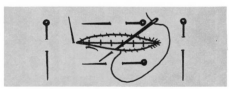

For a neater finish, slash facing to corners, as you did in turning the buttonhole. Turn in raw edges, and hem around buttonhole, again reinforcing corners.

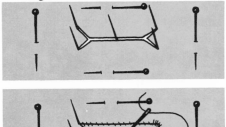

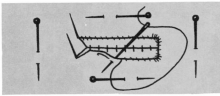

ORGANZA PATCH METHOD:

This is a foolproof buttonhole for loosely woven or bulky fabric. Cut a patch 1″ longer and wider than button from a crisp, sheer fabric like organza. Center patch over buttonhole marking; pin. Using small stitches, stitch ⅛″ from each side of marking; start at the middle and pivot at corners. Count stitches at ends for accuracy.

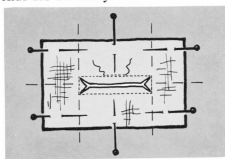

Slash as in Two-Piece Method. Turn patch to wrong side; and press seam allowances away from opening.

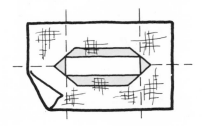

Cut two bias fabric strips 1½″ longer and wider than buttonhole; baste together along lengthwise center. Press basted seam open.

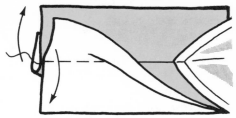

To form buttonhole lips, center strip under opening, keeping basted seam exactly along position line; pin.

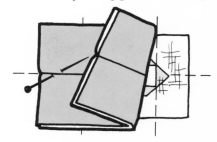

On inside, pin long seam allowances to patch and strips. Starting and ending ½″ from each end, stitch alongside previous stitching so organza does not show on outside.

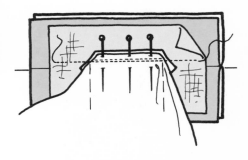

Secure ends, as in Two-Piece Method. Trim excess fabric from patch and strips; press. Finish underside of buttonhole as in Two-Piece Method.

HAND-WORKED BUTTONHOLES

Especially attractive on delicate fabrics or tailored garments, these buttonholes are made after interfacing and facing are applied.

HORIZONTAL BUTTONHOLES: Machine stitch a scant ⅛″ on either side of buttonhole position marking, and across both ends at length markings; slash along position marking.

Use buttonhole twist or matching thread coated with beeswax. Work buttonhole stitch along cut edge, using stitching line as a guide. Bring needle through slash to the outside and insert just beyond stitching line, keeping thread under needle as shown.

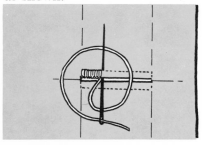

Draw thread up, but not too tightly, to form a purl on slashed edge. Repeat, keeping stitches close and evenly spaced.

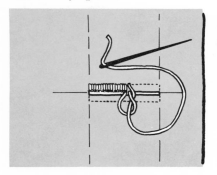

Fan stitches at end closest to garment edge.

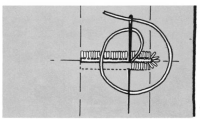

Place a bar tack at remaining end (see Thread Loops).

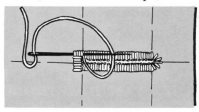

VERTICAL BUTTONHOLES: Make bar tacks at both ends. These are explained in Thread Loops.

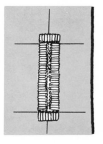

KEYHOLE BUTTONHOLES: To make these favorites on man-tailored clothes, punch a hole at buttonhole end nearest garment edge with an awl. Work buttonhole stitch around hole and slash. Complete like a hand-worked buttonhole.

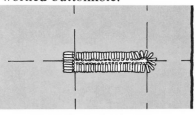

EYELETS: Simply round holes, use these with many fastenings. Sew small running stitches around marking. Make the proper size hole with an awl or small scissors. Work buttonhole stitch around cut edge.

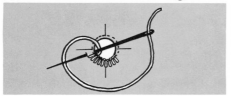

Commercial kits with metal eyelets are explained in Notions. Follow manufacturer's hints carefully.

MACHINE-WORKED BUTTONHOLES

Best suited to casual, washable clothes, machine buttonholes are super-fast. Use buttonhole attachment or zigzag sewing machine. Read your machine manual for instructions, and test before beginning.

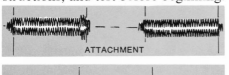

ATTACHMENT

ZIGZAG MACHINE

Make machine buttonholes after garment is interfaced and faced. Check placement carefully, because ripping buttonholes out damages fabric. Slash through center, then trim the cut edges carefully.

CORDED BUTTONHOLES

Prevent stretching and add body and strength by cording buttonholes.

BOUND BUTTONHOLES: Cord Two-Piece Method buttonholes by enclosing cable cord in fold as fabric strips are stitched. Use a regular or invisible zipper foot.

Zipper foot shown courtesy of Unique Zippers

For bound buttonholes made by other methods, draw yarn through lips before securing ends.

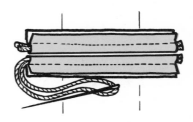

WORKED BUTTONHOLES: For hand-worked buttonholes, work buttonhole stitch over buttonhole twist which has been secured at one end with a pin.

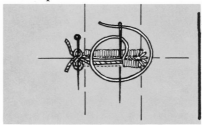

Bar tack the end before clipping the cord.

For machine-worked buttonholes, use a special foot; refer to your machine manual for instruction.

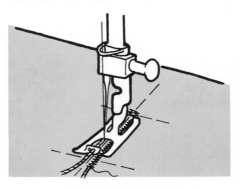

Pulling It All Together

The last-minute details—hems, belts, and pockets—are the ones you're the most likely to skimp on. Don't let yourself be lured by the temptation to get your new outfit done in a hurry. With a little more know-how, you can add the final touches with professional speed and skill.

WAISTLINE FINISHES

From now on your waistlines can fit and be comfortable at the same time! Skirts generally have ½" to 1" ease at waistline because the body curves out directly below.

Overlap waistband ends in the usual female way—right over left on side or front; left over right on back. Underlap extends at least 1¼".

STAY

A waistline stay prevents waistline from stretching as garment is worn; supports stretchy or heavy fabric; and controls a sheath, blouson, or princess style.

Cut a strip of ½"-1" grosgrain ribbon to fit waist, plus 2" for finishing. Turn ends back 1"; hem by machine and secure with hooks and eyes. Sew stay to seams and darts; leave 2" free on each side of zipper.

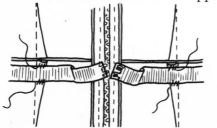

FACING

The smooth, no-waistband way to finish a skirt or pants is with a facing. Although often of self-fabric, a lighter weight fabric, lining, or ribbon can be used to reduce bulk.

FABRIC: Assemble facing unit and stay; lap one edge of ribbon seam binding or twill tape ⅛" over waist seamline. Pin facing to garment, easing garment to fit. Complete same as Shaped Facing, pages 190-191.

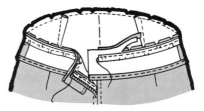

Turn in facing ends to clear zipper teeth; sew to tape. Secure top edges with hook and eye. Tack facing to garment seams and darts.

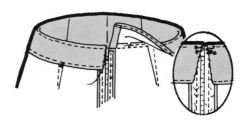

RIBBON: Shape ¾"-1" wide grosgrain ribbon by steaming and stretching the lower edge to correspond to waistline edge. Cut shorter edge of ribbon to waist measurement plus 1½".

Staystitch and trim garment seam allowance to ¼"; clip at even intervals. Lap and pin ribbon over garment so shorter edge is along seamline and each end extends ½"; ease garment to fit. Stitch close to ribbon edge.

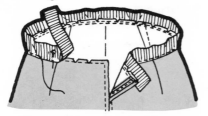

Turn ribbon to inside; press. Complete as for fabric facing.

CUT-IN-ONE: Make darts and seams in garment and facing. Slash darts and press open. Cut ribbon seam binding or twill tape to waist measurement plus 1¾".

Pin stay to waistline, keeping one edge along foldline and ends even with opening edges. Stitch stay to facing ⅛" from foldline.

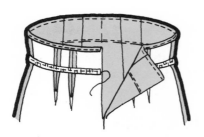

Turn facing to inside along fold-line; press. Complete as for a fabric facing after inserting zipper.

WAISTBAND

The classic waistband can be wide or narrow, straight or contour. Use the Sew and Go method for heavy fabric.

STRAIGHT: Cut on the lengthwise grain, this type is the most common. Interface notched half of waistband. Fold lengthwise, and stitch ends from

fold to within ⅝" of edge; trim and grade ends.

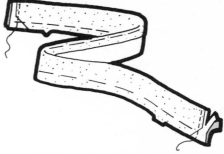

Turn and press waistband. Pin to garment, matching markings and easing skirt to fit; stitch, trim, grade, and clip seam.

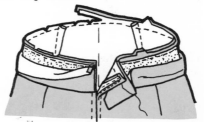

Press seam allowances toward waistband. Turn in remaining raw edge; sew over seam and across underlap. Secure ends with hooks and eyes. **OR . . .**

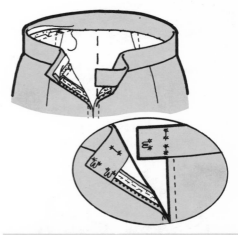

notches and symbols. Fold lengthwise so raw edge extends ⅝″ below selvage; press. Turn in long raw edge a scant ¾″ and end ⅝″; press.

Encase waistline edge of garment with waistband; pin fold over seamline. From the outside, edge-stitch all edges of waistband, catching selvage underneath in stitching; finish ends with hooks and eyes.

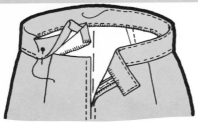

CONTOUR: Interface waistband. Stay both long edges of one interfaced section by lapping one edge of stretched bias tape ⅛″ over seamline (see Pre-shaping in Bindings); baste. Stitch upper edge and ends of waistband sections together, stopping ⅝″ from ends. Trim, grade, and notch seams.

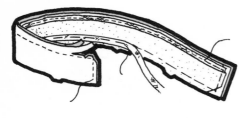

Turn and press band, then stitch to garment, easing garment to fit; trim, grade, and clip seam.

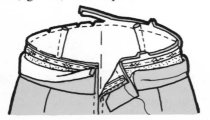

Press seam open, then toward waistband. Turn in remaining edge over seam. Trim edge to ¼″ and sew over garment seam and across underlap. Fasten with hooks and eyes.

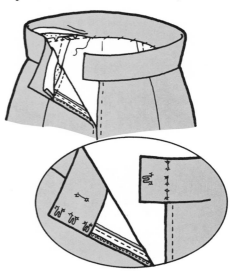

BELTS

Around the waist, down on the hip, in-between—laced, snapped, buckled, or tied, the belt is THE accessory to complete your garment.

PICK A BELT

Self-fabric belts are a luxury within reach—buy a commercial kit or create your own. Find waist measurement with belting or interfacing; wider belts must fit around rib cage. Add 7″ to this length for finishing.

STRAIGHT BELT is hand or machine sewn. Shape one end of belting for slide or prong buckle; leave ends unfinished for clasp buckle.

By Hand: Cut strip of fabric along selvage the length and twice the width of belting; add seam allowance to each long edge.

Fold fabric in half lengthwise. Stitch and trim end (1). Press seam open (2).

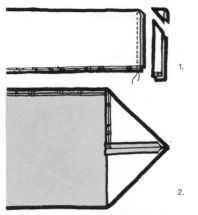

Turn stitched end to inside and fold flat. Insert pointed end of belting into fabric point; press (1). Pin raw edge over belting; press (2).

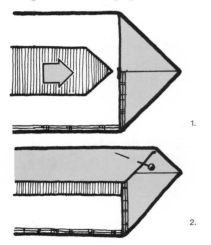

Pin selvage edge over belting; press. Sew edges and selvage in place.

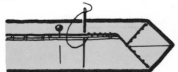

Press. Attach buckle to unfinished end as described on page 227.

By Machine: Cut fabric strip to length and twice width of belting; add seam allowance to each long edge.

Fold fabric over belting. Using a zipper foot, stitch close to, but not through, belting; trim seam to ¼″.

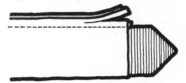

Slide seam to center of belting and press open with tip of iron.

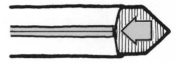

Pull shaped end of belting in position. Stitch close to belting; trim.

Remove belting and turn belt; do not press. Cup belting and slip into belt, shaped end first.

Attach buckle to unfinished end as described on page 227. **OR . . .**

SEW AND GO . . . extra easy: Cut strips—one of commercial belting and two of a fusible adhesive—the length and width of finished belt. Shape one end of each strip. Cut a fabric strip the length and twice the

225

width of belting. Place a strip of fusible adhesive under belting; center both on fabric strip. Follow manufacturer's directions to fuse layers. Cut and place triangular strip of fusible adhesive over belting. Fold fabric to form point; fuse point only.

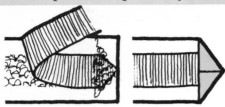

Fold in long edges; press. Open long edges and insert fusible adhesive. Refold long edges in, cutting away fusible adhesive which shows at end; fuse.

Attach buckle to unfinished end (see page 227).

CONTOUR BELT is cut in two pieces on lengthwise grain; all edges have seam allowances.

Pin together two layers of interfacing. Trace belt on one. Within outline, make rows of stitching ¼" apart along lengthwise grain. Cut along outline; stay long edges with stretched bias tape.

Staystitch belt and belt facing. Pin interfacing to wrong side of belt; fold seam allowances in.

Shape end and sew seam allowances to interfacing with long running stitches.

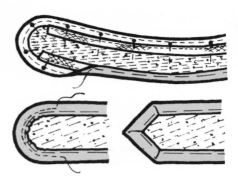

Turn in belt facing edges ¾"; baste and trim to ⅜". Pin facing to belt; slipstitch.

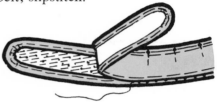

Attach buckle to unfinished end.

CORDED BELT is fabric-covered cord. Follow directions in Loops to make cording. Finish ends with knots, Chinese ball buttons, or other ornaments.

SASH BELT can be bias or straight. Cut fabric twice the finished length and width plus seam allowances; piece if necessary.

Fold sash in half lengthwise. Stitch ends and long edge (stretch bias as you stitch), leaving an opening. Trim and grade seams.

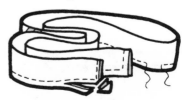

Turn sash through opening. Press, then slipstitch opening edges.

SIDELINE SUPPORT

Belts never look right if they're allowed to wander. Following are suggestions for keeping them put.

BELT LOOPS can be bold ones of fabric or nearly invisible ones of thread. Center them over the waistline at side seams.

Fabric: Cut a fabric strip along selvage long enough for all loops. The length of each loop equals belt width plus 1¼". Make strip ¾"-1" wide, depending on weight of fabric.

Fold long raw edge one-third to inside; press. Fold selvage one-third to inside; press.

Topstitch both edges. Cut strip into single loop lengths. Fold in ends ½" and press; machine or hand sew to garment.

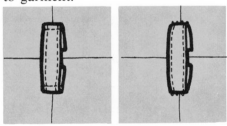

Thread: Use a double strand of buttonhole twist in color of belt. Make a thread loop or chain between markings as in Loops.

BUCKLES are of many materials—wood, plastic, metal, or fabric-covered. Commercial kits with instructions are available for doing the covering yourself. The three types of buckles are attached differently. Try on belt with buckle to find and mark correct buckle position.

Clasp Buckle: Slip unfinished belt ends through buckle. Turn ends to inside over bar at marks; trim to 2". Turn in raw ends and whipstitch to belt.

Slide Buckle: Slip unfinished belt end through buckle. Finish like clasp buckle; secure belt with snaps.

Prong Buckle: Stitch a rectangle through all layers on marking at center of belt. Make a slit between stitches for prong. Insert prong through slit, folding belt to inside over bar. Turn in raw edge, and whipstitch to belt.

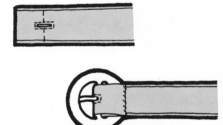

Make eyelets in appropriate positions on shaped end; use a commercial kit or make hand-worked eyelets as in Buttonholes.

Half buckles are similarly attached, but have a fabric loop to hold belt end. Make loop large enough for two thicknesses of belt. Position buckle and sew loop to inside of belt before sewing end to belt.

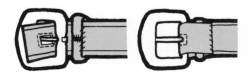

SLEEVE FINISHES

For a photo finish on sleeves, care is the key word. Match the moods of sleeve finish and garment.

Fit sleeves before finishing. Will sleeve plus sleeve finish be the right length? Don't include the turnback part of a cuff in this measurement. Is sleeve opening big enough? Is it in the back, and does it open toward the body? Whenever possible, complete sleeve finish before joining sleeve to garment.

CUFFS

Interfacing makes cuffs a little more rigid than the sleeve. Cut interfacing on the bias so it will curve smoothly around your arm. See Interfacing for quick methods.

BAND: Cuffs without openings must be big enough to slip your hand through.

Extended: Interface cuff; stitch ends together. Trim seam allowances to foldline and press open. Pin cuff to sleeve, matching markings. Adjust gathers, stitch, trim, and grade.

Press seam allowances toward cuff. Turn cuff up along foldline; pin. Turn in remaining edge as it falls over seam; slipstitch.

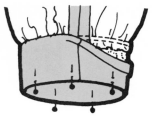

OR . . .

SEW AND GO . . . extra easy: Interface one half of cuff (fusing it is easiest); zigzag unnotched edge. Gather lower edge of sleeve.

Pin cuff to sleeve; adjust gathers. Stitch, trim, and grade seam. Press seam allowances toward cuff.

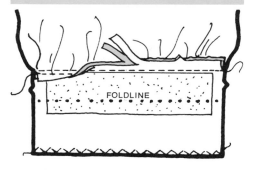

FOLDLINE

Pin baste underarm seam, then stitch sleeve and cuff in a continuous seam. Trim cuff seam allowance as shown. Press seam open.

Turn cuff up along foldline; pin baste remaining edge over seam.

With sleeve inside out, stitch on outside of cuff along seam through all thicknesses.

Turnback: Interface cuff; finish unnotched edge with ribbon seam binding. Join cuff to sleeve like extended band. Trim and press seam open.

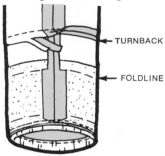

Turn cuff up along foldline; pin.

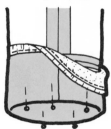

Making a fold below seam allowance, turn cuff back over outside of sleeve. Sew finished edge to sleeve. **OR . . .**

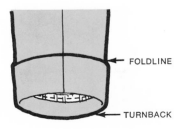

SEW AND GO . . . extra easy: Attach cuff to sleeve, then stitch a continuous underarm seam. This flat construction method is like the Sew and Go extended band cuff.

APPLIED: Interface cuff. Stitch sections together, leaving notched edge open; trim and grade.

Turn and press cuff, then machine baste it to sleeve. Cut single-fold bias tape 1″ longer than lower edge of sleeve. Open one fold of bias, and place crease over seamline on lower edge of basted cuff. Turn in ends ½″ to meet; stitch along seamline. Trim and grade.

Turn bias to inside, favoring cuff; press. Sew bias to sleeve and ends together.

229

WITH OPENING: Tight cuffs must have an opening for the hands. A placket in the sleeve provides extra room when cuff is opened. Caution: be sure that right and left openings are opposites!

Continuous Lap Placket: Reinforce slash area with small stitches along stitching line; take one stitch across point. Slash.

Cut a straight strip of self-fabric on the selvage; make it 1¼″ wide and twice the length of slash. Spread raw edges of slash open and place line of stitching ¼″ from raw edge of strip. Stitch strip to sleeve in a continuous line alongside reinforcement stitches.

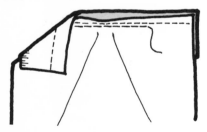

Press strip away from garment. Encase raw edges by turning selvage to inside so it covers stitching. Stitch in place through all layers.

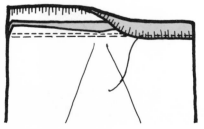

Turn lap to inside and stitch top diagonally.

Faced Opening: Cut self-fabric strip 2½″ wide and the length of opening plus 1″. Finish raw edges of sides and one end (1).

Center facing over slash marking. Stitch along stitching lines with small stitches; take one stitch across the point. Slash (2).

Turn facing to inside; press. Invisibly sew upper edge of facing to sleeve (3).

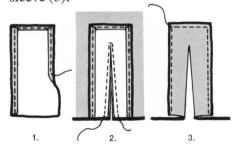

1.   2.   3.

Buttoned Cuff: Prepare opening in sleeve. Interface cuff. Make bound buttonholes now, or worked buttonholes when cuff is completed. Folding cuff lengthwise, stitch ends from fold to within ⅝″ of long edge; trim and grade.

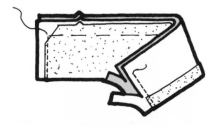

Turn and press cuff. Fold front lap of sleeve placket to inside; pin. For a faced opening, keep facing on the inside.

Pin interfaced half of cuff to sleeve; keep front edge of cuff and folded edge of placket even. Place remaining placket edge at marking on back edge of cuff. For a faced opening, attach cuff so edges meet when cuff is buttoned. Adjust gathers, stitch, trim, and grade.

Press seam allowances toward cuff. Turn in remaining edge and pin as it falls over seam. Slipstitch this edge over seam and edges of extension together. **OR . . .**

SEW AND GO . . . extra easy: No need for a sleeve opening, because this area is hemmed. Center a 3″ line of reinforcement stitches over slash marking on seamline. Clip 1″ from each end of stitching. Trim seam allowance between clips to ⅜″ (1). Narrow hem between clips. Stitch underarm seam and gather lower edge of sleeve (2).

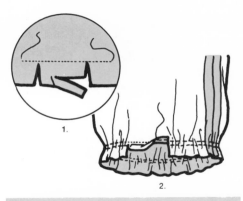

1.

2.

Interface unnotched half of cuff (fusing is fastest). Prepare cuff just as you would the buttoned cuff, then clip seam allowance to marking and finish long unnotched edge.

Turn and press cuff, then pin to sleeve. Match front edge of cuff to one edge of narrow hem and back cuff marking to other edge; adjust gathers. Stitch, trim, grade, and press seam allowances toward cuff.

Turn in and pin together edges of cuff extension. Lap remaining edge over seam and pin. From the outside, stitch in seam through all thicknesses; continue stitching to end of extension.

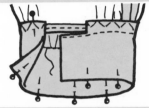

Complete with button and machine buttonhole.

ZIPPERS

Long, wrist-clinging sleeves are easily and neatly finished with a short zipper. Stitch sleeve seam above marking; press open. Mark hemline and finish hem edge with seam binding.

Baste seam below marking; press open. Clip to seam at hemline. Center closed zipper face down over seam, keeping zipper tab above hemline; baste. Trim tape at clips.

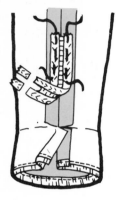

Remove basting from seam. Open zipper and stitch ¼" from each row of teeth and across top. Pin hem up, turning in ends to clear zipper teeth. Invisibly sew hem to sleeve and ends to zipper tape.

Hems, facings, casings, and ruffles are alternative sleeve finishes. For further information, see each of these sections. The shirt sleeve cuff and placket are in the **Men's** section.

CASINGS

Snug in new fashions with elastic or a drawstring in an easy-to-make casing. Some patterns have casings galore; others have only one.

Make drawstring openings before casing; openings for elastic are formed during application. See Tie or Stretch, page 234.

ZIPPER OPENINGS: End casing at seamline for slot zipper; extend casing ¼" beyond seamline for invisible zipper. Sew elastic or drawstring to each end of casing.

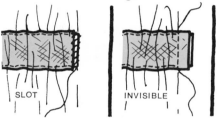

Apply zipper and sew seam allowances securely to casing.

CUTTING: Make casing ⅛"-¼" wider than elastic or drawstring to allow for thickness; add a ¼" seam allowance to each long edge. Cut length of an applied casing equals the area to which it will be stitched, plus ½" for finishing ends. Turn in long edges ¼" and press.

CUT-IN-ONE

This casing is a garment extension folded in like a hem. On a curved edge casing must be narrow; gently stretch or ease it while stitching.

AT EDGE: Allow for desired casing width. Mark and turn in edge along foldline for casing; pin. Turn in raw edge ¼"; press and edgestitch to garment (leave an opening for elastic).

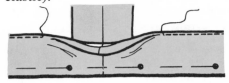

WITH RUFFLE: Allow enough fabric for casing width plus twice the finished ruffle width. Mark ruffle foldline and casing placement lines. Turn in fabric along foldline; pin. Turn in raw edge ¼″ and press; edgestitch to garment (leave an opening for elastic). Stitch along remaining casing line, overlapping ends of stitching where they meet.

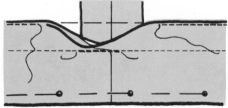

APPLIED

Bias or straight grain, self-fabric, or bias tape, an applied casing is a separate fabric strip stitched to a garment.

AT EDGE: Cut and press casing as explained in introduction. It may be necessary to piece the casing. Trim garment seam allowance to ¼″. Open one folded edge of casing. Pin casing to garment, keeping raw edges even. Where ends of casing meet, turn them in ¼″. Stitch ¼″ from raw edges.

Turn casing to inside favoring garment at edge along seam. Edgestitch remaining fold of casing to garment, overlapping ends of stitching.

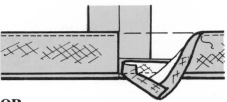

OR . . .

SEW AND GO . . . extra easy: Trim garment seam allowance to ¼″ and turn to inside; press. Pin bias tape to folded edge; turn in ends ¼″ to meet. Edgestitch both casing edges to garment.

WITH RUFFLE: Cut and press casing as in introduction or use bias tape.

For a *single thickness* ruffle, allow fabric for casing plus ruffle width and ⅜″ for a narrow hem. Mark casing placement lines. Finish seams to placement lines and narrow hem lower edge.

Pin casing over placement lines; turn in ends ¼″ to meet. Edgestitch both casing edges to garment.

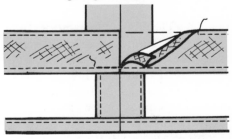

Use a *double thickness* ruffle on lightweight or sheer fabric. Allow fabric for twice the ruffle width plus a ¼″ seam allowance. Mark ruffle foldline and casing placement lines. Turn in fabric along foldline; pin.

Keeping raw edges even, pin casing over placement lines. Complete like the single thickness ruffle.

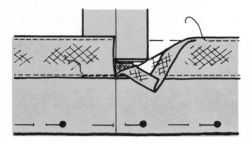

AT WAISTLINE: Cut and press casing as in introduction or use bias tape. Pin casing to garment so bottom edge is on waistline marking; turn in ends ¼" to meet. Edgestitch both casing edges to garment.

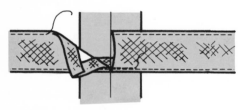

TIE OR STRETCH

The choice is up to you and your casing—drawstrings can be adjusted; elastic, expanded.

DRAWSTRING: Cord, fabric tubing, braid, leather, scarfs, and ribbons are all drawstring material when inserted in a casing.
Openings: Complete buttonhole or in-seam openings in garment *before* applying casing. Make two hand or machine worked buttonholes perpendicular to casing lines.

For in-seam opening, stitch seam, leaving an opening as wide as drawstring. Reinforce opening ends on wrong side by backstitching over small squares of seam binding.

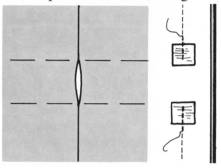

Insertion: After casing is completed, cut a drawstring equal to body measurement at casing position plus enough extra to tie a knot or bow. Use a safety pin to pull drawstring through openings.

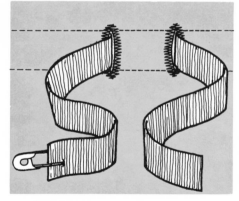

ELASTIC: Sleeve, waistline, neckline, and leg casings are sturdy and cónvenient when pulled in by elastic.
Openings: For a cut-in-one casing, leave 1"-2" of one folded edge open.

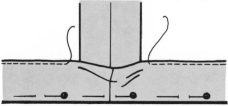

For an applied casing, leave ends open.

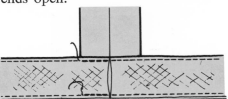

Insertion: Cut elastic ½″ longer than body measurement at casing position. Use a safety pin to pull one end of elastic through finished casing; pin other end of elastic so it won't slip into casing. Take care not to twist elastic. Lap ends of elastic ½″ and stitch securely.

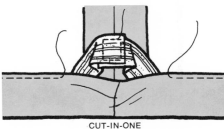

CUT-IN-ONE

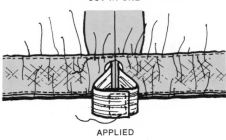

APPLIED

Finishing: Edgestitch opening of cut-in-one casing, stretching elastic as you stitch. Sew open ends of applied casing together.

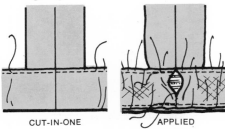

CUT-IN-ONE   APPLIED

POCKETS

Treat yourself to a pocket pick-me-up. Put decorative pockets almost anywhere on a garment; position functional pockets for convenient use. Be accurate: check pocket placement and transfer markings to right side of garment.

PATCH POCKETS

Add the final smash to your fashion with bold patch pockets, whether decorative or functional.

PREPARATION: Shape is the determining factor in making pockets. **Corners:** Miter by turning edges to outside along seamline. Fold excess at corner until seam allowances meet; stitch seam allowances from corner to edge (1). Slash and trim fold (2).

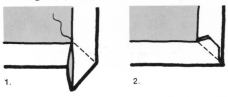

1.   2.

Press seam open (1). Turn corner to inside and press flat (2).

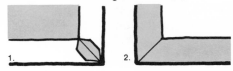

1.   2.

Curved Edges: Easestitch curves ⅜″ from edge (1). Turn in seam allowances and pull up ease threads; notch excess fabric and press flat (2).

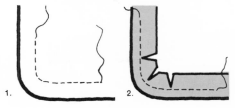

1.   2.

ATTACHMENT: With garment over a tailor's ham to prevent buckling, pin baste completed pocket over markings on garment. Edgestitch, topstitch, or combine the two to attach pocket to garment (1). Or, turn edges back and slipstitch pocket to garment (2). Reinforce opening edges with backstitches.

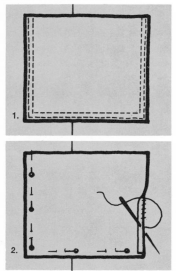

Press pocket from the outside, using a press cloth.

UNLINED: This is ideal on firm fabrics. Finish top edge of pocket. Turn hem allowance to outside along foldline and stitch from finished edge to fold; trim.

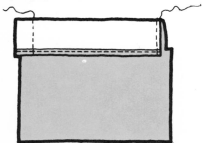

Shape corners or curved edge as previously instructed. Turn in and press hem and seam allowances. Invisibly sew hem to pocket.

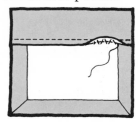

Attach pocket, using either method as explained.

LINED: Cut lining from foldline to bottom of pocket pattern.

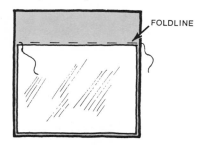

Stitch upper edges of lining and pocket together, leaving an opening.

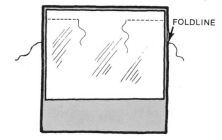

Turn pocket hem allowance down along foldline. Pin lining to pocket, keeping edges even; stitch. Trim.

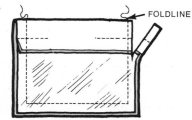

Turn pocket through opening; press. Sew lining to hem at opening.

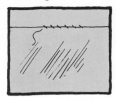

Attach pocket to garment as instructed on page 236. **OR ...**

SEW AND GO . . . extra easy: Cut pocket to width and twice length of finished pocket plus seam allowances. Make a 1½″ machine worked buttonhole or a 1½″ slash near one narrow end. Fold pocket in half. Stitch sides and bottom; trim.

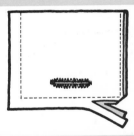

Turn pocket through opening; press. Whipstitch edges of buttonhole or slash together.

Attach pocket to garment by machine method, page 236.

SEAM POCKETS

Hidden in a seam, this pocket of lining fabric is attached to seam extensions. If fabric is stretchy or seam is bias, stay foldline with seam binding; stitches shouldn't show on the outside (1). Pin pocket sections to garment extensions; stitch (2).

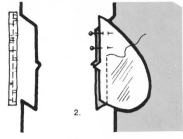

Press seam allowances toward pocket. Pin baste garment sections together along seam and around pocket section; baste along foldline. Stitch (1). Clip back seam allowance at ends of pocket extensions. Press pocket toward front and seam open above and below pocket. Sew clipped edges to front seam allowances (2). **OR . . .**

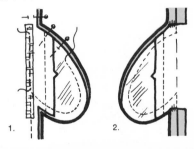

SEW AND GO . . . extra easy: Cut pocket in one with garment by lapping pocket and garment pattern pieces where they correspond (1). Pin garment sections together and around pocket. Complete like the regular Seam Pocket (2).

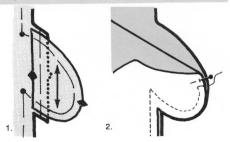

FLAPS AND WELTS

Alone or as decorative additions to a pocket, flaps and welts amount to the same thing used differently—welts are narrow, flat, and open at the top; flaps are wider and hang free at the bottom.

CONSTRUCT: Interface one half, extending interfacing 5⁄8″ past foldline. Fold lengthwise and stitch ends to within 5⁄8″ of long raw edge; trim, clipping or notching if needed.

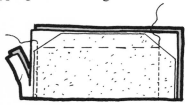

Turn and press. For welt, baste raw edges together along seamline. For flap, establish roll and pin raw edges together as they fall; baste along seamline of under layer.

Topstitch flap or welt before attaching to garment.

ATTACH: With seamline along garment placement line, place welt so raw edges point upward, or flap so raw edges point downward; stitch.

Turn back upper seam allowance and trim lower one close to stitching. To enclose trimmed edge, turn in 1⁄4″ on upper seam allowance

and fold ends in diagonally; edge-stitch.

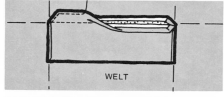

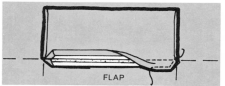

Fold and press welt up, flap down. Invisibly sew sides of welt to garment. Sew 1⁄2″ of upper sides of flap to garment.

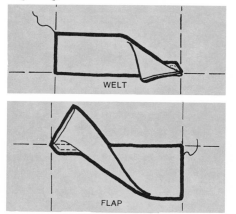

FLAP OR WELT POCKETS

Made of lining fabric, the pocket has a flap or welt covering its opening. Construct welt or flap as previously directed. Trim raw edges to within 1⁄4″ of basting.

PLACEMENT: For welt, place basted seamline over lower stitching line with raw edges up; baste. For flap, place basted seamline over upper stitching line with raw edges down; baste.

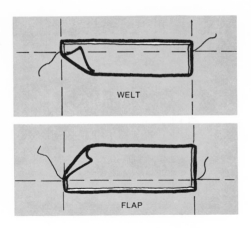

WELT

FLAP

Pin pocket to garment, matching markings. Stitch along stitching lines; backstitch ends. Slash between stitching to within ½″ of ends; clip diagonally to ends. Don't cut welt or flap.

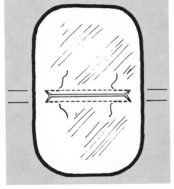

Pull pocket to inside, turning welt up or flap down.

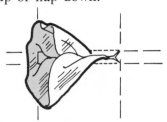

Press sections down so deeper portion is over shorter one; edges may not match. Stitch sections together, catching triangular ends.

Trim seam allowances and overcast edges.

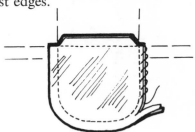

Using a press cloth, press pocket; keep brown paper under welt or flap. Press welt up; invisibly sew ends to garment. Press flap down; tack upper sides for ½″.

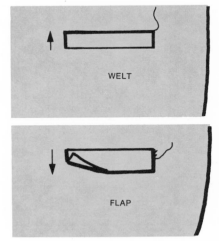

WELT

FLAP

To use a welt and a flap on the same pocket, or to make a buttonhole pocket, see the **Men's** section.

HEMS

Be an individualist—have a wardrobe of fashion hem lengths! The look of today is any length, provided it flatters *you*.

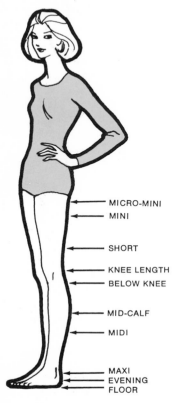

MICRO-MINI
MINI
SHORT
KNEE LENGTH
BELOW KNEE
MID-CALF
MIDI
MAXI
EVENING
FLOOR

There aren't any hard-and-fast rules for hem depth. Here are some suggestions of appropriate hem depths for common design features:

HEM DEPTHS	
⅜″	Blouses, ruffles, lingerie, extremely flared skirts
1″	Short sleeves, circular skirts
1½″-2″	Sleeves, jackets, pants, shorts, blouses
3″	Average hem width for dresses, skirts, and coats
2″-4″	Floor length garments
5″-10″	Full skirts in sheer fabrics

Hem lingo has a few universals to keep in mind:

- The heavier the fabric, or more flared the garment, the narrower the hem.
- Keep your height and hem depth in proportion—if tall, allow for a slightly deeper hem; if short, a narrower hem.
- Longer dresses need deeper hems unless a hand rolled or narrow hem would enhance an airy appearance.
- Let bias hang for 24 hours before marking hem.

PLAIN HEM

Edge finish may vary to suit fabric, but the hem is the same. Specialized hems are launched from plain hem beginnings.

Mark hem length (see Fitting), open hem over seams, and trim seam allowances below hemline to ¼″.

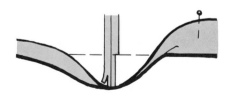

Pin baste ¼″ from fold; unpin raw edge. Measure hem depth and trim hem allowance evenly.

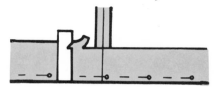

Press raw edge lightly, with brown paper between hem and garment; *don't* press over pins.

Finish raw edge, then pin in place, matching centers and seams. Invisibly sew hem with recommended stitch. Remove pins and steam thoroughly; hold iron 2"-3" above hem without touching fabric.

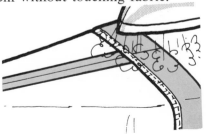

Mold fabric at hem fold with a pounding block or ruler. Pound heavily for a *sharp crease*, or pat gently for a *rolled edge*. Let garment dry thoroughly before wearing.

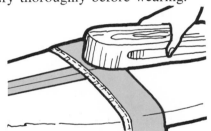

HEM FINISHES

There's bound to be a finish that's perfect for your fabric—an invisible one that won't make outside ridges after wearing and cleaning.

SEAM BINDING: On straight or slightly eased hems, lap ribbon seam binding ¼" over raw edge. Overlap ends, turning under top one; edge-stitch. Sew hem to garment with hemming stitch or slipstitch.

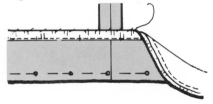

On curved edges, use bias seam binding. Open one folded edge and turn in end. Keeping raw edges even, lap bias over garment edge. Stitch along crease, stretching bias slightly as you work and overlapping ends. Turn bias up and sew to garment.

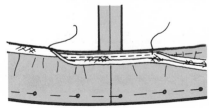

Press finished hem lightly.

STITCHED AND OVERCAST: This is a secure flat finish for medium or heavyweight fabric. Stitch ¼" from raw edge and machine or hand overcast. Turn back edge ¼" and blindstitch to garment.

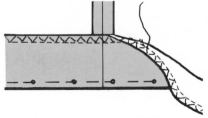

STITCHED AND PINKED: On non-ravelly fabrics, stitch ¼" from raw edge and trim with pinking or scalloping shears. Turn pinked edge back ¼" and blindstitch to garment.

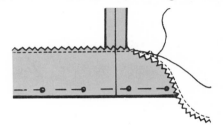

TURNED AND STITCHED: This is a durable finish for hems with very little ease in fabrics of light or medium weight. Turn under cut edge ¼"; machine stitch close to folded edge. Use a hemming stitch or slip-stitch to sew hem in place.

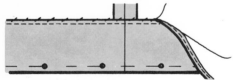

SPECIAL SITUATIONS

For an unusual hem, try some out-of-the-ordinary treatment—just modify plain hem techniques.

EASED: To adjust excess fullness in a slightly flared hem, stitch ¼" from raw edge with long stitches. Pull up ease thread every few inches.

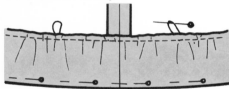

Press to shrink fullness, protecting garment with brown paper.

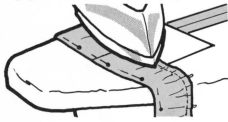

Complete hem with bias seam binding or stitched and overcast method.

CIRCULAR: Prevent sagging by hanging garments with bias or extremely flared hemlines for 24 hours before hemming. Trim hem allowance to 1"; complete like the Eased Hem.

FACED: Finish a circular skirt, lessen bulk in heavy fabric, or lengthen last year's favorite! Trim hem allowance to ½". For facing, cut a 2" wide bias strip of lightweight fabric or use commercial bias hem facing.

Shape bias to match curve of hem. Stitch facing to garment in a ¼" seam, keeping raw edges even and turning in ends ¼" to meet.

Turn facing to inside along hemline; press. Turn in raw edge ¼" and sew to garment; sew ends together.

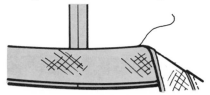

NARROW: Great for children's clothes and sportswear! Turn cut edge to inside 3/16", and again 3/16"; pin, then edgestitch.

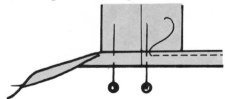

ROLLED: Use this one on scarfs and sheers. Staystitch ¼" from marked hemline; trim close to stitching. Turn in edge ⅛" and crease. Work zigzagging stitches ¼" apart over raw edge, picking up a thread on crease and alongside raw edge. Every 1" pull thread to tighten stitches and create the roll.

HORSEHAIR BRAID: This hem provides extra stiffness without extra weight. Steam creases from braid and cut to fit hem circumference.

Lap cut ends of braid ¾" and enclose in a fabric strip applied with two lines of stitching.

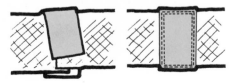

For **narrow** braid, trim hem allowance to ½". Pin braid in place on garment, keeping edges even; stitch ¼" from edge.

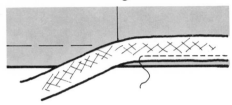

Turn braid to inside along hemline; baste close to fold. Sew free edge in place.

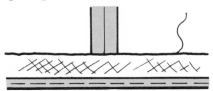

For **wide** braid, underlining your garment gives best results. Braid usually has one edge pre-threaded for easing; if not, easestitch along an edge.

Baste unthreaded edge of braid along hemline of garment. Place enclosed ends of braid over a seam. Turn up hem and pin to braid; check hemline.

Unpin hem and draw up ease thread to adjust fullness on upper edge of braid. Sew lower edge of braid to underlining at hemline.

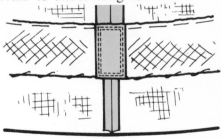

Complete hem by sewing finished edge to braid.

INTERFACED: Hold the curve of a hem with interfacing. Choose one with the finished effect in mind; lamb's wool or cotton flannel results in a soft rolled edge, while stiffer interfacings add body and can be creased or rolled. Underline garment to prevent hand sewing from showing on the outside. Mark hemline.

Cut bias strips of interfacing to width of hem depth and length of hem circumference plus ½" for lapping ends; piece if necessary.

Pin interfacing to garment, extending it ⅝" below hemline. Sew interfacing to underlining with long running stitches along hemline and long catchstitches at upper edge.

Turn up hem and baste close to fold. Finish raw edge and sew hem to underlining.

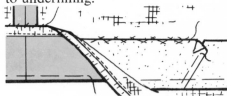

Press like the Plain Hem.

To hem pleated garments, see **Pleats.** For hems in knitwear, refer to **Knits.** Hems at corners are handled in **Tailoring.**

People Who Count

Something for Everyone

It's time to spread out the skills you've developed! Take the plunge and start sewing for the special people in your life—the young ones and your fellas. Combine what you know about sewing for yourself with some techniques developed especially for children and men. A bonus in the deal is that some of these special constructions are worth borrowing for your clothes, too!

THE SMALL SET

There's nothing more satisfying than making children's clothes with the built-in features that make them comfortable, durable, and fun for your child to wear.

GREAT BEGINNINGS

Careful selection of pattern and fabric paves the way for making great clothes for children.

FABRICS: For easy-care clothes, choose smooth, firm fabrics that can be machine washed and dried. Fabrics labeled durable press, permanent press, colorfast, shrinkage controlled, Sanforized, and washable wool are ideal. Polyester and cotton blends tend to spot unless treated with a soil-release finish.

Some perennial favorites for children's wear are denim, sailcloth, poplin, corduroy, terry, piqué, seersucker, organza, batiste, chambray, gingham, and broadcloth.

Knits are news because they adapt to the free-and-easy life style of active children. When buying bonded fabric, insist on quality.

Remember that children love bright colors, especially the primaries—red, blue, and yellow. Rollicking animals, pretty flowers, and bold stripes wandering across fabric can be made into fascinating clothes.

Make texture a factor in choosing fabrics, too. Children invariably prefer fluffy or pile fabrics. Velour and fake fur would be loved by any child—just be sure they're easy-care for you!

For very young children, select soft, smooth fabrics for greatest comfort. For older children, narrow the selection to several fabrics which meet your specifications, then let your child pick the one she likes.

SIZE: Oh, how children grow! Measure often for correct pattern size. Purchase patterns by inches, not age. Sizes run according to breast measurements for girls and toddlers, and chest measurements for boys. Size charts and measuring how-tos are in the section on buying patterns.

For children of **average** body contour choose the size nearest to breast or chest measurement. If measurements fall between two sizes, base choice on bone structure.

For **chubby** or **thin** children, arriving at pattern size in the usual way can result in poor fit at neck, armholes, and other key areas. Be sure that the design has fullness where needed and won't emphasize bad features. Purchase pattern according to child's frame and adjust circumference measurements.

PATTERN ADJUSTMENT

Butterick has figured out some easy adjustments to solve children's fitting problems. Begin with a review of pattern adjustments so you'll know how to make changes in pattern tissue.

Lengthen or shorten pattern along adjustment lines and/or at hem edges using "base of neck to lower edge" or "back waist length" measurements for dresses, blouses, jumpers, etc. and "finished side length" for pants. Whenever possible, locate adjustments so they won't interfere with darts.

Watch out for the fit of shoulders. Never make a huge dress in hopes that she'll grow into it!

AVERAGE: Increase or decrease pattern circumference at waist and/or hips as you would for an adult.

CHUBBY: Slash from shoulder edge to lower edge of front and back pattern pieces; spread each slash ¼ of the amount needed. Secure the adjustment with tape.

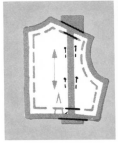 

THIN: Crease front and back pattern pieces from shoulder edge to lower edge making a fold ⅛ the amount needed to be decreased. Secure the adjustment with tape.

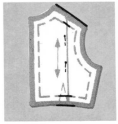 

For minor problems in making fabric conform to figure, turn to Fitting, pages 174-176.

A WORKING ORDER

Organization is the key to construction. With a system, you can whip up all sorts of clothes at a rapid fire pace. You may already be using a few short cuts; check out these economy measures anyway!

Keep your iron handy. Press after stitching as many darts and seams at one time as possible.

Flat construction is a great time-saver. Complete small details like collars, belts, and pockets before attaching to the garment. Add each detail to the appropriate garment section before joining major garment seams. Garment areas that normally require circular seams, like sleeves and cuffs, can be completed before joining side or sleeve seams.

For specific information, refer to the Sew and Go Set-In Sleeve, page 201, and the Sew and Go Band Cuff, pages 228-229.

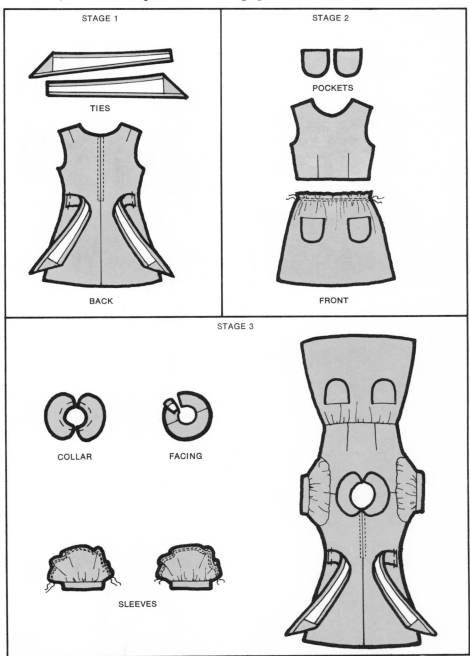

STAGE 1

TIES

BACK

STAGE 2

POCKETS

FRONT

STAGE 3

COLLAR

FACING

SLEEVES

SPECIAL HINTS

Some construction procedures have been planned to do a perfect job on children's wear.

SEAMS: Because they get a lot of use and washing, children's clothes must have sturdy, properly finished seams.

Self-bound seam encloses straight or slightly curved seam edges. It's ideal for ravelly fabrics. Stitch seam, then trim one seam allowance to ⅛″. Turn under other seam allowance and fold it down to meet the seam and encase raw edges; edgestitch.

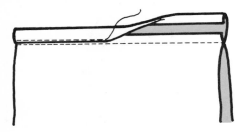

Plain seams finished with machine zigzagging are easy to do and almost indestructable. Although slightly more difficult, French seams or flat-fell seams in appropriate areas wear like iron. You'll find French seams in Seams. Turn to the Men's section for flat-fell seams.

Bind very curved seams with double fold bias tape (see Binding).

HEMS: Sturdy hems won't get pulled out during play. The turned and stitched finish or the narrow hem are two of the best (see Hems, pages 241-242).

For playclothes, the machine blindstitched hem is recommended. Read your sewing machine booklet for details.

CLOSURES: Plan to place closures in front so the child can dress without help. Use slightly larger buttons and zipper pulls.

Hammer-on snaps or snap tape won't pull apart during use. Eyelets with larger than average lacing can teach a child how to lace and tie.

For button closures, reinforce wrong side of fabric under button placement markings with a square of iron-on mending tape.

Use a continuous lap instead of a zipper to finish openings in seams. Stitch seam, leaving an opening for placket. Clip at end of opening and press seam open.

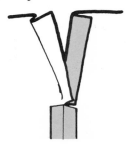

Cut a straight strip of light-weight fabric 2″ wide and twice the length of opening. Spread placket edges and pin to strip, keeping raw edges and ends even. Stitch, then trim and grade seam allowances.

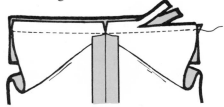

Press seam toward strip, then turn in remaining edges ¼″. Fold over seam; edgestitch.

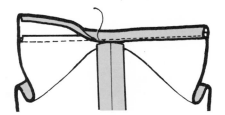

Fasten opening with hammer-on snaps, buttons, or nylon tape.

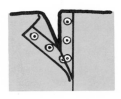

To cut a continuous lap along a selvage or to insert one in a slash, see Sleeve Finishes.

WAISTBANDS: Combine a no-dart waistline with a casing and you have another self-help feature—the elasticized waistband. Refer to Casings, pages 232-235, for directions.

FACINGS: You don't even need facings for those cute little sleeveless things. Use commercial bias tape wherever possible (see Facings).

Bind neck and armhole edges with color coordinated commercial double-fold bias tape; leave enough extra bias at ends to tie.

Reinforce ends by inserting seam binding in bias tape from garment edge to tie end.

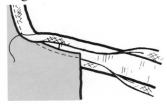

A self-fabric tie (see Binding) is also attractive.

POCKETS: Pockets are practical—they're handy and warm, and children love them.

Reinforce fabric at pocket markings with iron-on mending tape. Edgestitch pocket to garment, backstitching at opening corners.

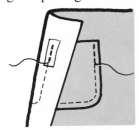

TRIMS: Don't be afraid to try trims—they add so much to the simplest little dress! Be sure they're washable, durable, and non-scratchy.

Children's clothes are a great place to try out fancy machine stitches, hand smocking, or embroidery. Go on a fringe, tassel, and pompon kick: make a pint-sized peasant dress with rickrack and bands, or add the masterful detail of shirring or tucks. Don't overlook appliqués, whether commercial or made-by-you. Give your imagination free rein and dream up creations that will be fun for you and your child.

PANTS: Reinforce knees before stitching leg seams. Cut two large rectangular bias patches about 8" long and wide enough to extend across front of each leg, seam to seam. Center patch over knee area; fuse or machine stitch to pants. Stitch leg seams.

GROW AND SEW

Build in a plan for growth adjustments so your child won't mind last year's dress or a sisterly hand-me-down. Make deep hems and add grow-tucks to bodice or skirt where suitable.

Use rickrack or braid to cover marks made when the tucks are released. If garment has faded, cover the tuck area with ribbon, lace, or braid trim.

Lengthen the waistline or the hem by adding or inserting contrast bands, lace, or trim to skirt or legs. Vary the width and amount of trim as needed, allowing for seam allowances.

MRS. FIX-IT

As every mother knows, wear means tear. Reinforce areas that get the most strain—knees, seats, and elbows. Use appliqués or iron-on patches for strength.

Mend tears by reinforcing the area on inside of garment with a fabric patch or machine zigzag stitch. Appliqué a larger fabric or iron-on patch to outside. Cut the patch in a cute decorative or animal shape to trim while you mend.

THE MEN IN YOUR LIFE

What man isn't proud to wear something his girl has made for him? Sewing for him is as easy as sewing for yourself.

You'll find men's and boys' size charts and measuring procedures in the section on pattern selection. Pattern adjustments are made like those for women; turn to that section for information.

SHIRT

Here's a collection of hints to remove your doubts about tackling a man-size project.

SEAMS: Durability is what's needed. The following special seams fill the bill.

Flat-Fell Seam: Stitch a plain seam with *wrong* sides together; press both seam allowances in the same direction. Trim underlying seam allowance to ⅛″. Turn in raw edge of remaining seam allowance ¼″ and edgestitch to garment.

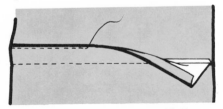

Make a simulated flat-fell seam by adding another row of topstitching to the Lapped Seam on page 170. **OR . . .**

SEW AND GO . . . extra easy: Make a plain seam; press both seam allowances in the same direction. From outside, topstitch ¼″ from seam and edgestitch next to seam. This is sometimes called the *double welt seam.*

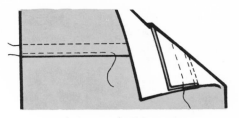

TAB FRONT: Pin tab to shirt opening edge; stitch in a ¼″ seam. Press seam open, then turn tab to outside along its seam allowance; press.

Turn in remaining tab edge along seamline; press. Pin in place, then topstitch ¼″ from both long edges to secure tab to shirt.

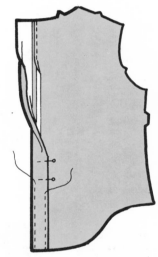

COLLAR: Shirt collars are sewn to a band which is then attached to the shirt. Measure neck size and make needed adjustments.

Prepare garment neck area. Interface collar, join sections, trim seam, turn, and press. On collar, topstitch ¼″ from collar edges and staystitch neck edge.

Interface one band section and pin to undercollar. Pin remaining band section to upper collar, clipping collar seam allowances to lie flat. Pin together ends of band sections.

Stitch ends and upper edges of band; begin and end stitching ⅝" from neck edge, leaving band neck edges open. Trim, grade, and notch seam allowances.

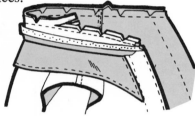

Press band away from collar. Pin non-interfaced band section to shirt neck edge, matching markings and clipping shirt if needed. Stitch, trim, grade, and clip seam allowances.

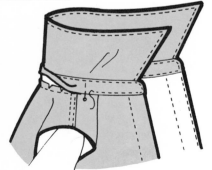

Press seam allowances toward band. On outside, turn in and pin remaining band edge over seam; edgestitch band.

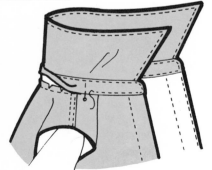

SLEEVES: Men's sleeves have wider, flatter caps than women's. Make the placket first, then insert sleeve in shirt, using the Sew and Go method on page 201. Use flat-fell seams.

Placket: Reinforce sleeve opening with small stitches; slash (1). Stitch

underlap to back edge of opening; trim seam allowances and press toward underlap. Turn in remaining underlap edge ¼"; press and pin over stitching line. Edgestitch through all thicknesses (2).

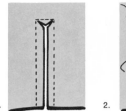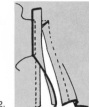

Stitch overlap to other raw edge of slashed opening; end stitching at top of opening. Trim seam allowances, then press them toward the overlap.

Stitch across triangular end alongside reinforcement stitches; catch underlap and one layer of overlap in stitching. Press stitched ends up.

Turn in overlap along seamlines and foldline. Baste close to edge and press. Pin overlap in place along folded edges (1).

Keeping underlap free, edgestitch along overlap foldline to top of opening. Pull threads to inside and tie.

Stitch through all layers across top of overlap as shown. Edgestitch remaining folded edge to sleeve; tie threads on inside (2).

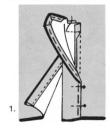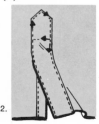

Cuff: Prepare cuff like the Buttoned Cuff, page 230. Stitch non-interfaced cuff section to sleeve, keeping placket and cuff edges even. Trim and grade seam allowances.

Press seam toward cuff. Turn in remaining long edge of cuff and lap over seam; baste. Edgestitch cuff; make a second line of edgestitching ¼″ from the first.

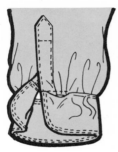

Finish with button and buttonhole closure.

PANTS

Fly closings and cuffs turn pants into menswear.

FLY CLOSING: Closings lap left over right. Trouser zippers are sturdiest.

Stitch and press crotch seam. Turn in front extensions along foldlines and baste. Place closed zipper face up beneath underlap, keeping bottom stop even with end of opening and folded edge close to zipper teeth; baste (zipper may extend beyond waistline edge). Position overlap, matching center markings; baste (1).

On inside, open overlap extension and stitch zipper tape in place; make this line of stitching close to teeth. Then make a second line of stitching ¼″ from the first. Keep the front free (2).

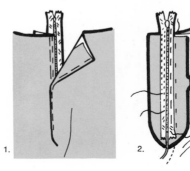

Turn extension back; baste. On outside, stitch along stitching line through all layers. Pull threads to inside and tie (1).

Stitch lining to fly section. Trim seam, notch curve, turn and press. Pin raw edges together. With zipper open, place fly over underlap extension. Stitch, keeping raw edges even and front free (2).

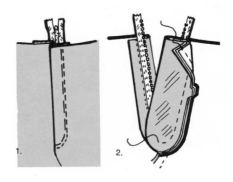

On outside, stitch close to folded edge of underlap through all thicknesses. Machine baste along waist seamline across zipper tapes; this prevents tab from being pulled off. Trim zipper even with upper edges. Machine zigzag or make a ¼″

hand-worked bar tack at lower end of fly opening.

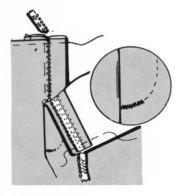

CUFFS: As fashion changes, so do cuffs. To add them to a cuffless design, lengthen pattern leg twice the desired cuff width. Complete hems, then turn cuffs up along markings, and press. Sew cuff to garment leg at side seams with a French tack or the Sew and Go method on page 191.

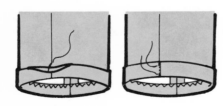

JACKET

Three criteria of man-tailoring are the handling of pockets, vents, and collars.

POCKETS: There are two types which you'll find commonly used on men's jackets and pants. The buttonhole pocket (a double welt pocket that looks like a buttonhole) and the welt pocket with a flap are classic tailored touches.

Buttonhole Pocket: Fold in long edges of strip to meet at center; press. Center strip, cut edges up, over pocket markings; baste.

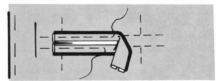

Slash through center of strip without cutting garment. Cut pocket from lining fabric and baste over strip between markings. Stitch next to basting lines; backstitch or knot ends.

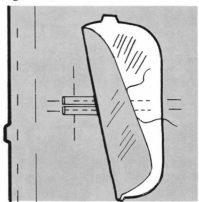

From wrong side, slash pocket opening as for a bound buttonhole. Pull strip and pocket to inside; press.

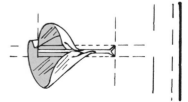

Baste lips together; then pin pocket edges together. Stitch sides and edges, catching base of triangular ends in stitching and keeping garment free.

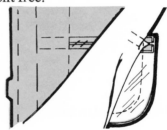

Invisibly sew upper edge to garment. Trim seam allowances to ¼″ and overcast edges.

Welt Pocket With Flap: Prepare and shape flap as instructed in Pockets. Trim seam allowance to ¼″. Baste flap to garment along upper stitching line.

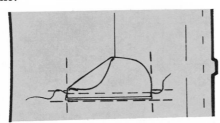

Cut pocket sections from lining fabric and stitch one to each long edge of welt; press seams toward pocket. On outside, pin welt over flap on garment, matching markings. Stitch along stitching lines; slash between lines without cutting flap.

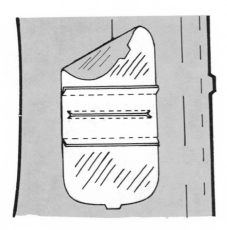

Turn welt and pocket to inside; press. To form welt, fold fabric over opening to within ⅛″ of upper edge. Baste close to fold and close to seam; press.

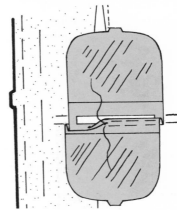

Stitch lower seam allowance at opening edge to welt along previous stitching, keeping front free.

Fold upper pocket section down along seam; pin welt and pocket sections together. Stitch, catching triangular ends in stitching. Trim seam to ¼″ and overcast.

On outside, turn flap down; press, protecting fabric with brown paper.

VENTS: Back openings are formed by overlapping extensions. For center vents, lap left over right; for side vents, center over sides.

Turn in seam allowances on underlap; baste. Stitch seam, pivoting at marking and stitching across upper edge of extension. Clip seam at top of underlap; press open above clip. Press extension in place. Invisibly sew upper edge to jacket.

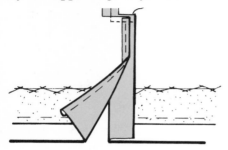

To hem, turn overlap to outside along foldline; stitch along hemline. Trim and grade hem allowance.

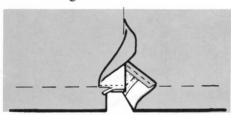

Turn and press overlap. Turn up hem, making underlap hem slightly shorter; baste close to fold. Invisibly sew underlap hem edges together. Sew overlap to hem. Invisibly sew long extension edges to jacket. Complete hem.

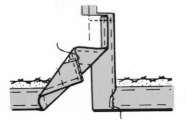

Insert lining as instructed in pattern, referring to Shaping, pages 179-181, for extra hints.

COLLAR: Complete jacket facings and lining before attaching collar.

Stitch undercollar sections together; trim seam allowances and press seam open. Fuse lightweight interfacing to undercollar or interface and padstitch undercollar as in Tailoring; shape undercollar (see Tailoring). Trim away undercollar seam allowances.

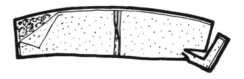

On upper collar interfacing section, trim seam allowances a scant 1/8″ inside seamline; fuse to upper collar. Pin upper collar to jacket neck edge; match markings and clip neck edge as needed. Stitch between markings; trim and grade seam allowances.

Press seam open, then toward collar. Turn in remaining seam allowances on upper collar, mitering corners; baste and press.

Pin undercollar to wrong side of upper collar, keeping neck edge along seam and outer edge $\frac{1}{16}''$ from upper collar edges; hemstitch in place.

If using a heavy-weight or loosely woven fabric, substitute felt or a firmly woven fabric in a matching color for the undercollar.

NECKTIES

Now that menswear has taken a turn toward fashion, ties have become the show-off accessory. Follow your pattern for construction and use these tips to help with finishing. For washable fabrics, use washable interfacing.

Cut long neckties on the bias and line the ends. For the "big" man, lengthen tie in the narrow center area so it will fit his neck and end in the proper spot. If no lining piece came with your pattern, cut one; use the same tie end shape, and make lining

5″ long for wide end or 4″ long for narrow end.

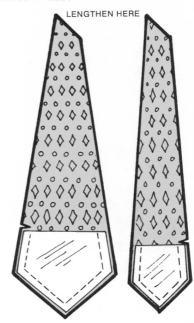

Hand stitches and seams should be invisible from the outside, so handle with care. Use a cardboard cut to size to prevent ridges when pressing tie; don't press edges. Add a label or ribbon to underside of wide end to hold the narrow end in place.

To teach someone the tricks of tying both long and bow ties, see **Bows and Scarfs**.

Your Own Thing

Trims And Trifles

Lovely to look at, mind-bending to plan, and fun to do—that, in a nutshell, is the trims story. As a general rule, trim simple garments elaborately, and elaborate garments simply. Never let trimmings destroy the balance or interfere with the design of your garment. Attach trims during construction or after the garment has been completed, depending on the type you've chosen.

SURFACE INTRIGUE

Move into the third dimension —round out the personality of an old fabric favorite by sculpting its surface with one of these techniques.

SHIRRING

Fullness drawn up on lines of stitching which are visible from the outside is called shirring.

The crosswise grain of soft or lightweight fabrics is ideal for shirring. Set machine for 8-10 stitches per inch; loosen upper tension slightly. Stitch along markings. Knot one end of each line of stitching on the underside, then pull bobbin threads to gather fabric. Tie remaining thread ends.

Press by working point of iron into and out of fabric puffs alongside shirring; never rest iron on shirred areas.

For added security when rows of stitching won't be caught in a seam, make a pin tuck and stitch over knotted ends.

Stay a shirred area when it might be subjected to strain. Use a flat piece of lightweight fabric or self-fabric. Stitch stay into garment seams as they are joined; or, turn edges in and slipstich.

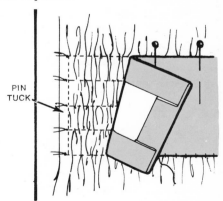

PIN TUCK

ELASTICIZED: Combine the beauty of shirred fabric with knit-like comfort! Use regular thread in your machine and elastic thread in the bobbin; hand wind bobbin until almost full, stretching thread to wind it firmly.

Set machine for 7 stitches per inch. Test shirring on a fabric scrap. Holding fabric taut, stitch along markings. As you work, stretch previously stitched rows to distribute shirring evenly.

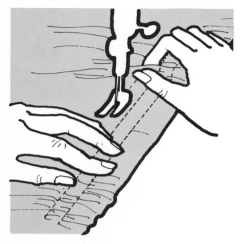

VARIATIONS: For puffy, grid-like **waffle shirring** make rows of stitching on the crosswise grain, then on the lengthwise grain. Elasticized thread makes it adjustable.

For **corded shirring,** encase cording or round elastic in fabric tucks, and draw them up to the desired fullness. Stitch across both ends to secure cord.

SMOCKING

Add interest and stretch to plain fabric, or individualize a simple design with smocking. These stitches are especially attractive on checked fabrics like gingham. Both hand and machine smocking require extra fabric, so always plan your work carefully before cutting and constructing your garment.

HAND SMOCKING: Thread needle with three to six strands of embroidery floss to match or contrast fabric color. Mark small dots on fabric to indicate points in the smocking pattern you have chosen. Secure thread on the wrong side of fabric, then bring needle out and work from the right side of your fabric.

Honeycomb: Working from left to right and pointing needle toward the left, do two rows at a time for the design.

Bring needle out at 1, then take a small stitch at 2 and another at 1; pull thread taut.

Re-insert needle at 2, and bring it out at 3. Repeat procedure at 3 and 4, and at 5 and 6. Continue until designated area is smocked.

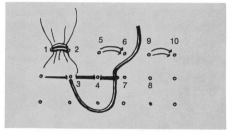

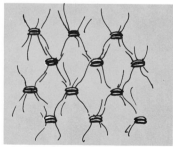

Diamond: Working from left to right, and pointing needle toward the left, carry thread from row to row on outside of fabric.

Bring needle out at 1. Take a small stitch at 2, keeping thread above needle; pull thread taut.

Take a stitch diagonally to 3. Then take a stitch at 4, keeping the thread below the needle. Pull thread taut.

Repeat at 5 and 6, keeping thread above needle. Continue this for two rows, then alternate the procedure for the next row. By doing this, you'll have two threads holding the fabric.

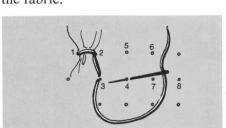

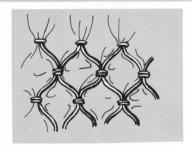

orative thread to match or contrast with your fabric. Stitch over shirring between the lines of stitching that are ⅛″ apart. Alternating zigzag stitch patterns can result in some really intriguing smocking.

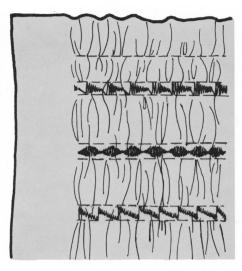

MACHINE SMOCKING: Easy-to-do shirring that looks like smocking! Use matching or contrasting thread, and loosen upper tension slightly. Make rows of stitches for shirring; as in hand smocking, work from the right side of your fabric.

Stay smocked area as explained in Shirring to prevent smocking from losing shape or tearing.

With Zigzagging: Make the first line of stitching for shirring ⅜″ from raw edge. Add a second line ¼″ away, and a third line ⅛″ from the second.

Make additional lines of stitching in groups of two, spaced ⅛″ apart. Space groups about ½″ apart, covering designated area. Gather fabric to desired width, and secure threads.

Select a zigzag stitch pattern to suit your fancy. Use regular or dec-

Simulated Hand: Shirr fabric as for smocking with zigzagging, spacing lines of stitching for shirring to accommodate embroidery stitches. Work a hand embroidery stitch between the lines of machine stitching —herringbone and fly stitches look great.

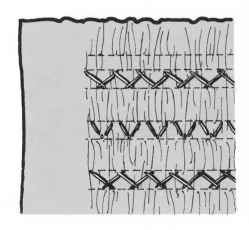

TUCKS

Mini pleats whose entire length is controlled by a line of hand or machine stitching, tucks are usually on the outside of the garment. They're an attractive addition to special blouses and dainty children's clothes. Tucks assume an air of elegance when used on evening wear.

In *Blind Tucks,* each touches or overlaps the next; in *Spaced Tucks* there is space between each tuck. *Pin Tucks* are narrow spaced tucks.

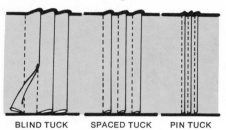

BLIND TUCK   SPACED TUCK   PIN TUCK

MAKE: Tuck folds are on straight grain. Use a notched paper gauge to indicate depth of tuck and space from fold to fold. Working from right to left, slide gauge ahead as you baste tucks.

Stitch tucks from the outside for maximum control and evenness. Use a regular length machine stitch or, on sheer or delicate fabrics, short running stitches.

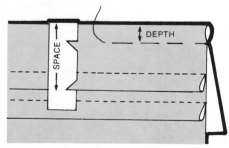

PIECE: Here's what to do when you'd love to make that great tucked design in a fabric that's not wide enough to accommodate it. Split pattern along stitching line of a tuck. Cut fabric, allowing a ⅝″ seam allowance on each edge to be pieced along with an additional tuck width on the overlapping layer. Mark and make tucks as usual; baste tuck that will cover piecing seam. Matching seamlines, lap fabric layers and stitch next to basting.

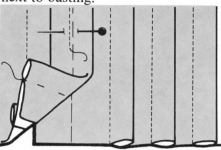

PRESS: After stitching each or all tucks, press the tuck crease from the underside of fold on the outside of garment. Then press tucks in desired direction.

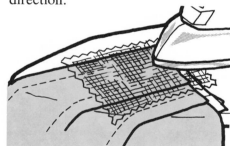

Press entire tucked area from the inside; use little steam, as this causes puckers. Touch up the outside of the tucked garment; use a press cloth over fabric and brown paper beneath fold of tuck.

ADD: Before cutting out pattern, determine placement, width, and spacing of tucks in relation to garment design and your figure. Make tucks in fabric, then pin pattern pieces over tucked fabric. Cut and construct garment.

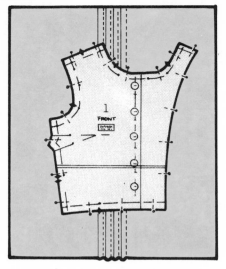

VARY: For **cross tucks,** use lightweight fabric. Stitch and press lengthwise tucks. Next, stitch and press crosswise tucks.

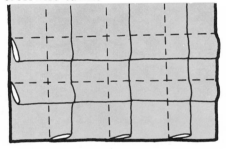

When tuck stitching ends to release fullness, a **released tuck,** or **dart tuck** is formed. Apply tuck principles and refer to page 183 of Darts for more information.

QUILTING

Stitch together two or more layers of fabric along the lines of a planned design. Lightly pad and back the wrong side of fabric for a soft puffy effect; pin and baste both layers to fabric before quilting.

Baste along edges and lengthwise grain at 6″ intervals. Test to determine tension, pressure, and stitch length. Use regular thread in a matching or contrasting color; buttonhole twist emphasizes stitching lines.

DIAGONAL: Crisscross lines of stitching form squares or diamonds. Use a quilting foot with space guide attachment for quilting; this can be purchased for your sewing machine.

Indicate the first line of stitching in each direction by marking two intersecting lines on right side of fabric; lines can be on bias or straight grain. Adjust space guide to width between rows of stitching.

From right side of fabric, stitch along one marked line. Space successive rows of stitching by keeping edge of space guide on preceding row. Stitch all rows in one direction, then stitch all rows in the opposite direction.

To quilt a large area, make first lines of stitching at the center of the area and work toward the edges.

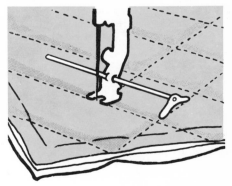

PATTERN: Use padding and quilting techniques to outline a print or plaid or to create your own free-form graphics with stitching.

APPLIQUÉS

Delicate or bold in shape and color, appliqués are individual fabric motifs applied to a larger fabric background. Contrast color or texture of appliqué and fabric background for effect.

HAND: Cut appliqué with ¼″ seam allowances. Stitch along outline of motif; trim seam allowances to ⅛″. Pin and baste appliqué in place.

Work small blanket stitches along edges, using thread to match or contrast (1). Or, for an invisible finish, turn edges in along stitching; press. Slipstitch appliqué to garment (2). **OR . . .**

1.   2.

Choose fabrics for appliqué which have the same weight, durability, and cleaning requirements as the background fabric. Avoid fabrics that ravel easily.

SEW AND GO . . . extra easy: Cut out appliqué, eliminating seam allowances. Use a fusible adhesive to attach appliqué to garment; follow manufacturer's instructions. Zigzag or overcast edges if fabric ravels. Or, cut colored iron-on mending tape in fun shapes and fuse to fabric.

MACHINE: Cut appliqué with a ¼″ seam allowance. Back soft stretchy fabric with a stiff lightweight fabric. Pin appliqué to garment. Match thread to color of appliqué.

Stitch along motif outline and lines within the design. Trim raw edge close to stitching, then enclose the edge of the design and the stitching with a close zigzag stitch. Use matching or contrasting thread. Pull threads to underside and tie.

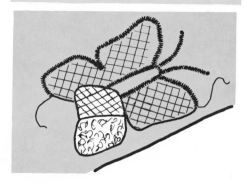

PATCHWORK

Fabric potpourri! Blending patches of diverse fabrics is the most fun, but be sure they're similar in weight. Avoid bulky, ravelly fabrics.

Create a patch shape and use heavy paper to make a pattern the size of the finished patch plus seam allowances on all sides. Cut enough patches on the straight grain to arrange the design.

Work on a flat surface with enough patches for two or three horizontal rows and arrange fabrics. Pin patches together in strips; stitch, then press seams open.

Pin long edges of strips together. Match intersecting seams of uniform patches. Stitch; press seams open.

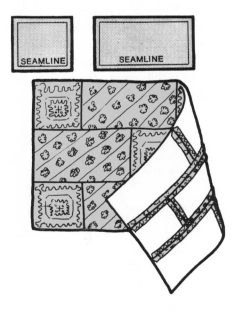

Repeat procedure until patchwork fabric can accommodate your pattern pieces. Pin and cut pattern as you would with regular fabric.

Think outside the square—piece together rectangles of different sizes. Pad and quilt patchwork following instructions in Quilting.

SEQUINS AND BEADS

Space age glitter, shimmery beads and sequins are glamourous and exclusive. The rewards of wearing a beautifully trimmed garment make your time and energy well spent.

Choose or create a design to transfer to batiste. Pin batiste, design side up, to inside of garment. Thread trace design to outside; use silk thread if fabric mars. To trim a design already on your fabric, use batiste for backing only.

Unless trimming a small area, complete garment before applying trims or trimmed sections. For motifs on fabric which doesn't mar, hold fabric taut in an embroidery hoop while working.

Use a fine or special beading needle and transparent nylon thread or matching thread coated with beeswax. Never pull stitches so tight that fabric puckers. Instead, secure beads or sequins every few inches with a backstitch.

When pressing, never touch trim with iron, as steam and heat can cause considerable damage to beads and sequins. With a dry iron and using a press cloth, press around trim on the inside of the garment. Use a towel as your pressing surface to protect both the trim and your fabric.

SEQUIN application depends on type and time.

Single Sequins: Backstitch from center hole to edge (1). Or, attach each sequin with a bead. Bring needle up through hole, string bead, and return needle through hole (2).

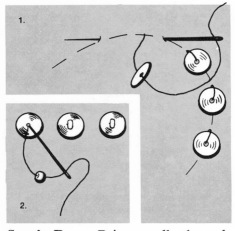

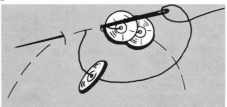

Sequin Rows: Bring needle through hole and backstitch to edge of preceding sequin. Bring needle forward for next sequin, which will overlap its predecessor and conceal thread.

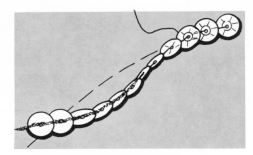

Paillettes: These are large sequins with hole at edge rather than center. Backstitch from hole to edge or attach each with a bead. Apply rows like sequin rows.

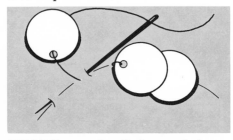

BEADS come in all sizes and shapes for scattering or grouping.

Single Beads: Bring needle to the outside of garment. String bead, and backstitch to garment.

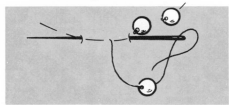

Rows of Beads: Bring needle to the outside of garment, string several beads and sew from group to group with a running stitch. Don't string so many at a time that thread droops.

Pre-strung Sequins: Invisibly sew through strands of sequin backing; take extra stitches at ends.

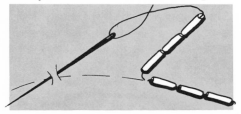

Bead Loops or Fringe: Bring needle to right side, string beads, and return needle to wrong side. Secure each loop singly for added strength.

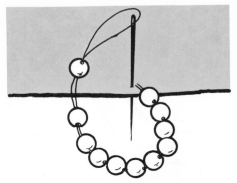

For fringe, string small beads, a large bead, and an anchor bead if necessary; return needle through same or another series of small beads and anchor to garment. If thread is drawn too tightly, stiff, rigid loops or fringe will result.

Pre-Strung Beads: Attach these as you would pre-strung sequins. Carry the needle and thread on the wrong side of the garment. **OR . . .**

SEW AND GO . . . extra easy: Purchase beaded or sequinned bands or appliqués; these have a foundation of thread chains, elastic, or organza. Turn cut ends under and secure with transparent tape, nail polish, or glue to prevent raveling. Sew edges and ends invisibly to garment.

STITCHOMETRY
Occupy your TV time with some sewing handiwork! Linear or solid stitch patterns add up to a big plus for the geometric in fashion.

TOPSTITCHING
High fashion stitchery, topstitching is the designer's darling and the machine approach to fine hand sewing.

Although a completed garment can be topstitched, it's often easier or even necessary to topstitch individual or large areas during construction. Always make fitting adjustments before topstitching seams.

Use buttonhole twist, a size 16 needle, and 6-8 stitches per inch. Test machine tension on fabric sample, adjusting if necessary.

Stitch slowly along markings for topstitching; use an appropriate guide—a seam guide or quilting foot is most convenient to use as you work. Take extra care at curves, corners, and other tricky details, because messiness here could spell disaster! Marking and basting before stitching reduce the chance of error. Always leave thread ends long enough to be worked to the underside with a needle and tied.

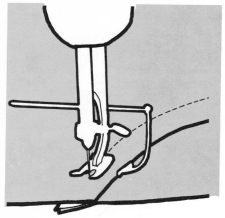

For heavy fabrics, make two lines of topstitching very close together. An extra-rich look results from running yarn through topstitched areas to pad out the space between stitching and seam. Or, pad area with bias strips of self-fabric before topstitching (see Quilting).

SADDLE STITCH

Subtle and elementary, saddle stitching is usually done parallel to the edges or seams of a garment. Use buttonhole twist, embroidery floss, heavy thread, or yarn in matching or contrasting colors to make continuous running stitches along edges or seams. Space stitches evenly and make them at least ¼ " long.

DECORATIVE TACKS

When custom tailoring is the byword, emphasize pockets, pleats, and the beginnings of slits with special tacks. For either type, mark a triangular shape. Use buttonhole twist secured with small backstitches to make the tack.

ARROWHEAD TACK: Bring needle out at 1, and take a small horizontal stitch at 2. Insert needle at 3, bringing it out just inside 1. Continue until entire tack is filled; secure thread with small backstitches.

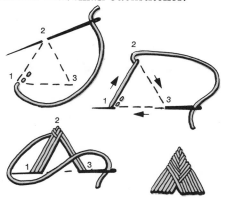

CROW'S FOOT TACK: Bring needle out at 1, and take a small horizontal stitch at 2. Then take a small diagonal stitch at 3, and another at 1. Continue until tack is filled; secure thread with small backstitches.

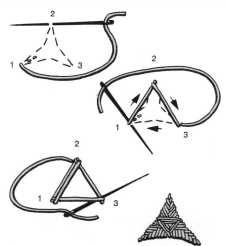

MONOGRAMS

Personalize your clothes with a monogram. Choose whichever of the following methods is best for your fabric.

Trace the design for monogram lightly on right side of fabric with chalk or pencil. If fabric is very soft, apply a backing of crisp, lightweight fabric. Hold fabric taut in an embroidery hoop.

MACHINE: Adjust machine for a zigzag stitch; test stitching on a fabric sample to determine appropriate stitch width, spacing, and tension. Stitch monogram, keeping design lines centered under needle. When monogram is complete, pull threads to underside and tie. Trim excess backing close to stitching; press.

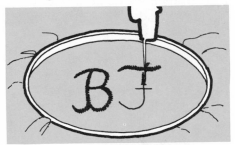

HAND: Apply backing if necessary. Then, satin stitch the monogram. Secure thread on underside and trim backing close to stitches; press.

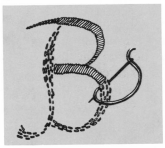

FABRIC APPLIQUÉ: Trace and cut your monogram from fabric which either matches or contrasts with that of garment. To apply, follow one of the methods discussed in Appliqués which is appropriate for your fabric and garment.

EMBROIDERY

A favorite pastime in years gone by, embroidery enjoys renewed popularity as a distinctive clothing accent and creative bit of handwork. Mark your design with chalk and thread tracing. Use three or six strands of embroidery floss, yarn, or a heavy decorative thread.

THREAD NEEDLE: Wrap thread end *tightly* over needle and hold; pull needle away. Squeeze thread tightly between finger and thumb. Push eye of needle onto fold of thread, rather than pushing thread through needle. Then pull thread end through needle.

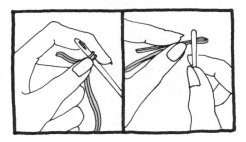

BLANKET STITCH is often used over edges, but can be worked from left to right between two lines. Bring needle out on lower line. Re-insert needle a little to the right on upper line. Bring needle out directly below on lower line, keeping thread under needle. Draw needle through loop which was formed and pull thread taut. Continue in this manner.

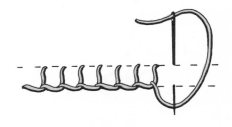

OUTLINE STITCH is a slanting backstitch worked from left to right in a single line. Follow each stitch with a short backstitch to the right side and close to the previous stitch.

SATIN STITCH consists of close parallel stitches worked over an area that has been padded with tiny running stitches. Slant the stitch for straight lines, and fan it on curves.

CROSS STITCH is the classic sampler pattern. Bring needle out at 1, carry thread diagonally to 2, and take a stitch from 2 to 3. Carry thread to 4, and take a stitch from 4 to 5. Continue until all stitches are taken in one direction, then work in the opposite direction, crossing over each stitch and keeping the points together.

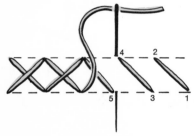

HERRINGBONE STITCH begins by bringing needle out at 1. Carry thread diagonally to 2, and take a stitch from 2 to 3. Carry thread diagonally to 4 and take a stitch from 4 to 5. Continue until row is finished.

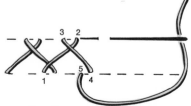

FLY STITCH is worked from left to right between two lines, like the blanket stitch. Bring needle out at 1. Holding thread down, stitch from 2 to 3. Take a tiny stitch over thread at 3 and bring needle out at 4 on upper line for next stitch.

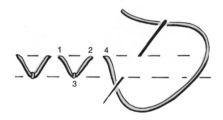

CHAIN STITCH begins by bringing needle out at the end of the line. Carry thread across line and take a stitch next to the first one; needle will cross thread. Pull thread taut to form a loop. Repeat procedure, beginning each stitch in the previous loop.

270

LAZY DAISY STITCH forms a flower when grouped. Bring needle out at center of flower. Keep thread under needle as you take a stitch next to the first and bring needle out at opposite end of petal. Pull thread taut to form a loop, then take a tiny stitch over the loop to form the petal, bringing needle out at central pivot area to begin next petal.

FEATHER STITCH is worked along four lines. Bring needle out at 1. Insert needle at 2, bringing it out at 3; keep thread under needle. Insert needle at 4, bringing it out at 5; again, keep thread under needle. Continue, alternating stitches.

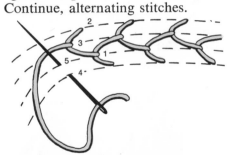

FRENCH KNOT begins by bringing needle out at mark. Holding thread taut, twist it around needle three or four times. Return needle to wrong side near point at which it was brought out; pull thread through loops and fabric until only a small knot remains.

FROU FROU

Nineteenth century opulence reborn . . . tassels and fringe vibrate along edges, and ruffles and lace do their bit for portraiture. Make use of these perennial leaders of the fashion parade in your latest creation.

FRINGE, TASSELS, AND POMPONS

Flippy and diverting, fringe is a fashion favorite. It can be made of self-fabric or applied as a separate strip of yarn, leather, or other crafty material. Snugged-in fringe forms tassels and pompons. Sew tassels on frogs for an extra-fancy closure, or polish off a tie belt with pompon ends.

SELF-FRINGE: Choose a woven fabric that is soft, thick, heavy, or nubby for beautiful fringe. Straighten ends by cutting across fabric exactly along straight grain. Determine depth of finished fringe and pull out a thread within fabric to act as a guide.

Stabilize fringe by machine stitching along pulled thread. Remove fabric threads below stitching; pull them out one at a time and in the same direction.

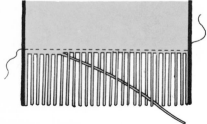

PURCHASED FRINGE: Countless styles and colors are available, most with a heading to stitch to your fabric. Use a single row of stitching or sew invisibly.

KNOTTED FRINGE: Usually this is a yarn trim applied to a loosely woven fabric. Determine depth, fullness, and spacing of fringe. Cut a cardboard strip to depth of finished fringe plus 1″ for each knot. Wrap yarn around cardboard to appropriate fullness, then cut one end of the strands.

Use an awl to make a small hole about ½″ from finished edge of garment. Insert crochet hook through hole from wrong side. Center appropriate number of strands over hook, and pull them through the hole to form a loop. Work ends through loop and pull to tighten. Continue process along entire edge.

For additional rows of knots, tie the halves of two long adjacent tassels; plan length of strands accordingly. Use a cardboard gauge to space knots evenly.

TASSELS: Cut a strip of cardboard to desired tassel depth. Thread needle with an 18″ double strand of heavy thread or buttonhole twist. Place thread along top edge of cardboard. Wind yarn around cardboard and double strand to appropriate fullness. Tie double strand at top (1).

Remove cardboard, and wind strand several times around tassel, about ½″ from the top. Slip needle inside wound portion and bring it out at top. Cut loops at lower end and attach tassel to garment (2).

1.   2.

POMPONS: Shorter and much thicker than tassels, pompons are made in a similar manner. Cut cardboard half the diameter of pompon. Hold a separate double strand of heavy thread or buttonhole twist at top edge of cardboard, and wind yarn around cardboard and strand until full enough for pompon. Tie separate strand and cut across other end (1).

Remove cardboard and shake pompon to make it fluffy. Spread, shape, and trim strands to form a ball (2).

For an extra thick pompon, insert a second pompon in the center of the first and tie them together at the center.

RUFFLES

Simple or frilly, ruffles are always feminine. Make them of matching or contrasting fabric for a most appealing accent. Stay curved garment areas before applying ruffles.

STRAIGHT: Plan to make ruffle strip 2-3 times longer than garment area to be trimmed; wide or sheer ruffles look best when very full. Strip can be on bias or straight grain; piece if necessary, stitching seams in bias ruffles on straight grain.

For a stronger gathering thread, use nylon or silk thread in the bobbin. At inward corners, allow less fullness than in the rest of the ruffle; at outward corners, more fullness.

Ruffle width depends on type and finish. **Single ruffles** have one free edge; **double ruffles** have two free edges. Finish a single-layer strip with narrow hems, a double-layer strip with folded edges.

Cut **single ruffle** in one of two ways: (1) for single-layer strip, allow desired width plus 1″ (⅝″ for seam allowance, and ⅜″ for narrow hem); (2) for double-layer strip, allow twice the desired width plus 1¼″ (two ⅝″ seam allowances).

Cut **double ruffle** in one of two ways: (1) for single-layer strip, allow desired width plus ¾″ (⅜″ each for two narrow hems); (2) for double-layer strip, allow twice the desired width.

Finish Edges: For **single ruffle,** (1) narrow hem one edge of single-layer strip, or (2) fold double-layer strip in half lengthwise and pin.

For **double ruffle,** (1) narrow hem both edges, or (2) fold raw edges in to meet where gathers will be placed.

Make: Stitch gathering rows as directed in Gathers, page 184.

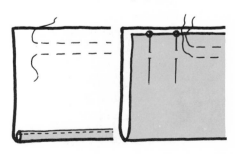

SINGLE RUFFLE

When both free edges of ruffle will be the same width, place gathering rows ¼″ apart at center of strip, or ⅛″ on either side of raw edges.

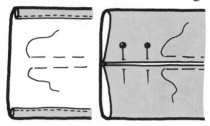

DOUBLE RUFFLE

When one free edge will be narrower to form a heading, place gathering rows ¼″ apart the desired distance from edge, or ⅛″ on either side of raw edges.

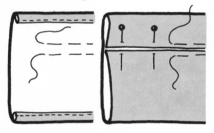

DOUBLE RUFFLE WITH HEADING

Attach: For a **single ruffle,** pin to garment and draw up bobbin threads to form gathers; distribute fullness evenly and baste. Press seam allowances flat, as in Gathers, page 184.

Enclose ruffle seam allowances by applying a shaped or bias facing when stitching ruffle to garment (see Facings).

Self-finish hem edges by stitching ruffle to garment; trim ruffle seam allowance to ⅛″. Turn in garment seam allowance ⅛″, then turn it over ruffle seam allowance; edgestitch fold in place. Turn ruffle away from garment. **OR . . .**

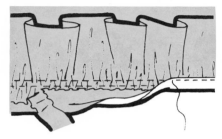

SEW AND GO . . . extra easy: Stitch ruffle to garment, then trim seam allowances to ¼″ and bind with double-fold bias tape. Turn ruffle away from garment.

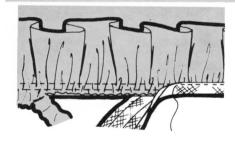

For a **double ruffle,** finish free-hanging ends or seam ends to be joined.

Applied finish is made by pinning ruffle in place and drawing up threads to form gathers; distribute fullness evenly, and baste. Stitch to garment along both gathering lines.

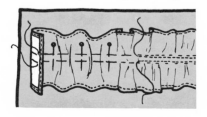

Self-finish hem edges by trimming garment hem allowance to ¼″ and pinning ruffle to inside of garment; keep bottom row of gathering stitches even with hemline. Draw up threads to form gathers; distribute fullness evenly, baste and press.

Stitch close to bottom row of gathering stitches. Press garment away from ruffle, then turn ruffle up over raw edge and baste to outside of garment. Stitch close to second row of gathering stitches.

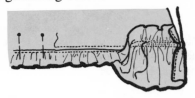

CIRCULAR: For ruffle, draw a circle equal in circumference to garment edge on wrong side of fabric. Establish ruffle width by drawing another circle around the first. Add a ⅝″ seam allowance to each circle. Draw a line along the straight grain to connect the outer and inner circles. Cut along edge of outer circle, straight line to inner circle, and edge of inner circle.

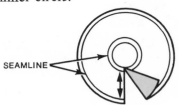

For ruffles which will be applied to long edges, cut several circles and join them with narrow seams on straight grain.

Finish Edges: Complete outer edge of ruffle with a narrow hem or a self-facing of corresponding circles. For self-facing, stitch outer edges together and trim seam allowances (1). Turn and press ruffle; staystitch inner curve (2).

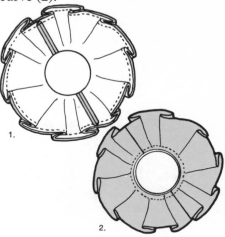

Attach: Pin ruffle to garment, clipping seam allowance so it will lie flat; baste.

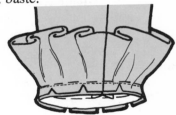

Complete with any of the finishes recommended for the straight single ruffle, page 274.

Refer to **Lace** for gathered lace ruffling.

LACE

A favorite trim for centuries, lace retains its popularity today.

Cotton, nylon, wool, and acetate, singly or in combinations, are used to make lace. Let fiber content and the openness of the lace be your guides in determining its application and care.

TYPES: When shopping for lace, you'll have to choose between *edging,* with one straight and one decorative edge, and *insertion,* with two straight or decorative edges.

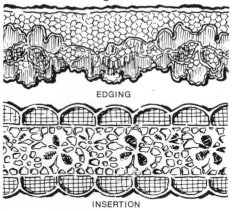

For **gathered lace,** you've got two options: either use commercially pre-gathered or pleated lace edging or gather flat lace edging yourself.

For the latter, cut a piece of flat lace edging 2-3 times the finished length. Machine or hand stitch close to straight edge of lace. Pull up bobbin thread to form gathers; distribute them evenly and secure threads before applying lace.

Some laces have been made with a gathering thread along the straight edge; all you have to do is pull!

ATTACHING: This can be done by machine or hand; the latter is invisible, delicate, and time-consuming.

Applied Edging: Use this method to trim an unfinished edge with flat or gathered lace.

To apply by machine, position lace on garment so straight edge is 1/8″ beyond seamline or hemline in seam or hem allowance; stitch. Turn to inside along seamline or hemline, clipping curved seam allowances; edgestitch. Finish raw edge as desired.

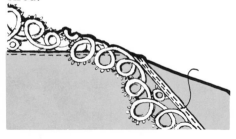

To apply by hand, make a machine or hand rolled hem, then overhand or whipstitch lace to edge of garment. **OR . . .**

SEW AND GO . . . extra easy: Trim seam allowance to 1/4″. Machine zigzag edge and turn it to inside. Lap edge 1/8″ over lace; edgestitch.

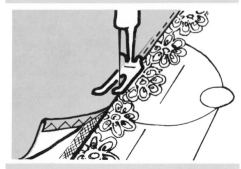

Or, apply lace using the narrow hemming or edgestitching foot attachment for your machine. A third quick way is to overhand edges of lace and garment together.

Enclosed Edging: Sandwich lace between the layers of fabric in collars, cuffs, and ordinary seams. Place heading or gathered edge of lace over seamline in seam allowance. Machine baste next to seamline, then pin second fabric layer over first. Stitch alongside basting; trim and grade seam allowances. Turn and press, or press seam open and turn lace in desired direction.

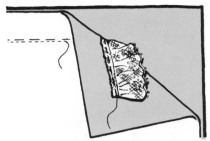

Insertion: Baste edges of insertion along markings. Cut fabric between basting lines; trim seam allowances to ¼″, finish raw edges, and press away from lace. Stitch or overhand basted edges of lace to garment.

On extremely curved edges, don't press after trimming. Lace insertions can also be applied using techniques explained in Appliqués.

Insertion With Edging: Baste insertion over edging. Stitch or loosely overhand edges so lace lies flat.

Apply as above, or as a band trim.

FINISHING: Problem areas, such as corners and ends, can be handled quickly and easily once you've got some inside information.

Corners: For flat ungathered lace, miter corners. Fold lace around corner; machine stitch or overhand diagonal fold (1). Or, stitch across diagonal fold, and trim excess close to stitching (2).

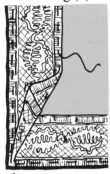 

1.   2.

For gathered lace, allow extra fullness at the corner for lace to spread.

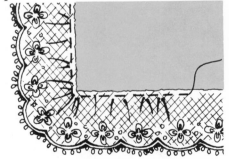

Ends: For free-hanging ends, make a narrow hem, and edgestitch or blindstitch in place.

277

For enclosed edging on a collar or cuff, taper lace where it meets the garment.

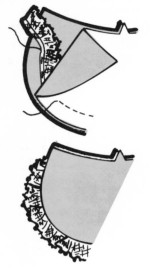

FEATHERS

Apply a boa-like band of feathers along neck edge, sleeve, hem, or anywhere it will enhance garment design.

To join ends, make a French seam, or appliqué along a motif. To appliqué by machine, lap ends, and edgestitch motif with fine zigzag stitch. Trim excess of both layers close to stitching.

To appliqué by hand, lap ends, whipstitch around motif, and trim.

For more information about lace, turn to Laces in the **Special Fabrics** section.

Cut feather strip to desired length plus 1″; lap ends ½″ and whipstitch together. Attach to garment with a loose overhand stitch through cord-like shaft of trim. Make stitches tight enough to support trim. With a large blunt needle, pull feather barbs out from under threads.

Make easy-to-remove feather trims on garments which require frequent cleaning. Sew small thread loops along placement line. Space them several inches apart, and make just large enough for trim to be pulled through. Insert feather strip by passing it through loops like a belt. With a large blunt needle, work feather barbs out to conceal loops.

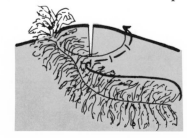

FUR

Pick a fur—whether fun or serious—and you can probably find it available as a trimming strip or in pelt form.

TRIMS: Made in a number of widths, fur trims are usually backed with fabric to make attaching them all the easier. Just decide where you want to put your trim, then simply cut it to the proper length. Whipstitch the ends singly or together, and sew fur trim to garment with strong, invisible running stitches.

Removable fur strips are handy on garments which need frequent cleaning. Apply trim with large snaps sewn to garment and fur. Space snaps to adequately support the weight of the trim.

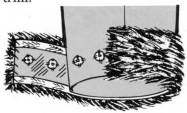

PELTS: When you want more than a simple band of fur, you'll have to start working with pelts. Purchase new ones or plan to use the soft flexible part of an old fur coat. Creating a fur collar is a logical beginning because it involves the techniques needed to make many other fur trims. Then branch out into making a variety of fur accessories.

Trim seam allowances from upper collar pattern. Place pattern on the fur side of an attractive area of the pelt. Outline pattern with pins. If collar requires piecing, be sure that pelts have similar texture, coloration, and direction of hair.

Remove pattern, turn fur to skin side, and mark the pattern outline indicated by pins with pencil or tailor's chalk. Cut along the marked line with a razor blade from the skin side, lifting pelt as you work to avoid slicing hairs.

Join pelts with an overhand stitch through skin only. Use strong waxed thread and work from skin side. Push hairs aside as you stitch. If you do catch hairs in your stitches, work them out with the point of a needle. Reinforce the seam by sewing twill tape over edges with running stitches.

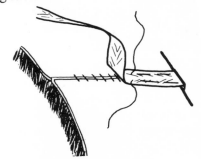

Finish the edges of your collar with twill tape. Place tape on fur side and sew to edge of collar with small overhand stitches. Ease or stretch the tape around curves and miter at corners.

Cut lightweight interfacing and flannel from collar pattern. Back fur with these two layers of fabric, placing flannel next to skin. Sew them to the skin with long running stitches made 1/4" from the collar edge. Turn tape to skin side over the interfacing and sew in place with long running stitches.

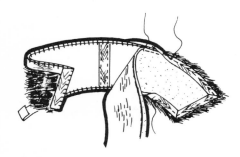

Slipstitch fur collar to finished collar of garment.

To make your fur collar a separate accessory, sew a hook and eye to the ends so they meet at neckline. Cut lining from collar pattern. Attach by turning in edges and slipstitching to tape.

LINEAR FROLIC

Track down edges with braid and binding, or follow the seam with bands and rickrack. The accent is on line, and the key word is emphasis.

BINDING

Use contrasting or self-fabric or commercial double-fold bias binding. Staystitch 3/4" from edge to be bound; trim away 5/8" seam allowance.

CUTTING: First determine method of application (see pages 281-282.) Cut binding on the true bias (see the section on fabric preparation).
Width: For single binding, cut bias strips four times finished width plus 1/4"-3/8" for shaping. For double binding, cut bias strips six times finished width plus 1/4"-3/8".
Individual Piecing: For a small amount of binding, fold fabric corner with perpendicular grains on true bias; cut along fold. Mark strips the necessary width and cut apart. Cut the same slant on all short ends.

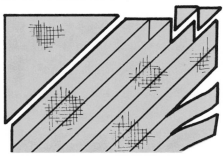

Join short ends on straight grain until bias is required length; press seams open.

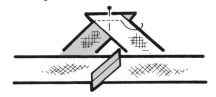

Continuous Piecing: For a large amount of binding, you'll need about ½ yard of fabric that's at least 35″ wide; cut raw edges on the straight grain. Fold one corner on the true bias and cut along fold. Mark consecutive lines the necessary width parallel to fold; cut along the last line. On each end, mark a seamline ¼″ from the raw edge.

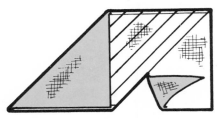

Matching markings, join seam so one strip width extends at each side; stitch and press open. Cut in a spiral along marked line.

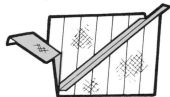

MAKING: Fold strip in half lengthwise; press lightly.
Single: Turn in cut edges of binding so one side is a scant ⅛″ wider than the other; press. Re-fold center crease; press.

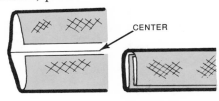

CENTER

Double: Fold strip in thirds so the section with the original lengthwise fold is a scant ⅛″ wider than the

other section; press binding.

PRE-SHAPING: To remove slack, stretch and press bias gently.

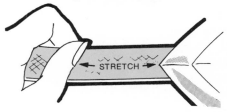

STRETCH

Shape bias to match garment edge. On an **inward curve,** stretch the two folded edges, on an **outward curve,** stretch the one folded edge.

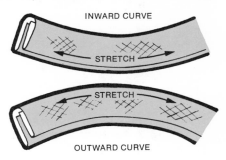

INWARD CURVE

STRETCH

STRETCH

OUTWARD CURVE

When using commercial bias tape to stay a seam, press open all folds as you remove the slack. Cut strip in half lengthwise, and shape.
APPLYING: Allow 2″ extra binding for finishing ends.
Single: Open and pin narrowest edge to garment; keep raw edges even. Stitch along crease.

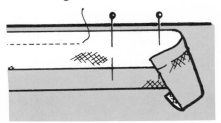

Turn binding to inside and pin over seam, keeping folded edge along stitching. Sew folded edge to seam. **OR . . .**

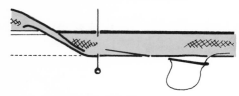

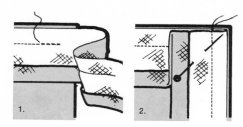

> **SEW AND GO . . . extra easy:** As you turn your binding to the inside, pin it so that the long folded edge covers the line of stitching. From the outside, stitch in the seam to catch the folded edge.

Turn binding to inside over seam, forming a miter on outside (1). On inside, form a second miter in opposite direction. Pin binding over seam; then sew binding and folds of miters in place (2).

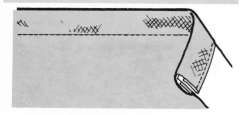

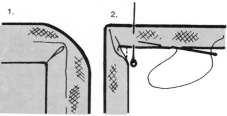

Double: On sheers, use double, or French binding. Opening strip, pin the binding to garment so raw edges are even; stitch and finish as for single binding.

Inward: Reinforce and clip corner(1). Spread clipped edges to apply binding; stitch from garment side(2).

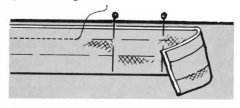

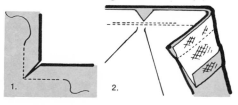

CORNERS: It's easy to bind corners when you've got inside information on mitering.

Outward: Apply binding, backstitching at corner pivot point (1). Fold strip diagonally to go around the corner; pin. Stitch the adjoining edge along crease from the edge of the garment, through corner, to the end of the strip (2).

On the outside, miter binding at corner. Pull fold of miter to inside through clip and turn binding over seam (1). On inside, make a second miter in opposite direction. Pin binding over seam, then sew binding and folds of miters in place (2).

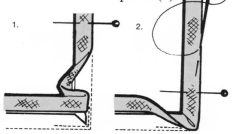

JOININGS: To seam ends of binding during application, extend them at point to be joined and break stitching 1″ on both sides of this point. Fold garment so strips are at right angles. Stitch ends on straight grain close to garment; trim.

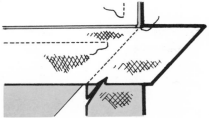

Press seam allowances open. Complete application.

OPENINGS: Apply facings and closure before binding. Pin binding to garment; at opening, turn in and trim ends to ¼″. Stitch, then trim garment seam allowance diagonally at opening. Complete application, sewing ends together.

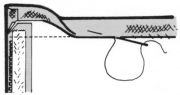

COMMERCIAL BIAS BINDING: Purchase double-fold bias binding; pre-shape, then apply (see Seam Finishes, page 169). Join ends on straight grain; turn in one and lap over the other.

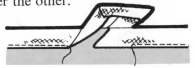

At openings, turn in ends even with garment as you apply binding.

See the section on **Children** for a binding with tie ends.

BRAIDS AND BANDS

Texture, color, width, and style are the variables. Singly or in rows, braids and bands hug edges or play the middle of the road.

Let the flexibility of the trim be your guide in its application to either straight or curved lines. Braids are always flexible; bands are either rigid or flexible.

STRAIGHT: Pin or baste trim to garment. Finish ends as for lace. To attach trim, stitch along both edges or through the center.

To miter, stitch both edges of trim to garment, ending stitching at opposite side of corner (1). Fold trim back and crease, then fold at a right angle to stitched section; press. Open trim and stitch along diagonal crease (2). Fold trim to finished position and stitch both edges in new direction (3).

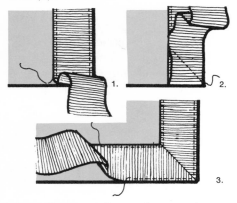

FLEXIBLE: Pin or baste trim to garment, finishing ends as for lace. To attach trim, stitch along both edges or through the center. At curves, stretch edge of trim which must be longer; stitch. Never ease trim to go around a curve.

Soutache Braid: Mark design, then pin or baste soutache in place; begin and end braid in a seam. Stitch along center of braid; or, hand sew braid to garment invisibly.

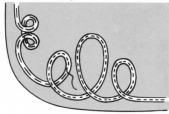

Fold-over Braid: The top half of braid is slightly narrower. Apply to either finished or raw edges. To prepare raw edges, staystitch ¾″ from edge and trim away ⅝″ seam allowance. - Pin or baste braid in place; edgestitch or hand sew.

At curves, stretch braid to fit the longer edge; never ease it to fit the shorter edge.

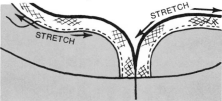

At corners, miter as in Binding.

RICKRACK

Curves and corners are easily turned by flexible rickrack. Place an outward point of the trim on the corner for an attractive little touch.

WITHIN GARMENT LINES: Pin or baste, then stitch along center of trim.

AT EDGES: Apply by enclosed method; usually only the points show when finished. Center rickrack over seamline; pin or baste. Attach facing, stitching through all layers. **OR . . .**

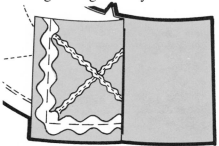

SEW AND GO . . . extra easy: Stitch rickrack to finished garment edge. For the entire trim to show, pin rickrack along finished edge; stitch along center of trim (1). For only the points of the trim to show, pin rickrack along inside of edge; edgestitch from outside (2).

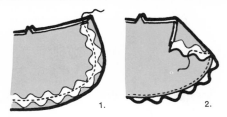

ACCESSORY BASH

Put yourself on the variety circuit—long live the wardrobe of accessories! Since more is necessarily better, make several perfect complements for the clothes you've sewn. Add the perfect accent to a beautifully basic outfit by trimming it with a detachable collar and cuffs, a belt, a scarf, or a frog and Chinese ball button closure.

DETACHABLE COLLAR AND CUFFS

Inside necklines or sleeve hems or over an existing collar or cuff, detachable collars and cuffs are a practical and decorative trim. Ideally easily removed and washable, they shouldn't be interfaced.

COLLAR: Cut detachable collar from collar pattern piece. Add slightly to length and width at outer edge when cutting the overlay type because it must be large enough to go smoothly over all thicknesses. Make collar neck edge small enough to fit smoothly inside garment neckline.

Construct, turn, press, and shape like the flat collar on pages 195-196; eliminate interfacing. Stitch neck edges together ½" from raw edge of undercollar; trim to ¼". Clip seam allowances to stitching every ½" so the neck edge can spread to fit garment neckline.

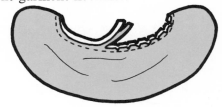

Cut single fold bias seam binding to neckline length plus 1". Apply as a single binding to collar neck edge, shaping binding and collar neck edge to fit garment neckline.

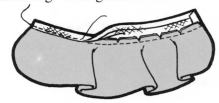

Pin collar to finished neckline of garment, matching seamlines. Mark placement of snaps to secure binding to neck facing in this manner. Sew snaps in place, or sew binding loosely to neck facing.

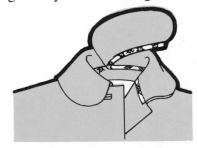

CUFFS: Cut detachable cuffs from cuff pattern piece. If you plan to make your cuffs the turnback kind, add to their length and width at outer edge as you cut them. A note of caution: make sure that the inside edge of cuffs is small enough to fit neatly inside the sleeve hem. Construct, turn, and press like the applied cuff in Sleeve Finishes on page 229. Baste raw edges of cuff together next to seamline in the seam allowance.

Cut a strip of double-fold bias tape 1″ longer than the measurement of the raw edges of cuff. Encase upper edge of cuff with binding; edgestitch (see Seam Finishes, page 169, for further information).

Pin cuff inside finished sleeve, mark to fasten with snaps, or sew binding to sleeve hem.

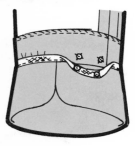

Roll the folded edge of turnback cuffs to outside and bar tack corners to garment.

FROGS AND CHINESE BALL BUTTONS

Opulent or just plain fun, frogs and Chinese ball buttons are easily added to dressy and casual clothes. Use filled or corded self-fabric tubing, made according to the instructions in Loops.

FROGS: Follow the diagram to form frogs. Keep the tubing seam on top as you work, and as you make each successive loop of the design of your frog, tack it with small hand stitches.

Make two halves for each frog. Attach halves of frog to appropriate garment edges with small invisible stitches; keep seam of tubing against fabric. Sew button to largest loop of frog section on garment underlap.

Form frogs in intricate shapes on paper, holding shape with masking tape. Baste to garment. Tear away paper and tape, and sew invisibly. **OR . . .**

SEW AND GO . . . extra easy: Buy commercial frog closures and sew to garment. Or, follow procedure above, using purchased braid or tubing to form frogs and buttons.

CHINESE BALL BUTTONS: Cut a piece of tubing 16″ long. Follow diagram for loop formation, keeping seam on top and loops open as you make the button.

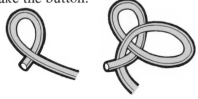

Draw up ends of tubing to pull loops closer together. Ease and shape loops to form an attractive button. Trim excess tubing and fasten ends to button with small stitches.

BELTS

A handcrafted belt made from materials which accent your fabric is an ideal way to customize your fashions and to set yourself apart from the crowd. Make several belts to go with each garment you make. Creativity is the key word here—get started and let your imagination run wild!

DECISIONS: Figure out where you'd like to wear your belt—high, low, or in-between—and find a self-belt in a Butterick pattern which can be customized to suit your creative ideas. Contour your belt if you wish, or design the edges in interesting swoops and curves.

Always measure the area to be belted—and remember to add enough to cover the knots, bows, or other closures you're planning.

MATERIALS: The look of your belt depends a great deal on what it's made of. Some crafty suggestions should inspire you!

Leather, Suede, and Leather-Look-Alikes: These are a good beginning because the results are almost instantaneous. Make clean, even cuts so your edges will be smooth and non-wavering. If you want a double-thick belt, cut pattern twice from the same or a different leather. Interface belt if leather is soft.

Use a glue for fabric or rubber cement to glue the sections of your belt together; trim cut edges so they're even. Edgestitching can be a great final touch; use a wedge-shaped needle made for leather. Complete fastener.

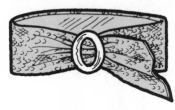

Felt: Because it has no grain to worry about, felt is handled like leather. Felt can be glued or stitched, but an even easier construction solution is to bond belt together with a commercial fusible adhesive used according to package directions. Try your hand at designing a landscape scene or Art Deco motif.

Ribbon: Printed, striped, or solid color ribbons in velvet, grosgrain, or satin make a gorgeous belt for a special dress. Cut color-matched felt or other non-woven backing to the length and width of your ribbon.

Follow package directions on a commercial fusible adhesive to attach belt to backing. Finish ends appropriately. Or, pin and edgestitch belt to backing, turning in and stitching ends. Complete fastener.

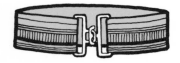

Trims: Ropey trims turn into beautiful belts with a little imagination. Try knotting and braiding drapery cord in different color combinations.

Or, combine the techniques of patchwork, appliqué, binding, rickrack, quilting, or beading with those of belt-making for a really unique creation.

FASTENERS: There are plenty of ways to cinch that new belt. **Tying** and **buckling** it are explained in Belts; **snaps, loops and buttons,**

hooks and eyes, and **nylon tape fasteners** are good closures too, and are fully described in sections of their own.

Borrowed from the shoemaking industry, **grommets and lacing** are a perfect way to tie up a belt. Buy commercial kits for metal grommets or eyelets; larger sizes are needed for thicker belts. Read package directions for the type you're using. Your belt should be firm enough to support the closure without extra interfacing.

If you'd like to stiffen the closure area anyway, fuse a piece of interfacing or firm lightweight fabric to the wrong side of one belt section over grommet markings. Complete belt construction.

Insert grommets through all layers, following manufacturer's instructions for the type you're using.

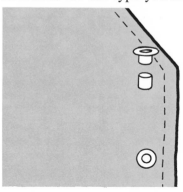

Insert lacing to complete closure.

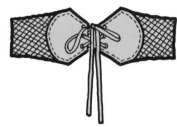

BOWS AND SCARFS

Tricky tying makes the bow you learned as a child an interesting and exciting fashion accessory. Begin with ribbon-like trims or a strip of contrasting or self-fabric. Fashion scarfs in super colors and prints are another way to add the softness of a bow to your outfit.

If you plan to make a bow from your fabric, prepare it as follows. Cut a strip of fabric the length needed for the finished bow; add a ⅝″ seam allowance to each end. Make the strip twice the desired finished width plus a ⅝″ seam allowance on each long edge.

Fold strip in half lengthwise. Stitch long edges in a ⅝″ seam, leaving an opening for turning. Trim seam allowances (1).

Bring seam to center of strip and press open with tip of iron. Stitch ends in a ⅝″ seam; trim (2). Turn strip through opening and slipstitch shut; press (3).

1

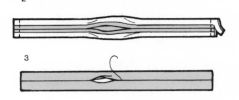

2

3

Use your completed fabric strip to tie the bow of your choice.

STANDARD BOW: When your pattern calls for that perfectly tied bow at your throat, waist, or wrist, here's how to achieve the look.

Fold a rectangular scarf in half lengthwise—square scarfs don't lend themselves to this bow, so beware!

Make a single knot, keeping both ends of tie or scarf even. For the first loop, use the lower section. Then bring the upper section down and carry it around your first loop to form a knot (1).

Hold the first loop in place and make a second loop from the upper section. Then pull this second loop through the knot (2).

Pull both loops tight and adjust them so that they are equal in size and the ends are equal in length. Puff out the bow and the ends and be sure the knot is rather square and flat (3).

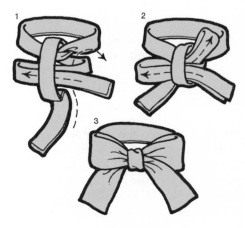

TAILORED BOW: Cut ribbon twice the length of finished bow. For the knot, cut ribbon twice its width plus ½″. Form bow by folding long ribbon in half, as shown, and stitching from edge to edge slightly less than halfway from ends. Secure with back-stitching (1).

Center fold over stitching line; tack and press very lightly. For the knot, fold the smaller length of ribbon to a suitable width and wrap around center of bow (2).

Lap one end over the other at the back of the bow and sew in place. Tack knot invisibly to finish (3).

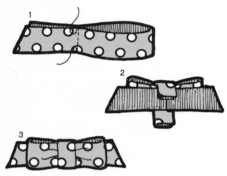

To use a fabric strip, follow above procedure. Then make a fabric knot for your bow by cutting a rectangle of fabric twice the desired width plus seam allowance and the necessary length plus ½″. Fold rectangle in half lengthwise, stitch, press, and turn. Bring seam to center and press. Attach knot as in ribbon version.

ASCOT TIE: Simplest of all, just loop one end of scarf or fabric strip under and over the other end. Both ends can be even, or you can make the top one shorter. Spread the folds of your ascot apart at the neck to expose several inches of fabric for a luxurious look.

NECKTIE: Borrowed from the men, this is a great way to wear long scarfs and ties. Fold a rectangular scarf in half lengthwise (not shown).

Fold a square scarf in half diagonally to form a triangle; fold the lower ends to one side (1). Then fold the scarf in half parallel to the folded edge so the pointed ends are inside (2). Repeat this procedure until scarf is desired width (3).

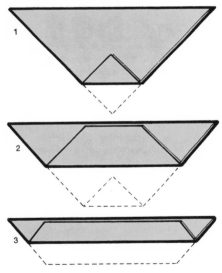

Place your scarf or tie around your neck, letting one end fall longer than the other in front of you (1). With one hand, hold the shorter end taut; with the other hand, loosely wrap the longer end twice around the shorter one (2). Then bring this longer end up from behind and pass it down through the knot formed by the last wrap (3).

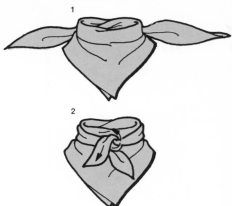

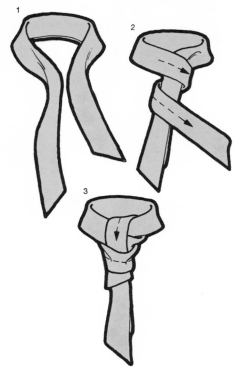

With the same end, tie a second single knot around the other (1). Pull the ends to make them even. Spread the ends apart and straighten the knot (2).

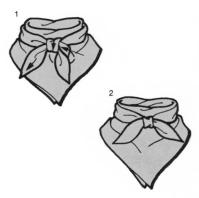

You may have to experiment a bit with tying the scarf before you know the best lengths to let the ends fall in the beginning. Pull the underneath section down to tighten it while raising the knot to the desired level.

SQUARE KNOT: The classic sailor's knot is shown here with fashion's cowboy bib. This is one of the prettiest ways to wear those big square scarfs. Begin by folding your scarf in half diagonally to form a triangle. Loop one end of the scarf over the other end at the back of neck (1). Bring ends directly in front of you; be sure they're the same length. Put one end over the other and tie a single knot (2).

In addition to tying it with a cowboy bib, you can use the square knot as follows. Wrap a long rectangular scarf around your neck several times and fasten it with a square knot.

Or, fold a square scarf diagonally to form a triangle. With the scarf around your neck, tie the ends in a square knot in front of you so the larger portion of the scarf is on your back. In all cases be sure to straighten the knot so it's smooth and flat.

Tailor It Yourself

*Having that suit or coat that's just **perfect for you** becomes a reality when you start to tailor. Don't panic—what's involved doesn't need any extraordinary skills or talent. To get to the point: tailoring is using shaping materials, with an organized progression of additional pressing and hand sewing techniques, to mold and stabilize fabric so your fashion will look as intended by its designer.*

DECISIONS

Begin tailoring by making some choices about the kind of project you'd like and are prepared to tackle.

- **TYPE:** Tailoring falls into two categories—completely tailored garments, and garments with tailored details (like the collar and lapels).

- **STYLE:** Choose a pattern which demands tailoring techniques but which isn't totally beyond your previous sewing experience. Begin with a basic design, and graduate to a more difficult design with each successive tailoring project.

- **FABRIC:** Follow the fabric recommendations on your pattern envelope. Fabric should be pre-shrunk and be able to stand wear and cleaning. A medium weight, closely woven, and durable fabric will make your tailoring efforts worthwhile.
  Wool fabric is a natural for tailoring. However, if you're new at tailoring, avoid hard-surfaced fabrics like gabardine, and very fluffy or loosely woven fabrics like a wool-and-mohair blend. These can be difficult to handle and will present complications.

- **SHAPING FABRICS:** These with your fashion fabric must conform to the look intended by the designer of your pattern. Refer to the charts on pages 63-65, for help in making your choice.

- **NOTIONS:** Purchase the notions listed on the pattern envelope back. Also, get silk thread in a contrasting color to use for basting, buttonhole twist for buttons and buttonholes, and ribbon seam binding for applying your interfacing.

- **PRESSING EQUIPMENT:** Tailoring is easier if you have these, or their substitutes on hand: tailor's ham, seam roll, point presser, pounding block, press mitt, press pad, press cloths, sponge, sleeve board, point turner, and needleboard. See pages 78-79 and 173.

When fashion demands tailoring, there is no substitute. We've set out to steer you clear of a flop and toward a smashing success.

FIRST THINGS FIRST

Prepare your fabric and lining (see pages 119-121). Test press a scrap of your fabric to see how heat and moisture affect it. Pre-shrink underlining, interfacing, tape, and notions that you plan to use, as the great amount of steam used in tailoring and subsequent dry cleanings will have an effect on these.

FITTING YOUR PATTERN: Be absolutely sure that your pattern fits before cutting your fabric. Make the same adjustments or alterations you'd make on a dress or skirt. If you're very unsure of fit, make and test-fit your jacket or coat in muslin (omit facings and hems). When fitting, pay particular attention to the waist and hip areas. Taking a little extra time and effort now can prevent a sad and costly mistake.

Style ease and wearing ease are built into all Butterick patterns. Jackets have enough room to go over a blouse and skirt, or a dress. Coats have enough room to go over a suit or dress. Retain this ease when you adjust or alter your pattern.

Cut-off versions of a design—a coat cut off to a jacket, for instance—can't be worn one over the other, as ease for this purpose doesn't exist.

CUTTING AND MARKING: From your carefully fitted pattern, cut and mark your fashion fabric first. On all pattern pieces, make all seam allowances but those of neckline and armhole 1″ wide instead of the standard ⅝″. Transfer pattern markings to fabric.

Thread trace lengthwise grainlines at center front and center back and crosswise grainlines at bust and hip on all major pieces for use as guides in fitting.

Cut lining from appropriate pattern pieces, making the same seam allowances 1″ wide, as before. Mark lining pieces.

UNDERLINING: This optional procedure requires more time, but has definite advantages. It stabilizes fabric and provides a surface to which construction lines and symbols can be easily and clearly transferred.

Much of your sewing can catch the underlining layer only without showing on the outside of the garment. Underlining acts as a cushion, preventing interior construction (like seam allowances and darts) from imprinting the fabric. When underlined, some fabrics wrinkle much less during wearings.

Select a suitable underlining fabric with the help of the chart on pages 63-65. Cut underlining from garment pattern pieces after cutting your fabric; make underlining seam allowances 1″ wide as you did those of your fabric.

Transfer seamlines, construction lines, and symbols to underlining with tracing wheel and paper. Mark center lines on underlining so they can be matched to the thread tracing on your fabric.

Pin underlining to wrong side of corresponding fabric sections; see page 178 for complete instructions on handling underlinings.

SKIRTS AND PANTS: Make either of these first so your jacket can be fitted over this finished garment. A tailored skirt or pair of pants isn't a major job—they're like regular garments, but should be lined and have a hand-sewn zipper. These easy-to-do extras add a special custom touch to basic sewing methods.

You're probably familiar with most of the construction techniques involved. Make skirt or pants according to your pattern instruction sheet. Follow directions on page 209 to finish the zipper, and pages 179-181 to finish the lining.

Finish pants hems, but leave a skirt pinned to an approximate length, with the lining ½" shorter than skirt. Complete the skirt and jacket of your suit before finishing both with interfaced hems. Hems are sewn last because they must be planned so they are in proportion with each other and your figure.

JACKETS AND COATS

Jackets and coats differ very little in construction procedures. Variations between the two will be discussed as they occur.

INTERFACING

A pre-requisite of tailoring, interfacing should support garment shape without disturbing the character of your fabric. Interfaced areas must look like they belong with the rest of the garment.

Neck, shoulder, finished edges like front openings and hems, and armhole areas of the jacket front and back are usually interfaced. Details like collars, cuffs, and flaps also require interfacing. Interfacing is easily attached to all garments, whether underlined or not.

Any alterations made in the garment must be repeated in the interfacing pattern pieces. Cut interfacing from appropriate pattern pieces. Mark seamlines and center lines on interfacing with tracing wheel and dressmaker's tracing paper. Eliminate all but the armhole seam allowances by cutting a scant ⅛" inside seamlines.

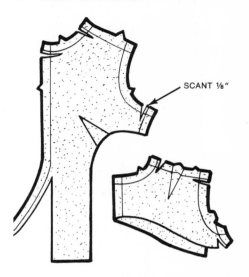

SCANT ⅛"

In the case of a foldline, extend interfacing ⅝" beyond foldline. Permanently stitch darts and seams in interfacing just before attaching interfacing to garment. On pages 177-178, you'll find several methods for making darts and seams.

FITTING SESSION: This is essential before permanently attaching interfacing. Baste and very lightly press jacket darts; add ease or gathering threads where needed. Staystitch neck edge of jacket. Baste interfacing to appropriate garment pieces, then baste garment pieces together.

Try on basted jacket over skirt or pants; lap right front over left, and pin jacket shut, matching centers and markings. Be sure jacket is correctly positioned on your body, and make any necessary adjustments in fit. Check top buttonhole placement

295

marking or point where lapels begin to roll.

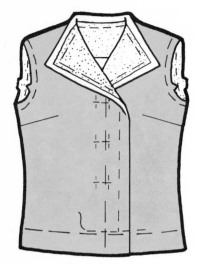

Noting any changes in fit, remove pins and interfacing from jacket to prepare it for permanent attachment. Make needed adjustments in jacket and interfacing, then stitch and press darts.

TAPE: When applied to interfacing, tape stabilizes finished edges and supports lapels. Tape substitutes for the bulky interfacing seam allowances which were cut away. The tape will be caught in the seam.

Ribbon seam binding is perfect for the taping job. All but armhole and long unnotched edges of jacket front and back interfacing are taped before interfacing is permanently attached to jacket.

Straight Edges: Place seam binding along edge of interfacing so one edge of seam binding extends a generous ⅛" beyond cut edge. Stitch opposite edge to interfacing (1).

Curved Edges: Evenly space scant ¼" clips along one edge of seam binding. Place seam binding over in-

terfacing as for Straight Edges, so unclipped edge extends a generous ⅛" beyond edge of interfacing; stitch clipped edges of seam binding in place (2).

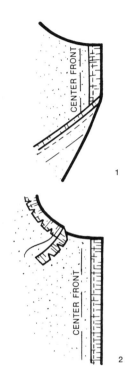

Foldlines: Place seam binding ⅛" beyond foldline in ⅝" extension. Stitch along both edges of the seam binding.

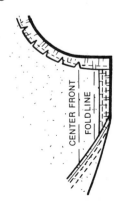

Tape the lapel area to support it. Extend ribbon seam binding over the interfacing from the point where the lapel begins rolling straight up to the shoulder seamlines at the neck edge. Stitch both edges of seam binding to interfacing.

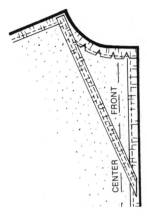

STABILIZE: The interfacing of collars or flaps which require extensive shaping can be stabilized by stitching. This method can also be substituted for taping, and works well on knits and other soft fabrics.

Staystitch interfacing ⅛" inside seamline (usually this is ¾" from raw edge); trim seam allowances close to stitching. Center and pin interfacing over garment piece; catchstitch, placing one row of stitches through interfacing only, and the other row just over the seamline in the garment seam allowance.

Catchstitches allow enough flexibility in the interfacing for it to be smoothly shaped over the garment piece.

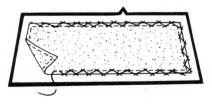

ATTACH: Pin interfacing to jacket, then baste alongside seamlines, center lines, and foldlines; seam binding will be caught when seams are stitched. Never sew long, unnotched edge of interfacing to garment (if garment is underlined, this edge of interfacing can be catchstitched to underlining).

DIAGONAL TACKING: After interfacing a garment which has been underlined, you must attach the entire surface of the interfacing to the underlining only. Use a long, loose, and permanent version of diagonal basting to accomplish this. Keep stitches ¾"-1½" apart, and work from the interfacing side.

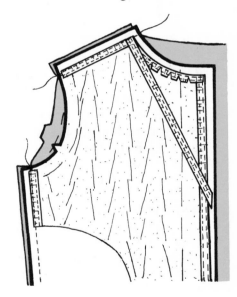

BUTTONHOLES

Bound buttonholes can be completed at this time. Choose the method you like the best for making these from the ones explained on pages 216-219. Worked buttonholes are made on the completed garment (see pages 220-221).

LAPELS

A super tailoring technique is to pad stitch shape into the interfaced lapels, and later into the undercollar. This small, permanent version of diagonal basting is done through all layers from the interfacing side. Catch only a thread or two of the fashion fabric.

Pad stitch lapels between roll line and seamlines. Space stitches ½″ apart, and work them along the lengthwise grain.

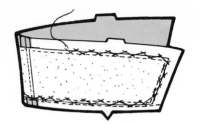

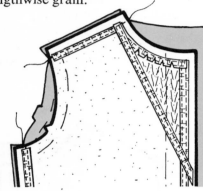

COLLAR

Notched with lapels, the classic tailored collar has shape stitched and pressed into it so that wear and cleaning won't take their toll.

FITTING: To see how the collar will look on your jacket, stitch undercollar sections together, trim seam allowances, and press seam open. Staystitch neck edge of undercollar. Prepare interfacing (see page 177) and stabilize edges with stitching.

Center and pin interfacing over undercollar between outer seamlines, with neck edge a scant ⅛″ inside neck seamline. Baste neck edges together. All other edges of interfacing should be a scant ⅛″ inside collar seamlines; if not, trim. Catchstitch interfacing to undercollar.

For fitting only, lap and pin undercollar to garment neck edge, matching seamlines and markings carefully; baste, clipping neck edges where necessary. Shape collar and lapels as they will be worn.

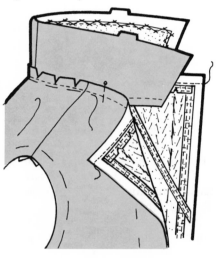

If your garment has extended facings, turn facings to inside at fold-line and baste along upper and lower edges before pinning collar in place.

Try on garment to establish roll of collar in relationship to lapels. Lap and pin right front over left, matching centers and markings. Collar should be close to the neck, evenly rolled, and symmetrical. Outer edge seamlines of collar should cover back neck seamline.

SHAPING: Pin along roll line of collar and lapels. Remove jacket and correct any fitting problems; transfer any changes to both undercollar and lapels. Thread trace roll line on collar and lapels. Remove undercollar from jacket.

Complete collar by stabilizing the roll: pin undercollar around end of tailor's ham; steam roll of collar, but don't touch iron to fabric. Work from center back to front, shaping the halves identically with fingers. Never crease the roll. Let collar dry thoroughly.

Holding undercollar in shaped position over fingers, pad stitch the stand area heavily between neck seamline and roll line. Space stitches ¼″ apart, and work along either lengthwise or crosswise grain.

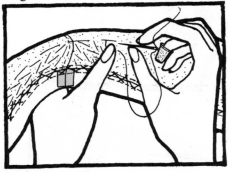

Pad stitch remainder of collar lightly with small stitches spaced about ¾″ apart, shaping collar over hand and working along grain.

Pressing undercollar blends pad stitches into fabric. Press from interfacing side on both sides of the roll. Use a damp press cloth, and be careful to retain shape of collar. With fashion fabric up, press again, protecting fabric with a press cloth.

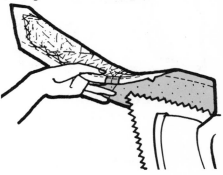

Shape and press lapels in same manner as collar, carefully retaining roll. Let collar and lapels dry thoroughly before handling again.

JOIN UPPER COLLAR TO UNDERCOLLAR: Special attention is given to making the upper collar mold smoothly over the undercollar, roll correctly, and cover the seam at the outer edge.

This is one of the most critical steps in your tailoring project. Follow all the Butterick techniques with great care because a beautiful collar can make a great tailored garment, or even save one that is less successful.

Pin a temporary tuck at center of upper collar neck seamline, tapering it to nothing at the outer edge.

This tuck allows enough ease for upper collar seams at outer edges to be favored when collar is turned.

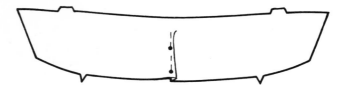

Pin upper collar to undercollar along neck edge, matching seamlines. Shape collar into finished position and pin outer edges together as

they fall; because it goes over the undercollar, upper collar seam allowances will be narrower. Baste alongside the undercollar seamline.

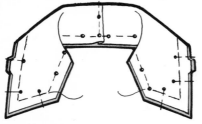
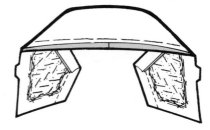

JOINING COLLARS AND FACING: Stitch from undercollar side, reinforcing and pivoting at corners, and ending stitching 5⁄8″ from neck edge. Trim, press, and turn like a regular collar, pages 195-196.

Press edge with a damp press cloth; don't flatten established collar roll. Use a pounding block to shape and flatten edge without causing shine. Let collar dry before handling

or joining it to garment.

Joining the collar and facing to your garment makes your jacket approach its finished look.

Join front and back facings at shoulder; trim and press. Staystitch facing neck edge between markings. Pin, baste, and stitch upper collar neck edge to facing between markings, clipping facing seam allowance as needed.

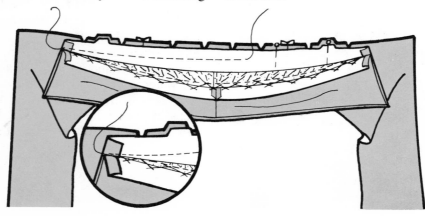

ATTACH COLLAR AND FAC-ING TO GARMENT: Pin and baste undercollar to garment neck edge between markings, clipping garment seam allowances as needed; stitch undercollar to garment neck edge in the same manner as you stitched the upper collar to the facing.

Pin a tiny tuck on facing at corner of lapel, for ease to favor edges. Pin facing as it falls to lapel of garment, and continue to pin along front opening. Edges won't be even at corner of lapel.

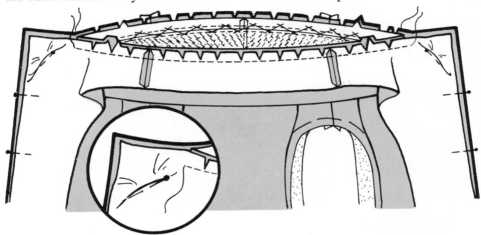

Baste facing to garment along garment seamlines. Stitch from garment side, beginning where facing meets collar. If fabric is bulky or heavy, you may not be able to start at this marking; in this case, leave thread ends long enough to hand sew to the marking later. Reinforce and pivot at corners; continue stitching.

Clip garment and facing to stitching at end of collar. Trim and grade lapel and front opening seam allowances. Trim upper collar and facing neck seam allowances; leave undercollar and garment seams as they are. Make additional clips in both garment and facing seam allowances if necessary.

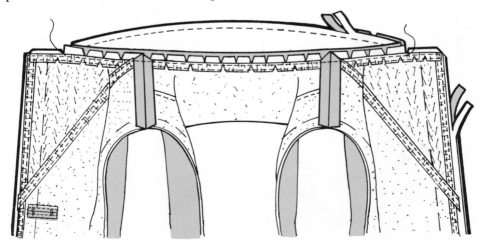

Press facing and collar seams open over a point presser. Turn facing to inside of garment and press; use diagonal basting with silk thread to keep edges in place. Favor facing side of lapels to point where lapel begins to roll, and garment side of jacket below this. Press lapels from underside first, using a damp press cloth; then flatten edges with a pounding block.

FINISH COLLAR: Check roll and pin it in place. Pin together layers of collar as they fall, about ¾ ″ above neck seams. Lift facing and sew neck seams together with long, loose zigzagging stitches; don't force seams together if they don't meet.

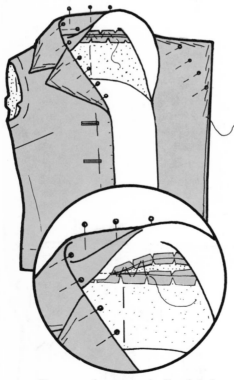

For very heavy or bulky fabrics, you may want to use the menswear tailored collar (see pages 256-257).

THE HALF-WAY POINT

You've just reached a milestone in your tailoring project—the half-way point. You're over the hump and on your way toward the finish line.

TAILORED FITNESS

Now you can get ready for a big fitting session. It's fun because you're at a point where a lot will happen all at once. Your suit will practically bloom before your eyes!

POCKETS, WELTS, FLAPS: Stitch, turn, and press any of these that are included in your pattern. If you need additional information about them, see pages 235-239. Pin and baste pockets, flaps, or welts over placement lines.

HEM: Pin up the hem of your jacket.

SLEEVES: Run a line of thread tracing along crosswise grain of sleeve cap, and two lines of machine stitches for ease between markings on sleeve cap. Baste and finger-press sleeve darts and seams.

Put sleeve in armhole, matching and pinning at notches, markings, and underarm seam. Pull up ease threads until sleeve fits armhole; wind thread ends around a pin. Adjust fullness and pin every ½″; baste sleeve in armhole. Pin up hems of sleeves.

FACINGS: Leave these free if you plan to attach lining by machine. If lining will be attached by hand, sew long free edge of facing to jacket and shoulder seam allowances and any other places that won't show on the outside. End stitching within 4″-6″

of lower edge of garment.

FITTING: This is the session where you take a careful look at all the things you've pulled together! Put your jacket on and pin the front edges shut.

Pockets, Welts, Flaps: Placement of these is your first consideration. Pockets which you intend to use should be at a comfortable height and position, while those which are for decoration only should be placed as featured in the design.

In either case, these details should look balanced. Pockets on either side of the center front are usually symmetrical, both ending the same distance from **center marking** and hem of jacket. Transfer any adjustments that apply to pockets, welts, or flaps, and complete them.

Sleeves: Thread traced grainlines in the cap should parallel the floor; if not, correct by shifting position of sleeve in armhole. Ease in cap should be where you need it. Adjust if necessary and mark new seamlines.

Be sure sleeves are roomy enough to fit over the sweater, dress, or, in the case of a coat, the jacket that will be worn underneath. Pad shoulders slightly if sleeve needs support, then check length and grain. Mark any changes on fabric, trace hems, and tie ease threads before removing sleeves from jacket.

SLEEVES

Because they are easier to handle singly, complete your carefully fitted sleeves before permanently joining them to the garment. Permanently stitch and press sleeve darts and seams. It's a good idea to stay seams if fabric is heavy or loosely woven: baste ribbon seam binding along one seamline so it will be caught in stitching as seam is joined.

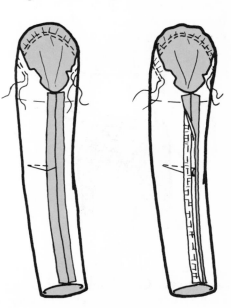

SLEEVE HEMS: Lower edges of sleeves are interfaced before they are hemmed. Lamb's wool or cotton flannel gives a soft hem edge, regular interfacing fabrics, a roll or sharp crease. Cut bias strips of interfacing material the length of hem circumference and the width of hem depth plus 1⅜".

Pin interfacing to sleeve, keeping one edge of strip ⅝" below hemline. Refer to page 306 for special interfacing technique if fabric is heavy or bulky. Invisibly sew interfacing to sleeve along hemline, upper edge, and ends. Turn up hem and sew to interfacing with catchstitches. Press hem over a sleeve board; use steam and pounding to get the desired edge.

JOINING SLEEVE TO GARMENT: This procedure is as much a pressing as a stitching story. Since you've already fitted your sleeve cap, you can get right to work on it.

Hold curve of sleeve cap over a press mitt, and shrink fullness by steaming the seam allowance. Don't press beyond stitches.

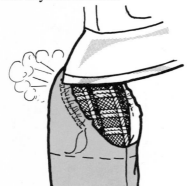

Turn in seam allowance along ease thread. Cap should be smooth; if puckers or pulling are evident, slide fullness along ease threads until it disappears. Steam again.

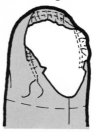

Pin and baste sleeve in armhole. Stitch with sleeve side up, beginning at the underarm; control fullness as you work. Make a second row of stitching over the first along underarm between notches. Trim this area to ¼" and clip to stitches at ½" intervals. Turn seam allowances toward sleeve, but don't press.

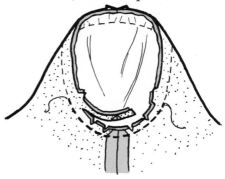

SLEEVE PADDING AND/OR SHOULDER PADS: These are sometimes needed to support and round out the finished sleeve and shoulder.

For padding, cut two bias rectangles of lamb's wool or heavy flannel. Each should be about 3" wide by 4"-6" long. Fold down 1" on one long edge.

Slipstitch folded edge along seam inside cap of sleeve.

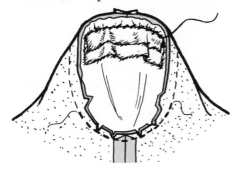

For shoulder pads, buy commercial ones in a thickness that won't distort the natural shape of the garment. Try on jacket to find exactly where you should attach pads; from the outside, pin pad securely on one side of the seam.

Turn jacket wrong side out, open facings at shoulders, and sew pads to seam allowances.

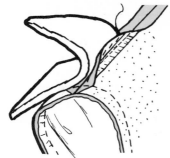

Loosely sew corners of shoulder pad to armhole seam allowance.

HEMS

Time to turn your attention to hems! Pin unfinished hems in place so you can analyze the proportion of jacket to skirt or pants on your figure. Jacket left front must be very slightly shorter than the right front so lower edge of left is concealed; inner folds of pleats and underlaps of vents must be shorter for the same reason.

Try on your garment exactly as you'll wear it—skirt or pants and jacket with blouse or sweater, belt, shoes, hosiery, accessories, and anything else you have in mind.

Lap and pin center markings of jacket, right front over left. Check button placement markings for accuracy; you may find that you need a snap, hook, or button on the inside to support the left front. Mark necessary adjustments.

Complete garment hems, using an interfaced hem in skirt and jacket (see page 243). When interfacing falls over seams in heavy or bulky fabrics, trim interfacing seam allowances generously; tuck cut edges of interfacing under seam allowances. If hem is shaped or eased, pre-shape interfacing to match garment contour before applying.

CORNERS: Hems can be handled in one of the following ways at a corner, depending on fabric weight, garment style, and the likelihood of lengthening the garment later. Press facing and garment seam allowances open within hem area.

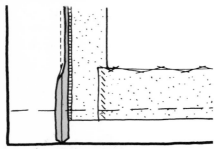

Turn hem allowance to inside along hemline, and clip seam allowances above hem. Taper facing hem slightly so it won't show from the outside. Pin, then baste close to fold.

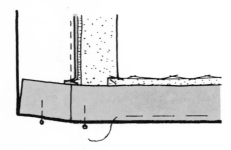

Adjustable Finish: This allows you to lower the hem later, should you choose. Trim facing hem allowance as shown.

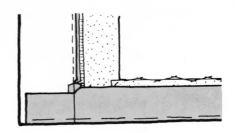

Permanent Finish: Ideal for very heavy fabrics, but this finish prevents you from lengthening the hem later. Mark hem where facing edge will fall.

Open facing and stagger trimming of facing and hem as shown. Trim hem of facing to ⅝″, ending at seam or foldline; cut down across hem to trimmed edge.

Then measure ½″ from marking toward facing. At this point, slash hem to within 1″ of hemline, and trim across hem to seam or foldline. Next to the seam, make a clip to the first trimming line.

Sew trimmed edges in place with long, loose catchstitches.

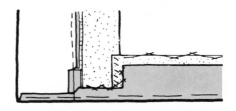

Completion of Hem and Corner: Catchstitch hem edge to interfacing. Press and pound the hem to get the desired edge. Then turn the facing to the inside of the garment and press and pound in the same manner as you did the hem.

Depending on the bulk and weight of your fabric, choose one of the following methods to sew the facing to the garment at the corner.

For non-bulky and lightweight fabrics, complete corner by making a ¼″ clip in facing at top of hem. Turn facing in below clip and pin (1).

Complete corner by loosely sewing lower edge of facing to hem; continue sewing up to the clip (2).

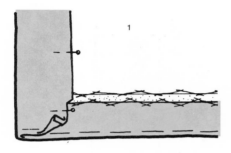

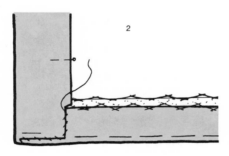

For heavy and bulky fabrics, complete corner by loosely sewing lower edge of facing to hem (1). Hemstitch raw edge of facing to hem (2).

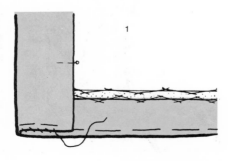

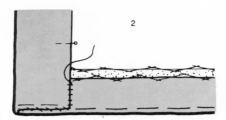

For either method, use running stitches to sew free edge of facing above hem to jacket interfacing; press.

PLEATS: End interfacing at seamlines and extend it ⅝″ beyond foldlines. Interface outer layer of pleat as you did the hem. Tape foldlines with seam binding to prevent stretching. To complete hem, see pages 188-189.

LINING

You're almost done — at last! Lining should complement fashion fabric in weight, durability, and cleaning requirements. Opaque lining prevents interior construction from showing through.

HAND APPLICATION: This is the finest finishing touch for your jacket or coat.

Prepare Garment Lining: Staystitch front, back shoulder, neck edges, and underarm edges between markings. Prepare lining for fitting by basting and finger-pressing darts, pleats, and seams.

Test-fit by lapping lining over facings and pinning into garment; match seamlines. Try on garment; lining shouldn't wrinkle, bubble, or interfere with wearing ease. Mark any adjustments.

Stitch lining underarm bust darts only. Other darts, pleats, and tucks should be secured by a large, loose cross stitch (page 270) through all layers.

Also use a catchstitch to secure the back pleat at neck, waist, and lower edge of jacket. Then stitch and press open major seams.

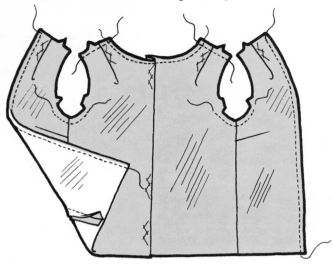

Attach Lining to Garment: Turn in front, back shoulder, and neck edges along seamline; clip or notch seam allowances so they'll lie flat. Baste, but don't press. Pin lining into garment, working from center back to front opening edges.

Sew each lining seam allowance to its matching garment seam allowance with long, loose running stitches, ending 4″-6″ from garment hem. Use this technique on all major vertical seams.

Pin armhole, shoulder, and edges of lining front in place. Keep back shoulder and neck edges free. With long running stitches, sew front shoulder edge to back shoulder seam allowance and lining to garment alongside front armhole seamline.

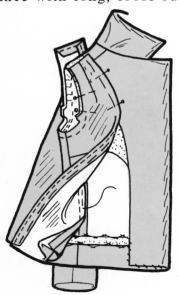

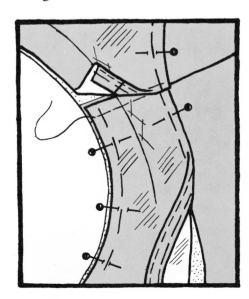

Finish Garment Lining: Slipstitch front edges of lining to facings to within 2″-4″ of garment hem. Space stitches at ⅛″ intervals; backstitch every 3″-4″ for extra strength.

Pin back shoulder and neck edges in place; slipstitch over front shoulder seamline. Trim and clip underarm between notches at ½″

intervals. Sew lining to garment back alongside armhole seamline.

To finish lining hem, use method on page 181, turning in lower edge of lining ¼″. Then release pinned tuck and sew remaining front edges of lining in place. For coats, you can also use the free-hanging hem on page 181.

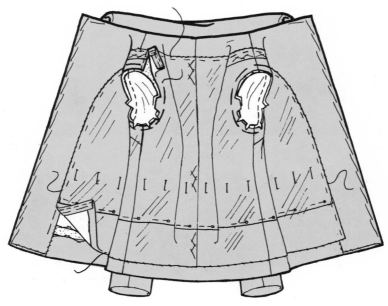

Sleeve Lining: Staystitch armhole edge. Add ease threads. Baste long underarm seam of sleeve lining. Ease lining sleeve cap as you did garment sleeve cap.

Clip lining underarm seam allowance between notches every ½″. Test-fit by lapping and pinning sleeve lining in armhole; baste in place. Try on jacket.

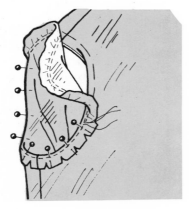 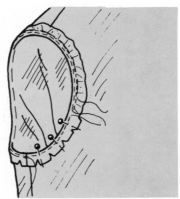

No wrinkles or bubbles should appear and lining shouldn't bind; lining and garment sleeve caps should mold together. Mark necessary changes; stitch and press seams.

Sew each sleeve lining underarm seam allowance to its matching garment sleeve seam allowance with long loose running stitches, ending 4″-6″ from sleeve hem. Turn lining back over sleeve by pulling lower edges of both through lining.

Turn sleeve right side out. Turn in seam allowances of lining armhole and pin to garment, matching seams and markings. Adjust ease and slipstitch, backstitching at 1″ intervals for strength.

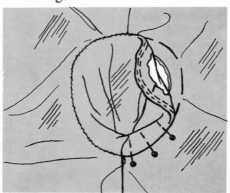

Put garment on a padded hanger or a dress form to complete sleeve lining hem. Hold lining in place with pins from the outside, then trim it even with lower edge of sleeve. For wearing ease, pin a ¼″ tuck 5″-6″ above lower edge. Turn lower edge of lining in ¼″ and pin to garment hem where it falls. Match seamlines of lining and garment. Adjust fullness, if necessary, and slipstitch lining to garment. Release tuck. The ease tuck is very important because it gives you enough room for freedom of movement.

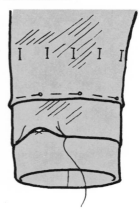

Lightly press all lining edges with the tip of your iron.

SEW AND GO . . . extra easy: You can apply a lining by machine! Enjoy the luxury of a lining without doing a lot of hand sewing. Finish sleeve hems, but don't finish jacket hem and corners. Leave facings free.

Prepare lining for a fitting. Baste and finger-press darts, pleats, and seams, including those of sleeve. Ease and pin sleeve into armhole; baste.

Test-fit lining by lapping and pinning it over facings. Lining shouldn't wrinkle, bubble, or inter-

fere with wearing ease. Sleeve caps
of lining and garment should mold
together. Mark any adjustments,
then remove lining sleeves.

Stitch lining darts or tucks as
instructed in sewing guide. Stitch
basted back pleat for 2″-3″ at neck,
waist, and lower edge. Press back
pleat to one side and baste in place
along neck and lower edges.

Stitch and press all lining seams,
including those of the sleeves. Pin
and stitch lining sleeve to lining armhole, easing as you did for the jacket.

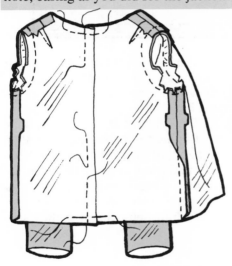

Turn jacket and lining right
sides out. Pin facing in place, lift lining, and sew facing seam allowances
to interfacing.

To attach the lining, open out
jacket facings. With right sides together, pin the long edge of the lining
to the free edge of the facing; match
shoulder seams and be sure to keep
raw edges even as you work.

Stitch from the facing side along
the length of the unnotched edge of
the facing. Be very careful not to mistakenly catch the body of either the
garment or lining in your stitching.

Begin and end stitching 4″-6″
from lower edges. This will enable
you to finish the hem of your jacket.
Press seam open, then toward lining.

Pull lining sleeves inside jacket
sleeves. Finish sleeve lining hems
as explained on page 310.

311

Then pin the remaining free edges of the lining in place over the jacket facing. Sew lining to facing; end your sewing at the lower corner of the lining. A fold of lining will automatically fall over the hem allowance to provide the necessary wearing ease.

To finish the jacket hem, use the interfaced hem on page 243. Turn in lower edge of lining ½" and pin to jacket hem, keeping raw edges even.

Finish corners, choosing an appropriate method from those explained on pages 306-307. Sew lower edge of lining to hem.

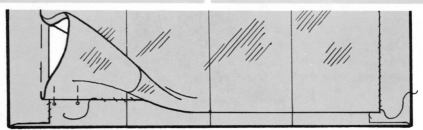

INTERLINING

When you want extra warmth in outerwear like jackets and coats, interlining is the answer. See the chart on pages 63-65, to pick a suitable type. When you interline, allow additional ease for it in fitting your garment, as interlining will use up needed wearing ease. Cut interlining from lining pieces, omitting center back pleats.

Attach interlining by pinning and basting to wrong side of lining as you would back or underline fashion fabric.

Treating the layers as one, construct lining for attachment by either the hand or Sew and Go method. Slash and press darts open. Trim interlining close to stitching at darts and seams; trim interlining close to staystitching before hand application.

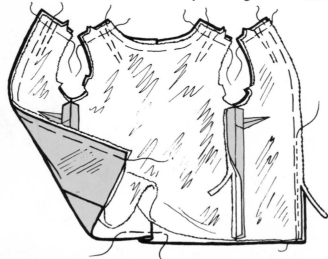

Sew lining and interlining unit to garment by chosen method. After machine application, trim interlining along neck and front edges.

PERFECT ENDING

A few simple and small finishing touches are in order. Do them carefully, because even at this point, haphazard work can spell disaster as far as a super-looking fashion is concerned.

- Finish the backs of bound buttonholes, or make hand-worked buttonholes.

- Sew on buttons.

- Attach covered snaps or hooks, or use small buttons with thread loops to give the extra support you found was needed in the last fitting.

- Sew lace or braid along front and neck edges where lining meets facing for a custom finish.

- Attach a gold chain weight along hem edge where lining meets hem allowance to keep a long jacket from riding up.

- Remove any stray basting threads.

At last you've finished, and you can be very proud to wear this newest tailored addition to your wardrobe. You'll experience the satisfaction of having done something above and beyond the call of duty, and done it well.

But don't stop here—you've only just begun! Developing your skills as a tailor is one of sewing's greatest challenges. You'll build up the knowledge that will enable you to express yourself in fabric, and have a marvelous wardrobe besides. Your coats and suits, and super dresses won't look as though they're off the rack, and will be exactly what you wanted.

You'll know too, that you're lots more than just someone who can sew. Tailoring is an ability that impresses people—not because of what they know about it, but because of what they don't know about it.

Let them be impressed by your talent, but never let yourself be persuaded that tailoring is difficult. It's a construction process like any other, only the units that make up the whole are smaller. No unit is hard, but each is absolutely essential, and must be completed in a certain order.

Everything you've learned will be used in future tailoring projects. With experience, you'll develop shortcuts to make the job go even faster. Now you've really got a good thing going!

Index

316

317